Movie Anecdotes

MOVIE ANECDOTES

Peter Hay

New York Oxford
OXFORD UNIVERSITY PRESS
1990

Oxford University Press

Oxford   New York   Toronto
Delhi   Bombay   Calcutta   Madras   Karachi
Petaling Jaya   Singapore   Hong Kong   Tokyo
Nairobi   Dar es Salaam   Cape Town
Melbourne   Auckland

and associated companies in
Berlin   Ibadan

Published by Oxford University Press, Inc.,
200 Madison Avenue, New York, New York 10016

Oxford is a registered trademark of Oxford University Press

Library of Congress Cataloging-in-Publication Data
Hay, Peter.
Movie anecdotes / Peter Hay.
p.   cm.   Includes bibliographical references.
ISBN 0–19–504594–7
1. Motion picture industry—California—Los Angeles—Anecdotes.
2. Hollywood (Los Angeles, Calif.)
—Social life and customs—Anecdotes.
I. Title.   PN1993.5.U65H38   1990
384′.8′0979494—dc20   89–49252

2 4 6 8 9 7 5 3 1

Printed in the United States of America
on acid-free paper

*For David Ambrose and Paul Jarrico,
good writers on and off the screen,
and my good friends in and out of Hollywood:
with constant admiration and my lasting affection.*

Acknowledgments

A compiler of anecdote books has almost as many people to thank as a winner on Oscar night. Some of you may not remember even how you have helped—by an encouraging word, lending or mentioning a book, giving a lead—or just by being a friend at a time when I really needed one:

Laurence and David Ambrose, Polly and Janos Bak, Lia Benedetti, Dennis Boutsikaris, Yurek Bogajewicz, Alan Brock, Raphael Buñuel, Didi Conn, Michael Donaldson, Marris and Rudi Fehr, Sidney Field, Syd Field, Hermine Fuerst-Garcia, Jacqueline Green, Nick de Grunwald, Richard Hatton, Leonora and David Hays, Patricia and Richard Herd, Jeffrey Henderson, Endre Hüles, Paul Jarrico, John and Donna Wong Juliani, Charles Kahlenberg, Joshua Karton, Barbara Keegan, Eva and Paul Kolozsváry, Kitty and Steve Kovács, Dana Kraft, Miles Krueger, Robert Lewin, Edward Maeder, Jenny Magid, Marcella Meharg, Elizabeth and Alan Mandell, Elisabeth Marton, Simon Mayo, Peter Medak, Julia Johnson Migenes, Virginia Morris, Hilda Mortimer, Cora and Oliver Muirhead, John Neshi, Eva Németh, Margaret Oberman, Ed O'Neill, Ethan (John) Phillips, Susan Roether, Deac Rossell, Don Rubin, Catherine Rusoff, John Sarantos, Marsie

Sharlatt, Roberta Sherry, David Shire, Howard Suber, Eve Siegel Tettemer, James F. Skaggs, Carol Sorgenfrei, Barbara Steele, Loren Stephens, June and Michael Szász, Adam Szőcs, Alex Uttermann, April Webster, John York, Vilmos Zsigmond.

My special thanks to Richard Kahlenberg for several suggestions and constant support; to Carol Channing, Judith Crist, and Sir John Gielgud for kind comments on my previous collections of theatrical anecdotes; to many friends and associates over the years at First Stage, the Sundance Institute, and the Eugene O'Neill Theater Center. I owe a great deal to conversations with knowledgeable bookstore owners, and to libraries, in particular: University of Southern California (especially Anthony Anderson), University of California at Los Angeles, the Los Angeles City Public Library (the Central branch and the Frances Howard Goldwyn Hollywood branch), the Glendale and Pasadena Library System, and the American Film Institute Library.

It is a pleasure to acknowledge—the third time around—the essential guidance of the staff of Oxford University Press in New York, especially my editor Sheldon Meyer, and Leona Capeless, Stephanie Sakson-Ford, Joellyn Ausanka, Vera Plummer, Laura Brown, Jeffrey Seroy, David Sartory, and others responsible for turning out such fine books. Richard Sansom at OUP in Oxford has also been most helpful.

Finally, my heartfelt thanks to my wife Dorthea Atwater, for her love and support—and for her expertise in preparing the index; and to my mother Eva Hay, for her lifelong encouragement, and for giving me the feeling that life is like an epic movie.

*   *   *

Every reasonable effort has been made to contact copyright holders to secure permission to include in this volume passages from works not in the public domain, and any omission brought to the publisher's attention will be remedied in subsequent editions. Grateful acknowledgment is hereby made for permission to reprint excerpts from the following works:

Bardot, Deneuve and Fonda by Roger Vadim; reprinted by permission of
    Simon & Schuster. Copyright © 1986 by Roger Vadim.
Blessings in Disguise by Alec Guinness; reprinted by permission of Alfred
    A. Knopf Inc. Copyright © 1985 by Alec Guinness.
A Child of the Century by Ben Hecht; reprinted by kind permission of
    Donald I. Fine, Inc.; special thanks to Roger Vergnes. Copyright ©
    1954 Ben Hecht.
Don't Get Me Wrong—I Love Hollywood by Sidney Skolsky; reprinted by

permission of Arthur Pine Associates. Copyright © 1975 by Sidney Skolsky.

Hello Hollywood! by Allen Rivkin and Laura Kerr. Reprinted by permission of Doubleday, a division of Bantam, Doubleday, Dell Publishing Group, Inc. Copyright © 1962 by Allen Rivkin and Laura Kerr.

A Hundred Different Lives by Raymond Massey; reprinted by permission of Little, Brown and Co., and McClelland and Stewart Limited. Copyright © 1979 by Raymond Massey.

The Jewish Mothers' Hall of Fame by Fred A. Bernstein; reprinted by permission of Doubleday, a division of Bantam, Doubleday, Dell Publishing Group, Inc. Copyright © 1986 by Fred Bernstein.

Ladies Man by Paul Henreid and Julius Fast; reprinted by permission of St. Martin's Press, Inc., New York. Copyright © 1984 by Paul Henreid and Julius Fast.

A Life by Elia Kazan; reprinted by permission of Alfred A. Knopf Inc. Copyright © 1988 by Elia Kazan.

One Reel a Week by Fred J. Balshofer and Arthur C. Miller; reprinted by permission of the Regents of the University of California and the University of California Press. Copyright © 1967 by the Regents of the University of California.

On the Set of Fellini Satyricon by Eileen Lanouette Hughes; reprinted by permission of William Morrow & Co. Copyright © 1971 by the Author.

The Parade's Gone By . . . by Kevin Brownlow; reprinted by permission of Alfred A. Knopf Inc. Copyright © 1968 by Kevin Brownlow.

Walt by Charles Shows; reprinted by kind permission of the Author. Copyright © 1979 by Charles Shows.

When the Shooting Stops . . . The Cutting Begins by Ralph Rosenblum and Robert Karen; reprinted by permission of Ralph Rosenblum and Robert Karen. Copyright © 1979 by Ralph Rosenblum and Robert Karen.

Contents

Introduction

Nicholas Schenck, president of Loew's which once owned MGM, reproached Howard Dietz, one of the famous writers at the studio, for always being late. "I can't deny it," Dietz is supposed to have replied, "but you must admit that I leave early." The anecdote does not appear inside this book, because the well-known original dates from at least a hundred years before. There the riposte is made by Charles Lamb in his famous stutter, and the English essayist employs it as an excuse to his tolerant boss at the East India Company. Of course, Howard Dietz could have reinvented Lamb's or adapted it to his own situation. That was certainly the case with "Honey, I forgot to duck"—Ronald Reagan's much-quoted line to Nancy after he was shot in 1981. The original (without the Honey) appeared on a telegram to Jack Barrymore from Jack Dempsey, after Gene Tunney defeated him as world heavyweight boxing champion in 1926. Epigrams and witticisms have an afterlife quite independent of their authors.

Then there are events which have taken place within living memory, such as the stealing of John Barrymore's body from the mortuary by some of his boon companions. They dragged it to Errol Flynn's house on top of the Hollywood hills and propped it up in his favorite chair. But who were *they?* Flynn wrote in his memoirs that the macabre prank had been organized by director Raoul Walsh. The incident is attributed to Peter Lorre by Paul Henreid; they were both acting in *Casablanca* at the time. My oldest friend from old Hollywood, Rudi Fehr, tells me categorically that the perpetrator was the actor Albert Dekker. Gene Fowler's biography of Barrymore, written soon after his friend's demise, does not even mention Errol Flynn. Proper allocation of credits has always been problematic in the movie business. And, as Otto Friedrich remarked in his *City of Nets,* "All the best Hollywood stories have several contradictory versions."

All three of the versions above at least agree that the prank took place. Paul Henreid tells another story, of Jack Warner's commissioning a portrait of his wife from Salvador Dali. When the painting was unveiled at a huge party at his mansion, Warner found his own likeness in the face of a monkey painted in the background; he is then supposed to have shut away the picture, as he did some of his motion pictures he did not want the public to see. Again I asked Rudi Fehr, who had been one of Jack Warner's closest associates for three decades; he called the monkey business pure fantasy—the mogul had the painting proudly displayed in his house. For a while I hesitated about including the story in this collection, but then I reminded myself that such scruples, taken to their logical conclusion, would result in a very slim volume, with more footnotes than text.

More importantly, it would no longer be a book of anecdotes. The genre is not about facts or history, though there might be more than a hint of truth to H. L. Mencken's definition of the historian as an unsuccessful novelist. With anecdotes, story is everything, and in this respect there is a happy coincidence with the craft of the scenarist. The material of life— most of it immaterial or antithetical to drama—has to be chopped up and fashioned into something that will hold large numbers of people entertained or in suspense. Facts and research become background; characters and episodes are transposed, eliminated, or invented; key moments, especially the ending, often changed. The best screenwriters and film-makers know that reality on the screen must be manufactured, not out of arbitrary judgment, but in order to serve the story. There is no pretense at objectivity; as with the camera, point of view creates the picture.

In the history of Hollywood movies, Ronald Reagan is of small importance, except perhaps for his tenure as president of the Screen Actors Guild during the period of McCarthyism and the breakup of MCA. From an anecdotal viewpoint, if Reagan had not become President of the United States he would also be minor: there are no witticisms from his Hollywood years that stand out, no stories that have not been told as well or better about others. But he did become President and so even minor incidents and casual sayings gain importance. They are embroidered by the tellers who thereby hope to garner greater significance. As Reagan grew to be a national and then world figure, everything he had said or people remembered about his Hollywood years (remarkably little, all things considered) was examined with a microscope and found to be prophetic.

Reagan proved to be also the most anecdotal President since Abraham Lincoln, and as several historians have begun to show, he believed more in jokes and stories from his old movies than in facts reported by his aides. So in a circular way, the Reagan anecdotes did become relevatory about the workings of Hollywood and of Washington, which is why he looms large in one chapter of this book.

A somewhat different distortion is caused by the innumerable stories associated with Samuel Goldwyn, who was indeed a giant figure in the first fifty years of Hollywood's history. He gained notoriety because of peculiarities in his language which reflected the even more peculiar way his brain worked. For the second half of his life Goldwyn ran an independent studio which was based on his taste and vision rather than on star actors, writers, or directors. That is why his press agents began to focus on his personality to fuel the insatiable publicity engine that sells movies. When they got everybody in Hollywood to laugh, Goldwyn tried to stop the machine and denied authorship of the mangled aphorisms attributed to him. But, as often happens with the dominant figures of any field in any age, anecdotes about more obscure people became attached to him, especially if a story or saying became so exaggerated through constant retelling that it required a larger-than-life personality. I felt it my obligation as an anecdotist to pass on as many of these famous Goldwynisms and stories as possible, rather than be pedantic about their origin. It is the story, as it typified an aspect of film-making, or of the Hollywood system, that interested me, not the casting in one particular remake.

Apart from gathering relatively large numbers of stories about a few of these archetypal figures and genuine wits, I have made no attempt to be comprehensive. Indeed, it would have been futile to do so; after all, what would constitute completeness? A story that pleases one, bores another. Also the volume of old material is staggering and, given the steady flow of new movie biographies and memoirs, must be endless. I have tried to include most of the classic anecdotes that movie-makers and buffs still tell each other, and find some lesser known stories that deserve to be remembered. But, despite the distinguished publisher, this is not meant to be a scholarly book. I give sources only when quoting directly; the same story crops up so many times that it would have been arbitrary to cite one provenance over another. I have built, of course, on previous collections (as they did, too), but the selection is highly personal. The groupings and order are meant to enhance and surround each anecdote with a context. For the same reason I provided in most cases a date, which must be taken as approximate, since the year a film is made, released, or given an Oscar, may all be different.

As in my two volumes of theatrical anecdotes, here, too, the past preponderates. This is in the nature of the beast. When you ask for somebody's best stories, they are likely to be of a vintage year, not last week's. Anecdotes about a golden age have a mythical quality, and it seems easier to be immortal, Goldwyn might have said, if you are dead. It is also safe to say that the ruthless egotists of the pioneer era were a good deal more colorful than the accountants, lawyers, and corporate executives who run the studios these days, often from New York or Tokyo. At the same time, I did include some stories about living, younger figures who are well on their way to becoming legendary. Although there is a great deal of amusing and tragic gossip associated with movie stars, which fill the tabloids, I avoided the purely sleazy and the merely scandalous.

Because the film community has always been global, I wanted to collect more anecdotes from Europe, Canada, Australia, India, Japan, but I must admit that these were swamped—as are the films of all foreign countries— by the product from Hollywood. The best stories took place in the movie capital, which of course has attracted talent from countries all over the world. In its heyday—from the twenties to the forties—Hollywood was an oasis where wit was more highly prized and paid than anywhere else since the days of Charles II in Restoration England; where more stories were told than in the Chicago newsrooms or the cafes of central Europe—often by the exiled habitués of these places. The movie colony is still a venue for fads and follies, but in those days the best wits from Broadway and the Algonquin Round Table recorded each wretched excess. A huge domestic and foreign press corps lived and died for items; columnists killed for exclusives; comedians trod on each other's gags. Even after that Hollywood died, aging show people have poured forth their memories on paper and on talk shows, retailing those same stories of long, long ago.

So this collection mainly consists of period pieces, some from the silent era, many in black and white, not colorized, I hope. Because I had collected the anecdotes out of sequence, I had to edit hundreds of bits and pieces into a montage of verbal images. They are taken from larger pictures and tell only part of the story. I selected the shots I needed for my continuity, with many scenes ending up on the cutting room floor. The result may not be Hitchcock, Bergman, or Fellini, but I will be satisfied if the reader said afterwards: *That's Entertainment.*

P. H.

Los Angeles
June 1990

Movie Anecdotes

CHAPTER 1

Past History

Visionaries

Auguste Lumière, who with his brother Louis invented modern cinematography, gave the following advice back in 1895:

"Young man, you can be grateful that my invention is not for sale, for it would undoubtedly ruin you. It can be exploited for a certain time as a scientific curiosity, but apart from that it has no commercial value whatsoever."

Adolph Zukor hired Edwin Porter in 1912 to make six pictures a year for Famous Players.

"There isn't that much talent in the world," said Porter.

When Warner Brothers shocked the film world with the announcement of *The Jazz Singer* (1927), the first feature film with sound, a reporter sought out Irving Thalberg on his honeymoon for comment.

"Novelty is always welcome," opined the all-powerful production chief of MGM, "but talking pictures are just a fad."

Not all the Warner brothers were behind the innovation which was adopted out of a make-or-break desperation by their studio. When Harry Warner heard about plans to break the sound barrier, he said:

"Who the hell wants to hear actors talk?"

Panic in the Aisles

D. W. Griffith has been credited, among many other technical innovations, with the invention of the close-up, although some historians attribute it to his cameraman, Billy Bitzer. Not everybody hailed this new development. When the financial backers first saw an actor close-up in the projection room, they were startled.

"It's murder," opined one of them. "Whoever heard of a face with no legs in sight?"

"Museums are full of masterpieces with nothing but large and arresting faces," Griffith retorted. "If the face tells what I mean it to tell, an audience will forget all about legs, arms, liver and lungs."

Henry Marvin, Griffith's boss at Biograph was even more blunt.

"We paid for the whole actor, Mr. Griffith," he is supposed to have said: "We want to see all of him."

Abel Gance, the French pioneer who sometimes has been called "the D. W. Griffith of Europe," also got into trouble with introducing close-ups into his film *Barberousse* (1916).

"What are these huge pictures supposed to mean?" asked his producer, Louis Nalpas, threatening to close down production. "You'll have people panicking in the cinema. They'll make for the exits!"

The Rest Is Silence

When Jimmy Durante's first picture, *Roadhouse Nights*, was released in 1930, his father Bartolomeo went to see his son on the big screen three times. Asked what he thought of the movie, the elder Durante adapted Hamlet's view of the world to the talkies. He simply said:

"Talk! Talk! Talk!"

Overnight Success

Ben Lyon came to movies from the theatre. The change to sound caught him in an endless project with Howard Hughes, called *Hell's Angels*

(1930), which took two years to make because Hughes was a perfectionist and he also insisted on making both a silent and a sound version. This was an era when studios were turning out pictures in four weeks, and by the time he emerged from *Hell's Angels*, Ben Lyon was practically forgotten. So when his friend Henry Duffy invited him back to act on the stage in a legitimate play, Lyon jumped at the chance to work. It was in a Los Angeles revival of *Boomerang*, a Broadway play Lyon had done ten years before, and since he was working for almost nothing, the actor invited everybody in Hollywood to remind them of his existence. The theatre was packed with directors, producers, and studio executives, and when Lyon made his first entrance and uttered his first line, there was a stir and a buzz that went through the audience, reaching him on stage:

"My god, he can *talk!*"

That week Lyon got three movie offers and he was a star again.

Read My Lips

There was much speculation in the silent era about what words were actually formed by the actors' lips. One story had a girl being carried by her lover to bed in a tender swoon, while her lips read: "If you drop me, you bastard, I'll kill you."

Conrad Nagel, one of the silent era stars, knew of one rehearsal in which an actor with a hangover was trying to lift an actress unsuccessfully from the floor.

"Use your breath," she advised him, "that's strong enough to do the job."

Bring on the Wits

As silent movies developed literary story lines, producers began to look to sophisticated wits who could write titles that "hit the back wall," as the jargon had it. Herman Mankiewicz, in the vanguard of the journalistic Broadwayites to be seduced by Hollywood, excelled at composing cards that packed a one-two punch. "Derely Devore, the star, rose from the chorus because she was cool in an emergency—and warm in a taxi," he wrote for a film called *Take Me Home* (1928). For *Three Week-Ends* (1928) Mankiewicz wrote: "I've got as much chance to wash in private as a six month old baby." Another title read: "Paris, where half the women are working women . . ." followed quickly by: ". . . and half the women are working men."

Fire

Joseph Mankiewicz, Herman's younger brother, recalled the panic stars felt in front of the microphone. One day there was a fire at Paramount, and Clara Bow ran out screaming:

"I hope to Christ it was the sound stages!"

Problem

Like many a worried silent star, Marion Davies went to see *The Jazz Singer*. She watched the first talking picture in quiet concentration. At the end the mistress of William Randolph Hearst turned to the MGM publicity man who had escorted her, and said:

"M-m-m-ister Voight, I-I-I have a p-p-problem."

A Sound Deal

The breakthrough of sound pictures caught most studios off-guard. MGM tried to get into the act by putting together an anthology of the greatest silent stars, and selling it with the slogan: "Hear the stars talk!" The most famous silent actor of course was a mime. Charlie Chaplin was asked if he would do two minutes of talking in front of the camera.

"I was in a jam," Chaplin later said, explaining how his reputation for being money-mad had come about. "If I agreed to do it I should have made a fool of myself, because I had never spoken on the screen and it could harm the picture I was making. If I refused, everyone would have thought me crazy to turn down the offer of good money for a couple of minutes. They went away muttering, but at least my reputation as a commercially minded film man was intact."

A Tramp Is Born

One of the important motion picture pioneers was William N. Selig, a young magician and showman, who was among other things responsible for the career of the great black comedian, Bert Williams. In the mid-1890s, Selig acquired a purloined copy of a Lumière Cinematographe, the French machine which could both take and project moving pictures. Up to his time the story of cinematography was mainly that of technological innovation. As Terry Ramsaye chronicles it in A Million and One Nights, *finally somebody became interested in what the new medium could do to provide entertainment.*

The early Selig pictures were made about the streets of Chicago and in backyards when it was desirable to escape the curious passersby. One of the classic first Selig productions was *The Tramp and the Dog*, a backyard comedy. It was nearly a hundred and fifty feet long. In this startling drama a tramp knocks at the back door for a hand-out and is chased off the premises and over the fence by the vigilant bulldog. An unforeseen happening added vastly to the success of this picture. As the tramp clambered over the fence the dog attached himself with great tenacity to the seat of the tramp's ragged pants. There was a brief struggle in which the genuinely frightened actor tumbled down the outside of the fence as the dog dropped back victorious with a large mouthful of pants in full view upstage, center.

The bulldog scene was a tremendous hit, just as it would be today. Here was the discovery for the screen of the basic humor of pants. Pants have always been a joke, despite all efforts to dignify them as trousers. Motion picture comedy without pants would be unthinkable.

Initiation

It is difficult to meet anyone with extensive dealings with movie people who will not have some horror story of having been cheated, bamboozled, or deceived. The early motion-picture business was lawless, cut-throat competition between trusts and robber barons, who ruthlessly exploited the original inventors or circumvented their patents. American film-makers moved first from Manhattan to Fort Lee, New Jersey, and then to California, primarily to escape the law. Fred J. Balshofer, one of the pioneer cameramen, describes, in One Reel a Week, *how he got initiated into the business in 1905 in the shop of Siegmund "Pop" Lubin, an optician turned entrepreneur.*

After two years with the Shields Lantern Slide Company, I had saved a little money, so I decided to take a vacation in south Jersey near Atlantic City. On the way home it was necessary to change trains in Philadelphia. I took the opportunity to take a few days to see the city. As I strolled along Eighth Street, my attention was caught by a store with the entrance between two plate glass windows. Gold letters on one window read "Siegmund Lubin, Optician" and on the other "Manufacturer of Moving Pictures." Moving pictures were now magic words to me, and on an impulse I entered the store. I hardly anticipated that this moment would change my career and start me in an industry where I would remain the rest of my working life.

After a moment Mr. Lubin came from the back of the store. He was a bald-headed, stoop-shouldered man, well over six feet tall, and when he talked he really mangled the English language. I told him I would like a job in his moving picture company. Lubin didn't say a word but looked me over like he was appraising a horse before buying it. I stood awkwardly embarrassed until he finally spoke. "You can vaste tousands of dollars if you don't know vat you are doing in diss moving picture business," was Lubin's first remark. "What makes you think I don't know what I'm doing?" I responded. "I know photography and I have been making illustrated song slides for the past two years." Mr. Lubin's sole reaction was a slight smile. Then I told him of my years with Underwood and Underwood. "You make money?" Lubin inquired. I told him I'd been doing just fine. "Then vy don't you stay in the singing business?"

I explained to Lubin that there had been a decline in the use of song slides and that I thought that moving pictures were a growing business. This seemed to make an impression on him and, after further conversation, we settled on a week's trial. I was so afraid I might not have a chance, even for a week, of learning something about the moving picture business that I forebore to ask Mr. Lubin how much he planned to pay me.

The real surprise was that for several weeks I never had the chance to photograph anything. I was kept busy in the laboratory in the basement of the store making duplicates of pictures that had been produced in France, by the Méliès company and Pathé Frères. We called them "dupes" from of course "duplicates." I simply printed a negative from a positive print and from that duped negative made as many positive prints as Lubin could sell to his customers. In those days each moving picture company had its own trademark which was usually placed in some prominent place in the picture to ensure its visibility. The Méliès trademark was a star, and Pathé used a rooster in a circle. I spent a lot of time blocking out the trademark on each individual frame under a magnifying glass, using a camel's hair brush dipped in opaque.

When customers came to the store to buy moving pictures, Mr. Lubin brought them down to the laboratory and I would show some of our duped pictures on a small screen. When the selection had been made, the customer paid in advance. Then I would make the prints to be shipped. It required little intelligence to know that this was shady business, but Mr. Lubin carried on the practice as if it were perfectly ordinary and completely legitimate. . . .

In my two years with Lubin, there is one incident I don't think I'll ever forget. He asked me to screen some pictures for a prospective buyer who didn't disclose his identity but said he was in the market to buy some films. As we sold to anyone who had the cash, Lubin hustled the customer into a small screening room where I was waiting to grind the projector, which was set up without a booth. After showing a few of the pictures made by Lubin without a sale, he had me run some dupes. Among them was *A Trip to the Moon*, one of Méliès's best pictures. Practice had made me quite expert at blocking out the trademarks, and the job on this picture was so good it was hard for our customer to believe his eyes. Suddenly he jumped up from his chair, shot his arm out in front of the beam of light from the projector, and shouted, "Stop the machine." Startled, I stopped grinding and turned on the light. Lubin stared at him wondering what was wrong. We found out soon enough when the prospective buyer shouted, "You want me to buy that film?" Lubin wanted to know why not. "I," the man bellowed thumping his chest, "I made that picture. I am Georges Méliès from Paris." The man, quite naturally, was in a wild rage. Lubin glared at him and, pointing to me, brazenly began telling Méliès what a hard time I had had blocking out the trademark. Lubin's defiant attitude stunned Mr. Méliès, and he stood there speechless. Lubin seemed to consider the incident a joke, and I was dumbfounded when he went out laughing. I didn't see the humor of the situation as Méliès was in such a rage he could have become physically violent, but he soon stamped out of the room. After that, whenever I was asked to run dupes for prospective buyers I was always a bit fearful.

The Past Is Prologue

The quest for originality in movies has a long history. One of the first pictures wholly made in Hollywood was *The Law of the Range* (1911), shot by Al Christie for the Nestor Company. After establishing a studio near the corner of Sunset Boulevard and Gower, Christie took a tour. He looked in on his scenario editor, and asked him what he was up to.

"I'm working on a scenario," said the writer.

"Do you think it will make a good picture?" asked the boss encouragingly.

"Why not?" the scenarist replied, "it always has."

The King of Comedy

The first satire about the movies, *The Small Town Idol* (1921), naturally found favor with the critics. One of them praised its producer, Mack Sennett, by likening him to Molière. The king of comedy was pleased and showed the review to his title writer, Johnny Grey, asking him:

"Who is this fellow Moly-something?"

D. W. Griffith, who happened to overhear the question, cut in:

"Molière was a smart French plagiarist who hired three men to do his thinking for him."

To Catch a Thief

D. W. Griffith, forgotten but not gone from Hollywood, was asked by journalist Ezra Goodman what he thought of Orson Welles's innovative *Citizen Kane* (1941). The veteran director replied that he "particularly loved the ideas he took from me."

Gold Rush Days

Although movies were made in many locations all over the world, and businesses sprang up in different countries, only one place became an industry town, coeval and synonymous with making pictures. Jack Hasty, an old-fashioned newspaperman, covered the second gold rush that began in California around 1910, which he recalled in his book Done With Mirrors *(1943).*

The mythical city of Hollywood had not as yet arisen out of the smoke of press agents' speeding typewriters. Where it is now presumed to stand was a dry and desolate area stretching north of Los Angeles, a dusty, discouraged expanse of terrain dotted with rubbish heaps, sign boards, dilapidated chicken farms, and the remnants of exploded subdivisions. The moving-picture business was scattered all over Southern California. Bronco Billy Anderson was producing the first horse operas at National City, close to the California-Mexico border. Lubin had a studio at Coronado in San Diego Bay. American Beauty Films were shooting in Santa Barbara. There were other studios in Burbank, and Culver City, and on the fringes of Los Angeles—studios which, if you were to mention them today, would draw only blank looks—Reliance, Peerless, World, Kalem, Christy. The industry was booming. There were opportunities for everyone, and with reasonable luck anybody could get a place in the Klieg light.

The Cinderella touch was everywhere. Sales girls became stars. A well-known "madame" landed as the head of a casting department, and for a time kept an eye on her former profession, as she didn't believe pictures would last. On the screens of a hundred thousand nickelodeons flashed names which only a few months before had appeared on factory and department-store payrolls. The legitimate stage was as contemptuous of the new art as in a later day the movies were contemptuous of radio; and performers came from almost every vocation except that of the theatre. Cullen Landis drove a truck; Edward Burns sold stocks; William Duncan ran a physical-culture school; George Walsh was a lawyer; Allan Hale was an osteopath. The top scenario writer of the period was a girl still in high school, a girl named Anita Loos. But an ex-sign painter ran a close second, and was fated to hold the highest paid scripting job in the City of Celluloid for a great many years.

These were the roaring gold-camp days. The pioneers, who with a dollar and an extra shirt had hit the trail westward, were striking it rich and spending it riotously. Life ran turbulently, played for high comedy and lurid melodrama. Few spots offered as many laughs as did the old Alexandria Hotel when a bunch of the boys and girls were whooping it up of a Saturday night. The evening commenced heavy with decorum and much polite flitting from table to table, exchanging compliments; but by eleven o'clock, when the crowd got down to serious drinking, you learned what picture stars really thought of each other. Waiters were run ragged escorting out drunks and breaking up brawls. Love making went on practically underfoot. It was '49 all over again, but in evening clothes and ermine. Gold! Gold in California! They had discovered it, and this was their night to howl. Like true pioneers, most of them died broke and not a few with their boots on— William Desmond Taylor, Olive Thomas, Thomas Ince—a long list of them. . . .

Pictures were a good source of copy, but the copy was not good. The Arbuckle party which resulted in the death of Virginia Rapp, the story of Wally Reid, the story of Blanche Sweet—these and other scandals made headlines throughout the world, headlines which hit the moving-picture business where it hurt most—in the box office. Through morality clauses in contracts it was possible to exercise some control over the private lives of picture people, but it was much more possible through well-organized press departments to exercise control over what was printed about picture people. And so typewriters began to click; typewriters building word upon word the mythical city of Hollywood.

Lunatics

United Artists was formed in 1919 by Mary Pickford, Douglas Fairbanks, Sr., Charlie Chaplin, and D. W. Griffith. When Richard Rowland, president of Metro, heard news of their venture he expressed the opinion of the whole industry: "The lunatics have taken charge of the asylum."

Like so many witty expressions of the period, the phrase may have originated with Wilson Mizner who described these early years of moviemaking circa 1916: "That was before the bankers had got into the saddle and the inmates were still running the colossal asylums—just where they were running them to was an immediate problem."

Several generations later, when stars wielded even more power in the film industry, some of the artists came to join the lunatic fringe.

"You spend all your life," Jane Fonda was once quoted as saying, "trying to do something they put people in asylums for."

Volunteer for the Asylum

Will Rogers, a big star on Broadway with the Ziegfeld Follies, *was actually living near a mental institution when Rex Beach advised Samuel Goldwyn to use the cowboy-actor for the lead in* Laughing Bill Hyde (1919), *based on one of Beach's novels. A few years later, Rogers himself described how he got into the movies.*

I didn't have any more intention of going into pictures than I had of being president of Yale. I was living quiet and peaceful down in Amityville, Long Island, where the insane asylum is, when Mrs. Rex Beach came driving down there one day.

She steps out of her royalty on *The Spoilers* and says: "Will, you're goin' into the movies."

I pointed over to the place where they kept the lunatics and told her chauffeur he had come to the wrong place.

"No, Will, I'm serious," Mrs. Beach says.

I told her my hair wasn't curly, that I couldn't roll a cigarette with one hand, and that I didn't aim to annoy more than one audience at a time.

"You've got to come, Will," she insisted. "The movies is the third biggest business in the world. Safety razors is first, corn plasters second, and movies third."

Well, I went in. Since then the movies has become the second biggest business in the country. Bootlegging is the biggest. The movies is the grandest show business I know anything about. It's the only place where an actor can act and at the same time sit down in front and clap for himself.

From Such Acorns

In 1923, when the name of Will Rogers was a great deal better known than that of the fledgling Warner Brothers, Jack Warner approached the cowboy vaudevillian about signing him for a part. Rogers sent back a wire that hung framed for decades in Warner's office:

I MIGHT FLY OUT OF HERE AND TO THE LEGION CONVENTION AND WORLD SERIES • BUT IF I DONT AND DONT GET A BETTER OFFER WILL BE GLAD TO BE WITH YOU • WHERE IS YOUR STUDIO?

The Warner brothers had begun in business by converting a storefront in Newcastle, Pennsylvania, into a theatre, borrowing the chairs from a nearby undertaker. When there was a funeral, the moviegoers had to stand.

The First Fifty Years

According to Arthur Mayer, living pictures were first used in vaudeville houses as "chasers" between acts to drive out the patrons. "Indeed," he wrote in 1953, "the history of motion pictures might well be summarized to date as starting with drive-outs and culminating with drive-ins."

Trendsetters

Theda Bara was the first star to have a screen personality specially tailored for her by William Fox, who did start his career as a tailor. "Is it only a coincidence," asked British film critic Stanley Walker, "that he, like some of his most powerful rivals, spent part of his early working life in the garment trade where success depended above all on creating new styles, then persuading people that they wanted them? Fox cut suit linings, Goldwyn sold gloves, Zukor was a furrier, Laemmle's family had owned an outfitter's."

Joseph P. Kennedy entered the movie industry in the mid-1920s and quickly rose to become chairman of Pathé. His business methods were greatly disliked by the founding moguls, and Marcus Loew remarked about the Irishman:

"What's Kennedy doing in pictures? He's not a furrier."

A Goldfish Named Goldwyn

Samuel Goldfish, who began his career as a glove-maker, formed Goldwyn Pictures in 1918 with the brothers Archie and Edgar Selwyn. When this venture failed, Archie Selwyn complained that his former associate had not only lost most of the Selwyns' money, but had also appropriated one-half of his name. Hollywood wits often wondered what would have happened if young Goldfish had taken the first half of the Selwyns' name and the last of his own. Then the famous malapropisms might now be called Selfishisms.

Day Care

Balaban & Katz were one of the early firms to make their fortune in the exhibition of motion pictures, starting in Chicago in 1917. They had to solve many problems as they occurred. Because in those days children under seven were admitted for free, it was difficult to police or verify the right age of every kid who claimed to be under seven. One of the younger Balaban brothers, Dave, decided how tall the average seven-year-old should be. He drew a chalk mark, and kids had to line up under it, in order to get free admission, regardless of age.

Arthur Mayer also relates, in his book *Merely Colossal*, that Abe Balaban set up a combination of valet/day-care service, to keep crying babies out of the picture palaces. The baby carriages were left on the sidewalk outside—in those more innocent days—allowing the mothers to enjoy the show inside. The buggies were numbered, and if one of the tots cried too much, the management would flash a slide on the screen:

"Mother Number 47, your baby is crying."

Rude Awakening

When Mary Pickford went to see Violin Maker of Cremona (1910), *one of her first pictures, she came up against the law:*

I glided proudly up to the theatre with the self-satisfying knowledge that I was a full-fledged motion-picture star, earning five dollars a day!

In front of the advertising display, I admired a picture of myself through a golden mist and tripped lightly over my dream cloud to the ticket window and clinked down a dime.

"Whatcha age, Goldilocks?" snapped the man, "you gotta be sixteen to get in here!"

Arguments failed. I walked away, a wilted lily—old enough to make movies, but not old enough to see them!

Sideshow

Most Hollywood studios are impregnable forts. The one exception has been Universal which discovered early that people are willing to pay money to peep backstage at how movies are made. King Vidor, who arrived in Los Angeles in 1915, remembered "a circus spieler was employed to escort the visitors through the studio and even during the filming of highly emotional scenes the sonorous voice of the professional guide resounded throughout the set and merged with the tinny raspiness of the portable organ employed to keep the actors in the proper mood. The visitors were charged twenty-five cents per head and the studio realized hundreds of dollars per day out of this annoying by-product."

Blind Justice

In the early days of Universal Pictures, Carl Laemmle had come through another round of litigation over patent infringement that was endemic to the industry. After the customary delays, the suit finally got to court in New York. Laemmle was on the West Coast, when he received a cable from his lawyer. It simply read: "JUSTICE HAS TRIUMPHED."

The mogul immediately wired back: "APPEAL IMMEDIATELY."

CHAPTER 2

Real to Reel

If You Must Know

Motion pictures, because of the enormous technical complexity involved, is the ultimate art form of our technological era. As Francis Ford Coppola once observed, very few inside the profession are familiar with more than one or two aspects of film-making. And, despite the avalanche of magazines, behind-the-scenes and interview programs, the whole process of how films are made remains a complete mystery to the average moviegoer.

Walt Disney was once showing a journalist around his studio, who asked:

"How do you stumble, Mr. Disney, on all those remarkable technical developments?"

Disney pointed to a building marked "Research Department."

"Well, you see," he said in his slow, deliberate way, "we maintain a Stumbling Department just for that purpose."

Director John Rich was taking some outdoor shots for a Western, filming one scene for the seventh time. In a break, while the shot was being set up again, a woman stopped her car to watch. She asked:

"Why do you keep taking the same scene so many times?"

"Madam," said the director wearily, "have you ever stopped to consider how many theatres there are in this country?"

Real Tinsel

Hollywood discovered early that genuine realism has to be staged. In 1914 Mutual Films, in search of documentary footage, signed up Pancho Villa, the populist bandit of Mexico, and accompanied him on one of his expeditions to fight the Federal troops. Villa agreed—for a consideration of $25,000—to fight all his skirmishes by daylight, and only after movie cameras had been put in place.

Villa kept his side of the contract, and his troops never went into combat unless they were accompanied by Mutual's crews bearing the emblem: "Mutual Movies Make Time Fly." However, when the studio executives viewed the footage, they found it too tame for their picture. So they decided to reshoot the battle scenes in a studio, where everything could be under greater control.

Arthur Mayer tells a similar story, when Paramount sent a crew to Nevada to shoot an atomic bomb test for *War of the Worlds* (1953). Finding the blinding flash and mushroom cloud inadequate, the special effects department was given the task of producing a more thrilling blast.

Comedies of Errors

The early studios cranked out movies at such a rate that errors were bound to occur. One day copies of a script were left accidentally in the mailbox for two directors, who went out and both shot the same movie. To prevent a loss, one of them was retitled and released a few months later, by which time nobody could remember whether they had seen it before.

Director King Vidor also recalled an incident when two studio drivers picked up each other's instructions and delivered their carloads of actors to the wrong location. Rather than waste half a day, the directors of each project simply recast their scripts as best they could and proceeded with the actors they had.

Through a Fog Darkly

Robert Newton's drinking sometimes made him confused. Once he was supposed to be working on a movie called *The Beachcomber* (1938); instead he turned up on the set of an English movie, called *Always in the Fog*.

'There happened to be a part for an adult delinquent, and since it was a low-budget movie, the director was delighted to have the services of a major star for free. Newton had shot four scenes before the producers from *The Beachcomber* had tracked him down and hauled him away.

Superstitious Natives

A film called *The Adventuress* (1946) was being made on the Isle of Man, and the cast was taken each morning by car to the set. Along the route a little bridge had to be crossed, where the native driver insisted that everybody had to greet the fairies to forestall disaster. Everybody in the crowded automobile complied, except Deborah Kerr, star of the movie. She refused to say "good morning" to the fairies, because she thought it was silly. The driver refused to cross the bridge. Clouds gathered and it started to drizzle. The stand-off lasted an hour, while both the producer and the director implored Miss Kerr to bow to tradition. Finally she mumbled "good morning" to the fairies—and the sky cleared and all was well with the world.

The Miracle

Occasionally in the making of a motion picture something actually turns out better than was planned. It is rare enough that such an event can be attributed to divine intervention. In appropriately awestruck prose, Richard Fleischer described how he lucked on to a shot while directing a biblical epic for Dino De Laurentiis.

On the morning of February 15, 1961, on a windswept hill near the medieval village of Roccastrada, some 120 miles north of Rome, the screen version of *Barabbas* began with the most unique sequence ever filmed.

The scene was so emotional and impressive, in fact, that hundreds of villagers who had gathered to watch the film company at work dropped to their knees and prayed, while most of the film crew hurriedly blessed themselves as they worked. It was a moving, unforgettable moment.

The unique sequence was the re-enactment of the Crucifixion of Christ against the total eclipse of the sun. This was a once-in-a-lifetime coincidence—the sun to be in total eclipse at the same time that a re-enactment of the Crucifixion was about to be filmed.

It took a producer with imagination to see the possibilities of this combination and then to make full use of it. Mr. De Laurentiis pushed this one sequence six weeks ahead of the scheduled start of actual production in order to take advantage of the unique lighting this natural phenomenon would offer, identical with that which must have prevailed on that fateful day, nearly 2,000 years ago, when, according to the Gospel of Luke, 23:44, "There came a darkness over the whole land. The sun was in eclipse."

This scene has made film history, for it is a real "first" in motion pictures. In fact, many of his own staff told Mr. De Laurentiis it couldn't be done; that it was impossible to shoot directly into the sun, and that when the eclipse was total there would not be enough light for the Technirama and Technicolor cameras. They insisted it was too costly a gamble.

But the producer decided to take the risk and sent a cast and crew to Roccastrada, to at least make an attempt to photograph the scene. That his insistence paid off is now history.

Chief Cinematographer Aldo Tonti had no precedent for this particular shot, so he was forced to rely on instinct. But his judgment proved perfect and he captured on film a moment that may never again be repeated. Later, viewing the results, everyone was amazed to see something on the screen that no artificial lighting on a sound stage could ever have duplicated. As the sun began to emerge from the eclipse, it sent rays of light up and out that formed a perfect cross of golden light in the sky, directly above the cross on which Christ was being portrayed. A miracle was provided by nature.

Even in the darkest moment of the eclipse, the outlines of the three crosses are still visible, adding drama to a scene already almost unbearable in its emotional beauty. It was during this darkest moment that the onlookers dropped to their knees and prayed. The combination of the eclipse and the re-enactment of the Crucifixion made it seem terribly real to the several thousand persons on that windswept hillside.

Cowboys and Indians

King Vidor was filming a Western near Gallup in New Mexico, with a group of Zuni Indians as extras. During one setup Vidor noticed some of the braves riding towards him, right up to the camera platform which towered above the horses. Leaning down, the director asked what they wanted.

"When do we go home?" their spokesman asked.

"Are you not satisfied with the food or your living quarters?" asked Vidor.

"Everything okay," said the brave. "But we are tired of playing cowboys and Indians every day."

John Ford employed real Indians in *Fort Apache* (1948), most of which he shot in Monument Valley. The director also got into the habit of finding out each morning what the local medicine man forecast for the day's weather. The predictions were remarkably accurate, and the film people came to rely on them more and more. One morning, there was no weather report. Questioned by Ford, one of the Indian actors told him that the medicine man did not have an answer yet:

"His radio broke down."

Smoke Signals

Another charming story told by Teet Carle and Richard Webb in their book *The Laughs on Hollywood* took place during one of the Westerns being shot by George Sherman in Navajo country. One particular scene involved the creation of smoke signals used for communication by the Indians. The special effects people had laid down a large quantity of explosive charges some five miles away, and these were set off when the director gave his order via a walkie-talkie. An enormous column of smoke rose behind the hills, and as the crew and cast stood in silent awe, one buckskin-clad Navajo actor was heard sighing:

"God, I wish I'd said that."

A scene in *The Fabulous Texan* (1947) required smoke signals sent by the local Indian tribe. Producer Edmund Grainger hired Indians from a nearby reservation to make sure it was performed correctly, and afterward congratulated them for a job well done.

"No problem," replied one of the Indian consultants, "we learned it from the movies."

In Darkest Africa

When MGM was making *King Solomon's Mines* (1950), they needed some scenes with primitive tribes. The moviemakers arrived in the Congo, the heart of the African jungle, and were appalled to find the natives wearing tennis shoes and Hawaiian shirts. Worst of all, their hair was slicked down and did not look right. Finally, MGM solved the problem by shipping two hundred Afro wigs from Culver City and the tribesmen agreed to wear them.

The Living Desert

Sometimes a director will ask for a small addition or change of the set at the last minute which will tax the ingenuity of the people around him. One well-known story about Oscar Lau, a legendary prop man, took place during the filming of *The Trail of the Lonesome Pine* (1936), one of Henry Fonda's early movies.

Henry Hathaway was directing the picture on location in the high desert about an hour and a half from Los Angeles. He was about to break for lunch, having set up the shot of a simple burial, when he casually mentioned to Oscar Lau that the freshly dug grave in the next scene would require fresh flowers. Hathaway had been a prop man himself and delighted in posing difficulties for his former colleagues. He now happily went off to lunch with his stars, leaving the panicked Lau with the problem of finding fresh-cut flowers in the middle of the desert in autumn.

After lunch, just as the stars were gathering around the grave, and Henry Hathaway was discussing the shot with his cinematographer, Oscar Lau arrived in a cloud of dust and with a dazzling bouquet of fresh flowers. The scene was shot, and the happy prop man told his story. He had remembered that a passenger train always stopped around noon for about half an hour in the desert town of Mojave to take on extra water. Driving at top speed, Lau had just managed to catch it, and by slipping ten dollars to the dining room steward, he could pick all the flowers he wanted from the tables.

The Rainmaker

Sometimes the preparations prior to production, no matter how meticulous, go to waste not because of a mistake or weather. During the making of *Shane* (1953) George Stevens thought it would be desirable to have a rainstorm during the cemetery scene at Boot Hill. Rain usually falls only when one does not want it, and the location in the wilds of Wyoming had no river or lake nearby to provide reliable and sufficient water. Scouting around the area a good three months before shooting began, Harry Caplan, who was unit production manager, found an animal watering hole. He brought in bulldozers to create a small underground reservoir almost seventy square feet. He bought several gas tanks of the type that are buried underneath your local gas station, and supplementing these with portable army reservoirs, he rigged up hoses to sixteen stands with nozzles which could spray water to simulate rain. Extra water would be trucked in.

A couple of days before shooting the scene, George Stevens visited the set. He inspected the terrain from a raised camera platform. All the elaborate rigging for the rainstorm was artfully hidden or outside the camera's range. After a few minutes, the director climbed down:

"Harry, I've decided to do something else. Scrub the rain," he said, walking away. Without another word, the stunned Harry Caplan began to dismantle the work of several months.

Nobody Is Indispensable

Frank Capra was having problems with a scene which had a parrot in the background. Unfortunately, the bird had picked up the constant megaphonic cry which precedes shooting on a movie set: "QUIET PLEASE!" Every time the director called "Action!" the parrot would ruin the scene by screaming "QUIET PLEASE! QUIET PLEASE!" When nothing worked to achieve silence, Capra fired the parrot.

And That's the Way It Is

While filming *Jaws* (1975) in Martha's Vineyard, Steven Spielberg became friendly with Walter Cronkite, still the CBS anchorman at the time, but who was on vacation and pursuing his favorite hobby of sailing. One day Cronkite watched the testing of the mechanical shark, when everything went wrong. Instead of leaping out of the water, the shark became twisted in the cable which controlled it from a hydraulic platform, and only the tail appeared. Seeing Spielberg's total humiliation, Cronkite remarked:

"Have you ever considered a career in broadcasting?"

Final Cut

Directors always fear that they might be removed from their pictures and the final cut would be made by the producer or some studio hack. Steven Spielberg, who shoots his films in such a way that no editor could make head or tail of the sequence of shots without his presence, likes to repeat a story told to him by William Wellman about the making of *Wings* (1927).

The director was falling so far behind schedule that the investors fired him. Faced with a mass of footage that cohered only in Wellman's head, they were forced to come back and rehire him. Wellman, whom James Mason once described as "a tough little bastard," enjoyed the discomfiture of his producers, and became more resolved than ever to shoot his films his own way.

The Director's Nightmare

One of the classic, and probably apocryphal stories about the problems of film-making has Cecil B. De Mille preparing for the biggest and costliest shot in one of his colossal epics. At a given signal from the director, high above the battle, thousands of chariots, horses, and extras are engaged in battle, which rages for quite a while, until De Mille shouts: "Cut!" The smoke and dust clear, the director turns towards his cameramen to see whether everything was okay, when he hears his cinematographer call out: "Ready, when you are, C.B.!"

Something fairly similar did occur when William Wellman was direct- ing Wings, *the first movie to win an Oscar. An enormous field outside San Antonio had been mined to re-create the battle of Saint-Mihiel of World War I. It was to start at a signal from a little red flag from the ob- servation tower, specially constructed, where the director stood with a large number of city officials to watch the awesome destruction. Producer Jesse L. Lasky was also up there.*

Acres of carefully planted TNT were set to go off in chain explosions. Two thousand soldiers—Americans and Germans—were standing by with guns in hand. Fifty Army planes, with engines idling, were ready to take off from nearby Kelly Field at the noise of the first blast. Everything was ready—*everything but the cameras!*

Up in the tower, the little daughter of one of the city dignitaries spotted a friend.

"Yoo hoo, Mildred! Here I am," she yelled . . . waving the direc- tor's red flag.

There was no stopping the futile battle of Saint-Mihiel.

Conversion

John Stahl, the first director whom Louis B. Mayer hired soon after his ar- rival in Hollywood as a young executive, refused to observe budgets or schedules and insisted on working at his own pace. This annoyed the fu- ture czar of movies, who began to call Stahl an uncompromising bastard behind his back. Unfazed, the more experienced director laughed it off:

"All is forgiven when you have a good preview."

Now for the Good News

Yankee Doodle Dandy had its principal day of photography on the day after Pearl Harbor. The actress Rosemary DeCamp recalled how she was listening with Walter Huston and Jeanne Cagney to President Roosevelt on the radio that the United States was at war with Japan and Germany. At that point director Michael Curtiz came on the sound stage with Jimmy Cagney, and they all listened in silence for the national anthem to finish. As the two women dabbed some tears from their eyes, and the men were deeply moved, Curtiz said in his best Hungarian accent:

"Now boys and girls, we have work to do. We have had bad news, but we have a wonderful story to tell the world. So let's put away sad things and begin."

Liberties

During World War II, after the Soviet Union and America became allies, there was a great deal of government pressure suddenly to produce pro-Russian films. That is how Jack Warner agreed to undertake *Mission to Moscow* (1943), based on Ambassador Joseph Davies's book of the same name. (A few years later, during the anti-Communist witch-hunt, this patriotic act came to haunt Jack Warner, who publicly apologized for making it.) The film was shot in a documentary style, which meant that an unusual amount of attention was being paid to historical and factual accuracy. The young Jay Leyda, later to become an important critic and film historian, was hired to do research, because he had worked with Eisenstein and knew the Soviet Union first-hand. Screenwriter Howard Koch remembers how Mike Curtiz, a director with typical Hollywood regard for authenticity, told Leyda at their first meeting:

"Your job is to make everything accurate, but don't forget I have to take liberties."

Technical Expertise

Aristotle may have written that drama is the imitation of action, but most movies take this bit of ancient wisdom quite loosely: stories based on real people's lives, or on carefully crafted fiction, end up on the screen bearing only the faintest resemblance to the original.

The King brothers, Maurice and Frank, independent producers of exploitation movies in the forties and fifties, tried to improve their image as people who really cared about accuracy and detail. They were planning to make a picture called *The Man in the Moon* and contacted Albert Einstein at Princeton as the ultimate expert about the secrets of the universe.

"Sorry," Einstein wired them back, "but I am not competent in this matter."

Tyrone Power was having problems grasping some of the symbolism in *The Razor's Edge* (1946), the novel by Somerset Maugham. After he had asked one question too many, Darryl Zanuck exclaimed:

"Do I have to bring my barber here for technical director?"

Early Tolkien

Samuel Marx was story editor at MGM in the forties. He was visited one day by a man who wanted a job as technical expert on mythical kingdoms.

"I spent most of my life in them and I know all about them," he claimed.

Grand Illusion

Film critic Judith Crist was devastated to learn from Mervyn Le Roy that the tornado in *The Wizard of Oz* (1939) was created by a swirling silk stocking in front of the camera.

"I've never forgiven him for telling me that," Crist has said, "and when I watch *The Wizard of Oz*, I know that it's *not* a silk stocking."

Made in Japan

In trying to make *The Yakuza* (1975) as authentic as possible, director Sidney Pollack became immersed in the culture of the Japanese underworld after whom the picture is named. As part of the price of getting the services of Takakura Ken, a star of Japanese gangster movies, Pollack undertook to shoot the film in a Japanese studio controlled by the Yakuza. One of the peculiarities in the code of honor of this Oriental equivalent of the Mafia (which becomes a plot point in Paul Schrader's script of *The Yakuza*) is the voluntary removal of a joint from one's finger for any mistake or dishonorable act. The joint is then wrapped up and presented as penance to the wronged party.

As soon as Sidney Pollack arrived at the studio in Japan, he noticed a number of employees walking around with hardly any fingers on any hands. And soon after work got under way, one of the transportation people made a mistake in picking up an American star arriving at the airport.

"Afterward," Pollack reminisced during a Tarrytown Film Weekend, "he came into the production office with the first joint of his little finger wrapped up in a handkerchief—and he presented it to the production manager as an apology."

Acting Is Where You Find It

Despite the careful details that go into preparing a film, some of the most memorable or telling moments come about by accident. Waiting for the sets to be built for *Rashomon* (1950), Akira Kurosawa was passing the time with the actors at a Kyoto hotel by running 16mm prints. He recalled that one of them was a Martin Johnson jungle film which had a fairly standard shot of a roaming lion. The director told his star, Toshiro Mifune, that he wanted him to be just like that lion. Then Masayuki Mori remembered another jungle film with a black leopard. They screened it, and when the large cat made its menacing appearance, Machiko Kyo hid her face.

"I recognized the gesture," Kurosawa told an interviewer. "It was just what I wanted for the young wife."

Given such inspiration, it is interesting that Kurosawa was criticized for making the acting technique in *Rashomon* "too traditionally Japanese."

Samurai Bergman

More frequently Kurosawa had been labeled as a Western-style director, in the tradition of Shingeki. As an example of how the few great directors in the world influence each other, Ingmar Bergman was asked about his opinion of *The Virgin Spring* (1959) some ten years after he made it. Bergman called it a "touristic, lousy imitation of Kurosawa." He said he made it when he was infatuated with the Japanese cinema:

"I was almost a samurai myself!"

Until Then—Ciao!

Luchino Visconti was an exacting perfectionist. If something had not been set up properly to his liking he simply went on strike. Burt Lancaster remembers arriving with the director to a Sicilian village during the making of *The Leopard* (1964), when Visconti noticed that some of the houses had anachronistic television antennas. Although he might have been able to shoot around them, he ordered his art director to remove every one of them.

"When they are down," he said, "we will shoot. You'll find me at my hotel."

Candid Camera

In making *North by Northwest* (1959), Alfred Hitchcock needed to film in the lobby of the United Nations building in New York. However, permission was refused on orders of Dag Hammarskjold, who instituted the ban after excessive disruption caused by *The Glass Wall* (1953). The director was forced finally to build a miniature of the lobby, but not for lack of trying.

"While the guards were looking for our equipment," Hitchcock told François Truffaut, "we shot one scene of Cary Grant coming into the building by using a concealed camera. We'd been told that we couldn't even do any photography, so we concealed the camera in the back of a truck and in that way we got enough footage for the background. Then we got a still photographer to get permission to take some colored stills inside and I walked around with him, as if I was a visitor, whispering, 'Take that shot from there. And now, another one from the roof down.' We used those color photographs to reconstitute the settings in our studios."

Hitchcock also sought in vain to get permission to shoot on location the famous chase scene over the monumental stone heads of the presidents at Mount Rushmore. He had to rebuild the landmark in the studio, as the Master recalled, "because to have Cary Grant get a sneezing fit in Lincoln's nose was considered an insult to the shrine of democracy."

Reality

Preparing to film *Sweet Bird of Youth* (1962), Richard Brooks was consulting the author of the play.

"Make sure you shoot it on the Gulf," Tennessee Williams urged, "because you can't find these locations anywhere else." Brooks spent some time scouting locations in New Orleans and along the Gulf states. On his return to California, he decided he could save a great deal of money by shooting in and around San Diego. Brooks did not tell Williams when he first screened the film for him where he found his locations.

"It just shows you," said the contented playwright, "when you have the real thing—how [good] it looks."

Fury and Sound

Like many German refugees in the 1930s, Fritz Lang arrived in Hollywood with a minimal knowledge of English. He gave authenticity to his first American script, *Fury* (1936), by copying suitable items from newspaper clippings. Under the studio system, once a script and its budget had been approved, no further changes were allowed without permission from the front office. Following a preview of *Fury*, the supervising producer, Joseph Mankiewicz, summoned Fritz Lang into his office and accused him of having changed the approved screenplay.

"How could I change the script," the director protested, "when I can't even speak English?" Mankiewicz sent for the script and began reading it.

"Damn you, you're right," he admitted, "but it sounds different on the screen."

Don't Try This at Home

In making the epic film The Bible *(1966), John Huston faced the problem of getting the animals to file into the ark two by two, as required in the Good Script:*

Finally I found a trainer who said it could be done, and he devised a way at enormous expense. We built a road that led through the ark and ditches on either side of the road. First the animals were led singly just around this circuit to the ark, and then two animals would be led, and finally when they had become used to this, nylon lines were attached to bridles and the men led them within the ditches. Then they would add another pair of animals, and each pair had been worked separately, at first singly and then in pairs, and then we added to the pairs, and finally came the time when the bridles were taken off and the animals walked altogether two by two around into the ark.

Dear Deer

Director Victor Fleming went on location to Florida to shoot some of the nature scenes in *The Yearling* (1946). When no footage was coming back, the studio sent a telegram telling him to speed things up. Fleming wired back:

JUST SAT DOWN AND READ SCRIPT AND YOUR TELE-GRAM TO DEER • FEEL SURE HE WILL DO BETTER HERE-AFTER.

Getting His Goat

Peter Lorre had to milk a goat in a scene, but he couldn't get the hang of it.

"Better get it right the next time," urged the animal's owner from the sidelines, "there's only one more take left in the goat."

CHAPTER 3

You Ought To Be in Pictures

Hobson's Choice

Allan Dwan, one of the pioneer film directors, found his career by accident. He was working as an engineer for a Chicago-based movie company, which sent him out to California to investigate a production in trouble. Dwan arrived in San Diego and found a bunch of actors waiting around for the director, who had disappeared on a binge. He telegraphed the home office, and a wire came back instructing him to take over the project. Dwan had never faced actors before, but he knew that somehow he must get them on his side. Calling together the cast he told them:

"Either I am a director—or you are out of your jobs."

Beginners

When Hal Roach, another Hollywood veteran, got his first directing assignment, he was afraid that all the technical staff would laugh at his inexperience. He was especially scared of Fred Jackman, his cameraman, who looked as though he had grown up in the business. On the first morning Hal Roach copied every gesture of Fred Jackman's, and was careful only to speak in the most technical jargon. They shot a scene that day in which Harold Lloyd rolled down a steep, rocky incline, but when they saw the rushes the next morning, it appeared as if he was going along level ground. The camera angle was such that it straightened out the incline, which meant that the whole sequence would have to be shot again, causing another series of bruises for Harold Lloyd. Tormented by his conscience, Hal Roach took his cinematographer aside:

"Fred," he said meekly, "I have a confession to make. I've never directed a picture before."

Jackman looked him manfully in the eye. After pausing for a second or two, he said:

"Hal, I've a confession to make, too. I never worked on a camera before yesterday."

Ogre

Josef von Sternberg, who almost gave definition to the tyrannical director, worked hard to gain his reputation as an ogre. The British actor Clive Brooks recalled sharing a room on a Welsh location, where the Austrian was working as an assistant director. One morning Brooks saw young Sternberg staring a long time at his visage in the mirror.

"Which is more horrible," he finally asked. "With or without a moustache?"

"What do you want to look horrible for?" asked the actor.

"The only way to succeed," said the director, "is to make people hate you. That way they remember you."

Later in life, on the university circuit, Josef von Sternberg was frequently asked by aspiring students what qualifications were needed to become a film director. He would tell them that a director must speak several languages; he must know the history of theatre and drama from the beginning of time. He must have some psychiatric training and be expert at psychoanalysis. Once a student asked:

"Mr. von Sternberg, did you know all that?"

"No," he replied, poker-faced. "But then I never asked anyone how to become a director."

Why I Became a Director

Director George Roy Hill is a fine amateur musician, who studied composition at Yale. David Shire had done for him the score for *The World*

According to Garp (1982), and they were chatting during a scoring session while the orchestra took a break.

"I wish I could be doing your job," the reticent director told the composer with frank envy. Shire, who is also a Yalie, asked why Hill had not pursued music further.

"I was in my senior year," George Roy Hill explained, "studying with Paul Hindemith. For my senior thesis I had composed a sonata for piano and violin. Several weeks after I had turned it in, I was summoned by Professor Hindemith. He was sitting in his office.

" 'Mr. Hill,' he said, 'I've looked at your sonata, and I also saw the excellent production of Gilbert & Sullivan you did recently at your residential college. I am prepared to graduate you, if you give me your solemn pledge that you will not write any more music.'

"It was at that moment," George Roy Hill concluded, "that I knew I was going to be a director."

In college John Badham wanted to be an actor but could never get cast. He noticed that there was a guy down in front of the stage always surrounded by girls.

"Gee," asked young Badham, "how do you get to meet all these girls?"

"Well," said the man, "you have to be the director."

Easy As One, Two, Three

Roger Corman is famous not only for his low-budget movies but also for giving a good many talented people their early break in pictures. Peter Bogdanovich was a *cinéaste* writing about film for *Esquire* and the Museum of Modern Art when he got a call from Corman asking whether he would like to try his hand at directing a picture. The producer told Bogdanovich that he could do absolutely anything he wanted within the following parameters:

1. Boris Karloff owed Corman two days' shooting, during which Bogdanovich should squeeze about twenty minutes of screen time out of Karloff, who was eighty years old and dying of emphysema.

2. To supplement it, there was another twenty minutes that Corman would let Bogdanovich have from an earlier movie he had made with Karloff called *The Terror* (1963).

3. "Then you get together a bunch of actors," Corman told the novice director, "and shoot for about ten days another forty minutes and you've got an eighty-minute Karloff picture I can release."

And that is how Peter Bogdanovich got to make *Targets* (1968), "his" first feature film, for $130,000.

Shoot First, Talk Later

Steve Kovacs began in movies working for Roger Corman. "I was production assistant at first, and soon became head of production," he recalls, "and the only difference was that with the second job I had access to a secretary."

One of his first assignments was to supervise *Deathsport* (1977), which was being shot near Agoura, some forty miles northwest of Los Angeles. One day, the first-time director began to be abusive towards the leading lady, Claudia Jennings, until David Carradine, the star, came to her aid by roughing up the man. It was a hot and dusty day, and all work came to an abrupt end. Kovacs called Roger Corman and told him what was not happening.

"Why don't you just go ahead," demanded Corman, "and keep shooting."

"The situation is very tense, Roger," Kovacs explained to the boss, "I think you'd better come out."

In about forty-five minutes Corman arrived in his Mercedes. He drove up right to the camera, got out, and said to the production manager and the cameraman:

"Let's set up the next shot."

Only after the scene was in the can did Corman take care of the human problem, which was all smoothed out by the evening.

Close Encounter

For those fascinated by the early development of great achievers, Leah Adler, the mother of Steven Spielberg, provides a stream of conscious information. Fred Bernstein interviewed her for his book The Jewish Mothers Hall of Fame *at her kosher restaurant "The Milky Way" in Los Angeles.*

Practically every day, someone at the restaurant—often someone who mistakenly addresses her as "Mrs. Spielberg"—asks her if she always knew that Steven was a genius.

Leah has an answer ready: "When he was growing up, I didn't know he was a genius. Frankly, I didn't know what the hell he was. I'm really ashamed, but I didn't recognize the symptoms of talent. I

did him an injustice. I had no idea back then that my son would be
Steven Spielberg.

"For one thing—and he'll probably take away my charge accounts
for saying this—Steven was never a good student. Once, his teacher
told me he was 'special'—and I wondered how she meant it.

"You see, Steven wasn't exactly cuddly. What he was was scary.
When Steven woke up from a nap, I shook." Long before *Gremlins*,
Steven was a master at creating terror. He practiced on his three kid
sisters. Says Leah, "He used to stand outside their windows at night,
howling, 'I am the moon. I am the moon.' They're still scared of the
moon. And he cut off the head of one of Nancy's dolls and served it
to her on a bed of lettuce.

"The first thing I'd do when we moved to a new house was look for
a baby-sitter," Leah says. "But it didn't work, because they wouldn't
let us go out for more than a few hours without taking Steven.

"Once," Leah remembers, "I took Steven to the Grand Canyon. He
said, 'This is nice,' and then he threw up. With Steven, you held on
for dear life.

"I mean, I didn't know how to raise children," Leah continues.
"Maybe we were more normal than I remember—but I sincerely doubt
it. Steven's room was such a mess, you could grow mushrooms on the
floor. Once his lizard got out of its cage, and we found it—living—
three years later. He had a parakeet he refused to keep in a cage altogether. It was disgusting. Once a week, I would stick my head in, grab
his dirty laundry, and slam the door.

"If I had known better," she says, "I would have taken him to a
psychiatrist, and there never would have been an *E.T.*"

. . . When he was fourteen, Steven made his first full-length movie,
a sci-fi flick called *Firelight*, and he got a theatre in Phoenix to show
it. It was Leah who put up the letters on the marquee. "I thought,
'This is a nice hobby.'" Incredibly, the film made money, and there
was no stopping Steven. Once, Leah says, "he wanted to shoot a scene
in a hospital, and they closed down an entire wing. Another time, he
needed to shoot at an airport, and they gave him a whole runway. Nobody ever said no to Steven. He always gets what he wants, anyway,
so the name of the game is to save your strength and say yes early."

At least once, she should have said no—early. Steven wanted to do a
scene (similar to one in *Poltergeist* twenty years later) in which something horrible came oozing out of Leah's kitchen cabinets. She not
only agreed but went to the supermarket and bought thirty cans of

cherries, which she cooked in a pressure cooker until they exploded all over the room. "For years after that," she jokes, "my routine every morning was to go downstairs, put the coffee on, and wipe cherries off the cabinets."

The Kid

George Lucas's first foray into the world of professional movie-making was a documentary he called 6–18–67 because of the date he finished shooting it. Columbia Pictures had given scholarships to four apprentice film-makers—two graduates each from the leading film-schools of the University of Southern California and the University of California at Los Angeles—with the idea that they would shoot short films about Carl Foreman's star-studded Western, *McKenna's Gold* (1968), which was being shot around the spectacular Canyon de Chelly in northern Arizona. Lucas avoided the trap of making a movie about the making of another movie; instead he filmed the landscape, the desert wildlife, with distant shots of the antlike activities of the Hollywood film crews. Foreman had opposed Lucas's idea, but the 22-year-old filmmaker refused to yield, saying that he was not interested in doing a promotional film under the guise of a training scholarship.

The veteran producer, who could be quite a bully, backed down and later openly admired the film. He also remembered Lucas's giving him a piece of advice. After one lunch-break, when the whole cast and crew were waiting around for the sun to come out, Lucas observed to Foreman that they could be rehearsing the scene while waiting, rather than wasting the light later. Foreman fought off his instinct to tell the young man to go wipe his nose, and went to ask the British director J. Lee-Thompson, another veteran, whether he had rehearsed yet. He had not, but thought that it was a good suggestion.

"I was both embarrassed and impressed," Carl Foreman later told writer Dale Pollock. "That director hadn't done something that the kid knew to do."

Discoveries

Every profession has its legend of how somebody was discovered or suddenly managed to get a lucky break. The most cherished Hollywood story concerns the 16-year-old Julia Turner, who was playing hooky from school and sat in a sweater sipping a strawberry malt. This historic event took place in 1936, though not, as has been retailed to generations of tourists, at the soda fountain of the late lamented Schwaab's drugstore, but a couple of miles to the east in Hollywood, at the Top Hat Malt on Sunset and Highland Avenue. There William Wilkerson, publisher of the *Hollywood Reporter*, who had been watching the well-developed teenager for some time, finally went up to her and popped the question:

"How would you like to be in pictures?"

Within a very short time, Wilkerson took the girl to Zeppo Marx, who ran a talent agency, and she was asked to think of a new name. She came up with Lana herself. Her first appearance in a sweater and a walk-on part in Mervyn Le Roy's film, *They Won't Forget* (1937), made her an instant star. Yet the first time "The Sweater Girl" saw herself on screen she was embarrassed by the garment she had made famous.

"I looked so cheap," she complained.

One block down from the Chinese Theatre is C. C. Brown, Hollywood's most elegant ice cream parlor, founded in 1929. This is the birthplace of the hot-fudge sundae and also the spot where agent William Demarest discovered Ellen Drew, selling chocolates. He took her to Paramount for a screen test, and when she became a star, Miss Drew returned to Brown's to help christen the Cinderella sundae in her honor.

Success Has Many Fathers

Orson Welles took credit for discovering Judy Holliday. In fact, she worked as a telephone operator at the Mercury Theatre, and Welles never suspected she had any talent.

Rudolf Seiber was assistant to the young Alexander Korda in Berlin and asked the director if his wife might get the tiniest bit part in their current movie. Korda told him that the lady had not the slightest potential as a film actress. Frau Seiber became better known as Marlene Dietrich.

Great Rejections

The movie world thrills almost as much to stories of rejection as to discoveries, provided that the rejected unknown consequently reached stardom. Looking at a screen test of Fred Astaire, some genius at RKO wrote a succinct report: "Can't act. Slightly bald. Can dance a little." Astaire, who disliked his own face and did not believe that the camera could keep his fancy footwork in focus, must have looked elsewhere to rebuild his confidence in the short period before he became, with Ginger Rogers, Hollywood's biggest box-office attraction.

Bette Davis did a test after Arthur Hornblow, Jr., saw her in *Broken Dishes*
(1929) on Broadway. Samuel Goldwyn, who was looking for a leading lady
in *Raffles*, watched the film and was reported to have yelled: "*Whom* did
this to me?" Davis was not surprised because, when she saw the test herself, "I ran from the projection room screaming."

Clark Gable was still trying for a career on the stage, even after he had
moved to Los Angeles. Discouraged with occasional work as a bit player
or extra, Gable told the talent scout who first offered him a screen test:
   "Why waste my time and your money? I've tried movie work often
enough to know I have nothing Hollywood wants."
   With the revolution brought about by talkies, stage actors were suddenly
in demand. Gable liked to tell the story how Lionel Barrymore, for whom
he had worked in the theatre, suggested that he make a test for a film
Barrymore was directing at MGM. As soon as Gable reported on the lot,
hairdressers curled his hair, he was stripped and given a G-string, a prop
man stuck a knife into it and put a hibiscus behind his ear. Barrymore told
him to creep through some bushes, as if looking for a girl. There were no
lines to speak. When Irving Thalberg viewed the test he called the director
and said:
   "You can't put this man in a picture. Look at him!" Lionel Barrymore
tried to stick up for his protégé:
   "He's young, but he'll be all right."
   "Not for my money, he won't. Look at his big, batlike ears."

A little later Clark Gable was tested at Warner by Mervyn LeRoy, and
overheard Jack Warner yell at him:
   "Why do you throw away five hundred dollars of our money on a test
for that big ape? Didn't you see those big ears when you talked to him?
And those big feet and hands, not to mention that ugly face of his?"
   Within a year the *Hollywood Reporter* announced to its readers that a
new star was born. "Never have we seen audiences work themselves into
such enthusiasm, as when Gable walks on the screen."

An Awkward Peasant Girl

On a visit to Berlin, Louis B. Mayer saw *Gösta Berling* (1924), a four-hour
film made by the Swedish director Mauritz Stiller, and was impressed by its
star, Greta Gustaffson. He invited her on the spot to come and work at
MGM, but only on condition that she take off some weight.

"We don't like fat girls in my country," he informed her through an interpreter.

When Greta arrived in New York in the summer of 1925, accompanied by her lover and director Stiller (he insisted that he be included in her contract), Mayer suggested to the front office that they meet the newest star in the MGM firmament. Major Edward Bowes was the only one who did and left wondering about Mayer's judgment:

"What an awkward peasant girl she is!" he said of the woman, who within a few short years would conquer the world. Meanwhile in Hollywood, Howard Dietz, head of the publicity department, called a meeting to decide what new name to give her.

"Garbo sounds too much like garbage," he said.

After arriving on the West Coast, Greta Garbo spent hours wandering around the MGM lot waiting for her first assignment. During one of these walks, noticing a fig tree outside the costume department, she picked a fig on an impulse and ate it.

"Those who saw her do it, gaped," noted Samuel Marx wryly; "no one had ever done that before. There was a widespread belief that fruit which grew inside a movie studio must be inedible."

What's in a Name?

Lucille Le Sueur was discovered by MGM executive Harry Rapf, who decided that her surname sounded too close to "sewer," so a nationwide contest was launched to find a better name. A woman in Albany, New York, won $500 for coming up with Joan Crawford.

Doris Day was born von Kappelhoff. Orchestra leader Barney Rapp changed her name, over her protest, after the song "Day after Day."

Anne Bancroft first appeared under her own name Anna Italiano, and then Anna Marno. She chose her current name from a list drawn up by Darryl Zanuck.

"Bancroft was the only name," she later said, "that didn't make me sound like a bubble dancer."

Actor Dane Clark was originally Bernard Zanville from Brooklyn, and received his less ethnic name when he signed on as a contract player with Warner. He was bitterly unhappy with his new name, and one day a fellow thespian played a cruel gag on him by saying that he had just been informed his name was being changed to Bernard Zanville.

"They can't do that to me!" screamed a.k.a. Clark, "that's my name!"

MGM publicist Howard Dietz once gave the following genealogical account of a typical Hollywood transformation:

"She was born Tula Ellice Finklea. Her baby brother nicknamed her Sid. She joined the Ballet Russe and became Felicia Sidarova. This was subsequently changed to Maria Estamano. She married and became Mrs. Nico Charisse. At the start of her screen career she took the name Lily Norwood. MGM changed that to Sid Charisse and she was fianlly billed Cyd Charisse."

Metro-Goldwyn-Mayer, in its golden age under Louis B. Mayer, once hired an actor named George Mayer. As usual, he was instructed to change his name.

"Mayer is not a good name for success in the movies," said one of the executives.

Maurice Joseph Micklewhite began acting on the English stage as Michael Scott. Soon he had to join Equity and the union already had a member with that name. After a discussion of the problem with his agent, the actor caught sight of the word "Caine" on the marquee of the big cinema on Leicester Square. The rest of the title was obscured.

"It's a good job the trees were in the right place," Michael Caine recalled, "otherwise I would have been called Michael Mutiny."

Just Say No

Even before Bette Davis arrived in California, the publicity men of Universal's office in New York told the stage star that she had a great name for a secretary, but it completely lacked glamour for the movies. Claiming that they had given the matter a great deal of thought, they told her that Bettina Dawes was the perfect name for her.

"*Bettina Dawes!*" Miss Davis exploded. "I refuse to be called 'Between the Drawers' all my life!"

Baptism

With the inevitable triumph of sound, Hollywood turned to Broadway to find actors who could talk and act at the same time. William Fox signed

Muni Wiesenfreund, the Austrian-born actor who had risen to stardom by playing old men in the Yiddish theatre of New York. As soon as the actor arrived in Hollywood, a Fox producer suggested that he make his first name his last.

"I like Muni for a last name," he opined. "It's short and catchy."

"So is Rin Tin Tin," the newly baptized actor retorted.

The studio immediately released the news that "Mr. William Fox has personally discovered the celebrated Russian actor, Paul Muni." On hearing this, the star told his wife Bella:

"I not only have a new name, I have a new nationality!"

"Russian," she explained to her husband, "is a polite word for Yiddish."

Sauerkraut

Joseph Schildkraut, another Austrian-born actor, was proud of having come from a line of great players. He was more than a little peeved at a Hollywood party when a woman compounded her failure to recognize him by suggesting:

"You know, you really should be an actor."

"Madam," he replied pompously, "my name happens to be Schildkraut!"

"Oh, that's too bad," said the young lady brightly: "but you can change it and nobody will know the difference."

What Was It Before?

Tony Curtis was brought to Hollywood by agent Joyce Selznick. His early career grew from the infertile soil of desert epics, in one of which, while riding on top of a dune with Piper Laurie, he uttered the immortal line: "Yonda lies the castle from my fodda!" In fact, Curtis was born Bernard Schwartz in the Bronx; and his father had come over from Hungary—lately the actor has established a fund in his father's memory to help restore the main synagogue in Budapest. As his career grew at Universal, Tony Curtis brought out his family to Hollywood. He was showing the studio to his father, when they came upon Oscar Brodney, a writer-producer. After being introduced, Brodney could not resist asking:

"Tell me, Mr. Schwartz, why didn't you like the name Curtis?"

If At First You Don't Succeed

Kirk Douglas knew that it would be hard to make his way in American society with the name he was born: Issur Danielovitch. So he changed his name to Izzy Demsky.

Patriarch

Kirk Douglas is as fiercely proud of his four sons—Michael, Joel, Peter, and Eric—as of any of his creations on celluloid over a career of fifty years. An old-fashioned paterfamilias, Douglas stayed close to his children over decades by writing to them constantly from every film location all over the world, proffering fatherly advice on every subject, whether they wanted it or not. All of them ignored his basic advice—to stay out of the movie business.

"They never had my advantages," the veteran actor said in an interview; "I started out poor."

The Answer to Every Girl's Prayer

Gabriel Pascal, the maverick producer of several Bernard Shaw films, was looking for a fresh face to play a young Salvation Army girl in *Major Barbara* (1940). He was telling his friend Richard Norton over lunch at the Savoy that he wanted a pure, innocent girl with a spiritual face.

"That's going to be difficult," Norton opined. Pascal scanned the dining room and his eyes rested on a girl having lunch at a nearby table with an older woman. He got up and went up to them, placing his hands on the girl's shoulder in a familiar manner.

"Are you a virgin?" the producer asked without preliminaries. The girl blushed, but before she could answer, Pascal explained who he was and about his mission.

"I have a feeling you can act," he said. "Please meet me in the lobby after lunch and recite something for me."

The producer was not far wrong. The young woman was a dancer at Sadler's Wells and did have ambitions of acting. She and her friend left their lunch and rushed for the ladies' room, where they rehearsed the only monologue the girl knew from a Spanish play called *Cradle Song*. When she began reciting it for Pascal, he stopped her almost immediately.

"Do you know the Lord's Prayer?" he asked. She nodded and her recital of it brought tears to the producer's eyes.

"You are the girl," he said simply, thus launching the career of Deborah Kerr.

The Scary Part

Not long after Peter Lorre came to Hollywood, he had been promised a part, but the producer had changed his mind. Lorre went to see him in the hope of reconsidering this decision. The Hungarian-born actor, who became famous through German films, was tongue-tied in English, so he just stood and glared at the producer with his bulging eyes. After about a minute of this, the man became truly frightened:

"Stop staring at me like this," he yelled at Lorre, "you can have your part."

Blondbeard

S. Z. Sakall, rotund comedy star who came to Hollywood just before the Second World War, was known in Hungary as Szőke Szakáll, or Blondbeard, a play on Bluebeard. He once explained his increased girth:

"Now I am a star but when I came over here I was just a starlet."

Playtime

Lucille Ball started in pictures as one of the Goldwyn Girls. She needed to stand out from a crowd of other beautiful chorines, so she devised a strategy of bringing herself to her boss's attention. She heard one day that Sam Goldwyn was meeting with his contract writers, so she drove the car up to the studio executive building and honked repeatedly. Finally, Goldwyn himself appeared on a second floor balcony and glared down at the pretty redhead, who smiled back at him as she asked disingenuously:

"Can the writers come out and play with me now?"

Better Late Than Never

George Cukor was speaking on a panel, which included Mike Frankovich, who was then production chief at Columbia Pictures. Cukor recalled how thirty years before Frankovich had wanted to break into pictures as an actor and Cukor had given him one line, which he kept fluffing.

"It was something really simple," said Cukor, "like—'Jack, your breakfast is ready.'"

"That wasn't the line," Frankovich rose to his feet. "It went, 'Your breakfast is ready, Jack.'"

Cukor glared at the executive for a moment and said:

"*Now* you remember the line."

CHAPTER 4

Cast to Type

There Are More Things in Heaven and Earth

Along with every other female star in the world, Katharine Hepburn coveted the role of Scarlett O'Hara. David O. Selznick terminated their interview quickly, telling the angular star:

"I can't imagine Clark Gable chasing you for ten years!"

Scarlett Fever

After David O. Selznick had announced that he must find an unknown to play Scarlett O'Hara, an unprecedented talent search got under way. One actress, after she had been rejected during a New York audition, followed George Cukor to Atlanta, where she boarded the train and tore through every carriage in search of the elusive director. Cukor had been warned and while the woman was forcibly held on the platform he clambered on to the coal wagon.

Meanwhile back at Selznick-International, a huge packing case was delivered, with a notice: "OPEN AT ONCE." As the secretary followed the instruction, a young beauty sprang out and ran into Selznick's office, where she began to strip while trying to recite lines in the character of Scarlett.

Irene Mayer Selznick, married at the time to David Selznick, recalls a truck bringing another large package to their Beverly Hills home on a Sunday morning. Inside, a giant facsimile volume of the cover of *Gone with the Wind* revealed yet another hopeful in period costume.

"Merry Christmas Mr. Selznick," she announced. "I am your Scarlett O'Hara."

The Real McCoy

As practically everybody in the whole world knows, it was David Selznick's brother Myron, an agent, who brought Vivien Leigh and her secret lover, Laurence Olivier, to watch the burning of Atlanta—the cumulated sets of previous pictures—on the back lot of Selznick-International. Since no Scarlett had been found yet, three pairs of stand-ins of different shapes and sizes were being used in silhouette against the flames which raged on thirty acres. Watching from an observation platform on that evening of the 10th December 1938 was David O. Selznick, surrounded by a few of his executives. As the red flames lit up Vivien Leigh's beautiful face—"hair stirred by the breeze," in the words of her friend Jesse L. Lasky, Jr., "eyes like fire opals beneath the circle of her wide-brimmed black hat"—Myron Selznick made the famous introduction:

"Hey, genius," he said with post-prandial joviality to his brother, "I'd like you to meet your Scarlett O'Hara."

Despite the legend that David O. Selznick later wove around this meeting ("I took one look and knew she was right,"), the reality was somewhat different. A "cold reading" was arranged on the spot with George Cukor, but she still had to have a screen test, which would follow final tests for Jean Arthur, Joan Bennett, and the front runner, Paulette Goddard. During Vivien Leigh's test with a bored Leslie Howard, who afterwards admitted that he had never read the book, Cukor warned her to cut out any temptation to sentimentality:

"She's not a fucking Peter Pan, darling," he cautioned. During the almost two weeks that followed, Vivien Leigh gradually gave up hope about her long-shot candidacy for the part of the century. There were many strikes against her. Although Hollywood likes to talk about fresh talent, it usually feels safer with a well-known star. Would the women of the South accept a Scarlett who was not one of them? Worse, one who was from Europe, a part of the world that an increasingly isolationist America was trying to ignore? And there was the possibility of a scandal, if the illicit relationship between Olivier and Leigh, each still married to somebody else, ever came to public notice. The young actress was under contract to Alexander Korda, the maverick Hungarian who was reshaping the British film industry, and who had put her under contract when she was twenty-two.

It was at George Cukor's crowded, noisy Christmas Day party in 1938 that the director told Vivien Leigh with a poker face that the matter of casting had finally been settled. Having armed herself against failure, the actress tried to sound indifferent:

"It must be a great relief to you, George."

"Oh, yes, vastly relieved," Cukor replied, and finally decided to put an end to her agony. "I guess we're stuck with you."

Postscript

One of the auditioning hopefuls for the part was Lucille Ball, then an unknown young actress on the RKO payroll. She had been drenched in a downpour on the way to Selznick-International and was trying to dry herself huddling in front of the fireplace in the producer's office when Selznick arrived. He gave her a scene to read, and only after he had thanked her, did Miss Ball realize that she had done the whole audition on her knees.

In a story typical of Hollywood fortunes, Lucille Ball and her husband Desi Arnaz later bought the studios of Selznick-International for producing their television series *I Love Lucy*. Out of nostalgia, or perhaps revenge served properly chilled, she chose for herself David Selznick's old office.

Cashing In

The search for Scarlett O'Hara resulted in 1400 interviews, of whom ninety were given screen tests, at a cost of $92,000. It had gone on so long and with such unprecedented publicity that Clare Boothe Luce wrote a highly successful Broadway comedy about it, *Kiss the Boys Goodbye* (1938). And Cecil B. De Mille told the press that he was launching a national search for a cigar-store Indian he needed in *Union Pacific* (1939). Later he got more publicity when he declared that he was forced finally to make the wooden statue in the studio's scene-shop.

All About Eve

Leo McCarey had commissioned a script about Adam and Eve from the novelist Sinclair Lewis. As word of this prestigious project began to spread around Hollywood, one of the famous silent screen stars came to the producer's office, dressed as an aging ingenue, wanting to play the part of the First Woman. McCarey looked at her and said ungallantly: "It's true I'm working on a new version of Adam and Eve—but not with the original cast."

(This story is often told of Cecil B. De Mille.)

Broken Nose

Charlton Heston apparently got to play Moses in the remake of *The Ten Commandments* (1956) because of his nose which he broke in college football. Doing his exhaustive research for the epic, Cecil B. De Mille noticed that Michelangelo's statue of Moses has his nose broken in the same place.

What About the Resurrection?

Cecil B. De Mille had a fierce loyalty towards old friends and people he had worked with. One who filled both these roles was the actor H. B. Warner, who had played Christ in De Mille's original version of *The Ten Commandments* (1923). Whenever Warner came to visit him, De Mille would cancel his appointments and spend hours talking about old times with his friend. Once, twenty years after they had worked together, the actor gently inquired whether there might be some role he could play in De Mille's current project.

"No," the director explained, "you played Christ so magnificently that the public identifies you with that part. It would be a terrible error if you ever accepted another part."

The Maid

For his ill-fated attempt to film Shaw's *Saint Joan* (1957), Otto Preminger personally auditioned three thousand young girls—out of eighteen thousand applicants. The 18-year-old Jean Seberg, a freshman from Iowa State College, was one of three finalists. After several takes during a screen test, she began to flag.

"What's the matter?" Preminger taunted her, "you want to quit?"

"I'll rehearse this until you drop dead," she hissed back at the bald tyrant.

Although Seberg both feared and hated "the terrible Otto," her next film with him, *Bonjour Tristesse* (1957), was described by François Truffaut as "a love poem from Otto Preminger to Jean Seberg."

Saint Joan was a flop and Mrs. Aki Hershey, who was a friend of both the director and the new star, said: "Actually, it was not Jean but Otto who played Joan of Arc."

Might Have Been

Sean Connery had quickly tired of his image as James Bond and began to hate the character that made him world-famous. George Lazenby replaced him in *On Her Majesty's Secret Service* (1969), but the public did not see the Australian as the sophisticated secret agent. The producers were desperate to find another Bond. At first they brought back Guy Hamilton, the director of *Goldfinger* (1964), who went on an international casting search in preparation for filming *Diamonds Are Forever* (1971), which Connery eventually and reluctantly did come back to do. But before that Hamilton happened to be watching an afternoon talk show in his hotel room in Los Angeles, when he saw somebody on the screen who seemed perfect for the part. He immediately called "Cubby" Broccoli, one of the producers:

"I've found James Bond." The fact that the man was an American did not worry Hamilton, and he quickly arranged a meeting with Broccoli, who was also impressed by the new face. The producer took the idea to a casting director at United Artists, who talked him out of it.

"He's just a stunt guy—he's going nowhere at all." The actor who almost became the new James Bond was Burt Reynolds.

Wanted—Dead or Alive

Burt Reynolds was approached repeatedly to play Clark Gable in *Gable and Lombard* (1976). He kept turning the producers down. Finally he told them:

"I'll play Tom Mix, because Tom Mix is dead. I only play dead people. But at night, when I turn on the television and I see Gable—he's alive."

No Pollyanna

Mary Pickford was among the first in a long line of movie stars who became prisoners of their own image. Even as she was making *Pollyanna* (1919), America's sweetheart was fighting her battle against what she called "that sticky stuff." In her late seventies she told the *New York Times* how during shooting that film "a fly lit on the tablecloth and I scooped it up and said, 'Do you want to go to heaven, little fly?' And I smashed it. 'Well, now you have, little fly,' I said. And they left it in the picture.'"

Not My Type

After making *The Sound of Music* (1965), Christopher Plummer was reported to have said that working with Julie Andrews was "like being hit over the head with a Valentine card."

And Moss Hart said about the star:

"She has that wonderful British strength that makes you wonder why they lost India."

When columnist Joyce Haber once wrote about Julie Andrews that "there's a kind of flowering dullness about her, a boredom in rowdy bloom," the star responded:

"She needs open-heart surgery, and they should go in through her feet."

Julie Andrews allegedly hates her wholesome image and has tried to shatter it with several roles against type. She even used to wear a protest button which read: "Mary Poppins Is a Junkie."

Pretty Boy

Early in his career Robert Taylor was labeled a "pretty boy" by the press because he played unmanly roles. His break came with *A Yank at Oxford* (1938).

"My picture was on the front page of every newspaper," the actor recalled, "with the caption: 'Taylor has hair on his chest.'"

The Curse of Dracula

Even though Béla Lugosi's career was entirely built on playing Dracula, he hated and despised this identification with the horror genre. He always described with proud exaggeration his beginnings as a star of the Budapest stage, and he longed to be considered a serious actor. Alan Brock, the Hungarian-born agent in New York who had arranged Lugosi's summer stock engagement in a 1948 tour of *Arsenic and Old Lace*, remembers the old actor confessing to him:

"I would never have accepted the original Dracula on Broadway if I'd known the dreadful and lasting curse it would have on my entire life and career. I could not escape the Dracula horror—ever! I'm ashamed, and sad!"

Almost Present at the Creation

Roland Young was starring in the Broadway hit *The Last of Mrs. Chesney* (1937), which was purchased by one of the studios. Since the success of the play was widely attributed to Young, he was brought to Hollywood to star in the screen version. He was soon put on a train back to New York, because it was decided that he was not the right type to play the role he had created.

Son of a Bitch

Rin Tin Tin, for long the top dog in Hollywood, never actually appeared in any of his films. On his first day at the studio, he took an instant dislike to Jack Warner and bit him on the backside. The mogul had the ungrateful hound banned from the lot. So it came to pass that an understudy, the son of Rin Tin Tin, stepped into the breach and won immortality.

Standing Tall

David O. Selznick poured his worries into his famous memos. Writing to Kay Brown in the story department about Ingrid Bergman, whom he had cast in *Intermezzo* (1939), the producer wrote:

"I note Bergman is five feet, nine and a half inches tall. Is it possible that she is actually this high and do you think we will have to use stepladders for Leslie Howard?"

Falling Short

The tall and heroic Christopher Reeve was telling Richard Dreyfuss, who is heroic but short, that he was thinking of playing one day the role of Fletcher Christian.

"What do you mean you're *thinking* about doing Fletcher Christian?" Dreyfuss burst out with indignation. "Give me your body for ten weeks and I'll *do* Fletcher Christian."

What We Do for Art

Putting on extra weight for a role is difficult because of the relatively short time an actor has to become fat, and the much longer time and discipline involved in taking off the weight. It also seems much harder on women than men. Robert De Niro entered the realm of legend when he put on fifty pounds for *Raging Bull* (1980), while poor Lynn Redgrave, who did the same for *Georgy Girl* (1966), has been forced to star in diet food commercials ever since.

Mistake

Originally Warner Brothers thought of *Casablanca* (1942) as a starring vehicle for Ronald Reagan and Ann Sheridan. But director Michael Curtiz wanted a tough guy to play Rick, and Jack Warner asked George Raft to do the part with Ingrid Bergman.

"Whoever heard of Casablanca?" said Raft in refusing to do it, adding graciously: "I don't want to star opposite an unknown Swedish broad." He later called it the biggest mistake of his life. Humphrey Bogart was the seventh choice in casting the part of Rick.

Lucky

The handsome Paul Henreid was listening to a fading actor complain about being pestered by female fans.

"You're lucky," sighed Henreid, who played the dashing Victor László in *Casablanca*, "you can send each one of them a lock of your toupee without endangering your appearance."

Age Cannot Wither

Ingrid Bergman said in an interview, when she was young, that she dreaded the years only between forty-five and fifty-five:

"Until forty-five I can still play a woman in love. After fifty-five I can play grandmothers. But between those ten years it is difficult for an actress."

Tallulah Bankhead was greatly annoyed by *Time* magazine's habit of always mentioning her age, along with everybody else's. She was complaining about the latest mention to her friend, the columnist Irving Hoffman, and asked him provocatively:

"Dahling, I don't look forty, do I?"

"Not any more," he said truthfully.

A Hungarian cartoonist by the name of Henrik Major was famous for his truthful portrayal of his subjects. But truth is not what movie stars necessarily desire, especially after they had reached a certain age. On a visit to

Hollywood, the artist captured Marlene Dietrich in a sketch, which the star found less than chivalrous.

"Your drawing shows me to disadvantage," she remarked frostily to Major, who replied:

"On the contrary, madam, my drawing has the advantage that you will still resemble it in twenty years."

Comeback

Marie Dressler had been a vaudeville actress and made some early movies, but by the late 1920s she was washed up and looking at want ads for house-keeping jobs in Hollywood. Then as now, it was difficult for an actress close to sixty (one who had called her autobiography *The Life of an Ugly Duckling*) to find any, let alone good parts.

However, her friend Frances Marion, the screenwriter, persuaded Irving Thalberg to cast Dressler in a silent comedy *The Callahans and the Murphys* (1927), and within four years she was voted the most popular actress and top box-office star in movies. MGM threw an elaborate party for the star's sixty-third birthday, causing the celebrant to remark:

"It's nothing special. I've been having birthdays for many years now."

Who's Counting?

William Meiklejohn, a producer at Paramount in the forties, once re-marked to a character actor:

"You gave your age here as forty. But I happen to know that you are at least fifty."

"Oh, no," said the actor, "I simply refuse to count the last ten years in Hollywood as part of my life."

The Role of His Life

Film is largely a naturalistic medium, and some directors have been both-ered that actors—just by being actors—may destroy the illusion that the movie is about real people. Luchino Visconti, one of the pioneers of Italian realism in the postwar era, became particularly well known for his efforts to find and cast people who not only had the right look but also were manifestly non-professionals.

Word got out that Visconti was about to make a movie, and an unem-ployed but enterprising actor managed to push his way to the director's office.

"Signor Visconti," he explained, "I realize that you are looking for non-professional people for your next film. I must tell you frankly that I am an actor, but I hardly ever get parts because I simply cannot act. My diction is laughable, my movements are awkward, I never know what to do with my hands. In a word, I'm a total amateur as far as acting is concerned—so perhaps you can use me!"

Visconti, who was visibly annoyed when the intruder began his soliloquy, broke into a smile and then into a laugh at his performance. He took a good look at him and said:

"Go to the casting director, and tell him that I want you to play the part of a terrible actor."

Real People

Vittorio de Sica also preferred non-professionals. He was always stalking the streets of Rome, on the lookout for the right type in his or her natural state.

"The good Lord has made people of every variety," he would say, "and if I search long enough I always find the one I'm looking for."

Once he followed an old man down the Via Veneto and startled him by offering him a role in his current project. The retired brigadier general said:

"You have insulted me, sir," and walked straight on.

During a trip to America, de Sica was asked what had become of the day laborer whom he had starred in *The Bicycle Thief* (1949).

"I'm afraid he has become an actor," the director replied contemptuously.

Back to Life

Federico Fellini is another Italian famous for picking faces he likes from the crowd. What happens to the lives of these amateur actors, after their brief moment in the Klieg light, is typified by this man described in Eileen Lanouette Hughes' behind-the-scenes diary of Satyricon (1969).

It is a cold, gusty day and Fellini, bundled in his sheepskin-lined jacket, his black fedora clamped firmly on his head, is directing the scene of Trimalchio and his cortege arriving at the entrance to his tomb. The guests are staggering down a dirt slope, some on foot, some being carried standing up in litters.

Finally, everything gets coordinated, and at two o'clock the funeral is over. Moro's acting career is also at an end and he can now go back to being plain Mario Romagnoli, the popular and proper Roman restaurant proprietor. The five thousand dollars he was paid was little enough recompense for the suffering he had to endure on the set and at home. "*Porca miseria!* Wretched misery!" grumbles Moro, "I got lumbago from lying on the triclinium and bronchitis from going around half nude with the toga. Do you know how many hours I had to lie on that damned triclinium? Two hundred and fifty hours, from nine until one and from two until six every day! Do you know what strength it requires to remain in that position, first on the right side and then on the left? From my thigh to my ankle, I haven't a hair left on my legs. There is absolutely nothing. They are smooth as if they had been shaved.

"And you know my wife wanted to repudiate me," he moans. "She is very religious and didn't like my being around all those nude women. And then, my son-in-law used to help me in the evenings to learn my lines, more than two hundred pages. Imagine how tiring! Once, without our realizing it, my granddaughter hid behind the door and heard some slightly off-color lines. She went right away to her mother and reported that her daddy and grandfather were telling dirty stories in the living room. It was the end of the world for my daughter, and my wife put on a long face. She said to me, 'For seventy years you lived a clean life and now, in your old age, you have ruined your reputation and become a dirty old man, kissing boys!' "

Life Imitates Art

Kam Tong, a Chinese-born American actor who later played on the television series *Have Gun, Will Travel*, began his acting career during the war as a Japanese villain in *Across the Pacific* (1942) with Humphrey Bogart. There was a shortage of real Japanese, because they had been deported and placed into camps as dangerous aliens. After a while Kam Tong became so convincingly Japanese that he found himself drafted into the OSS, the forerunner of the CIA, where he posed as a Japanese to steal secret documents.

Universal Pictures was looking for someone to play the role of Irving Thalberg in *Man with a Thousand Faces* (1957). By chance Norma Shearer spotted Robert Evans, who, she said, bore an uncanny resemblance to her late husband. Evans played the role so well that a few years later when the people at Paramount were looking for a top executive—somebody like the legendary Thalberg—they hired Robert Evans.

Tarzan Talks—Sort Of

Following his Olympic victories in 1924 and 1928, swimming champion Johnny Weissmuller was asked to make a screen test for the part of Tarzan, in the first sound version of Edgar Burroughs's saga. It was on that occasion that the future actor was supposed to have given birth to the line:
  "Me? Tarzan?"

Typecasting

Jesse Lasky contemplated making a film about the life of James Audubon, the ornithologist. He wanted to cast Errol Flynn in the role, saying that Audubon, too, "often pursued a specimen for weeks."

Staying in Character

During the filming of *The King of Kings* (1927), H. B. Warner took up with Sally Rand, an extra who played a slavegirl to Mary Magdalene. (A few years later she would cause a sensation with her fan dance at the 1933 Chicago World's Fair.) One day the two lovers arrived late on the set, and heard Cecil B. De Mille thunder from up on high through his megaphone:
  "Miss Rand, leave my Jesus Christ alone! If you must screw someone, screw Pontius Pilate!"

CHAPTER 5

No Acting, Please

Camera Shy

Sir Herbert Beerbohm Tree, the great English actor-manager at the turn of the century, consented to act in D. W. Griffith's version of *Macbeth* (1916). Unfamiliar with the medium, he turned up on the first day and pointed at the camera: "Take that black box away. I can't act in front of it."

Sarah Bernhardt was 67 when she played Marguerite Gautier in the film version of *La Dame aux Camélias* (1911). The Divine Sarah finally consented to appear on the screen because she wanted to be made immortal. But when she first saw her own Camille on the screen, Bernhardt fainted and spent some days ill in bed, from the shock of discrepancy between what she had felt in performance and how she looked.

"When I first saw my face on the screen," comedian Joe E. Brown once confessed, "in a closeup six feet high, I jumped up and yelled, 'It's a lie!' "

John Barrymore once said of film-acting:

"If you stay in front of the movie camera long enough, it will show you not only what you had for breakfast, but also who your ancestors were."

Who's Afraid of the Big Black Box?

Many stage actors have problems adapting to the camera. Louis Hayward, a Broadway actor who came to Hollywood in the late thirties, was so visibly shy of the big black box that after his first day on the set, as everybody was leaving, James Wong Howe invited him to stay behind. The veteran cinematographer had also asked his assistants to leave the camera behind, and he now proceeded to take it apart. Finally, the mysterious equipment was completely dismantled and lay with all its pieces in stacks in front of them.

"Now, Louis, take a look at this," Howe said. "Nothing but hunks of metal and glass. Are you really afraid of them?"

Sinking Low

A passionate admirer of Walt Whitman, the young D. W. Griffith wanted to be a writer. Trying to master the dramatic form, he was told by a friend to get some experience as an actor. According to Lillian Gish, when he informed his widowed mother of his intention to conquer the stage, she said:

"The Griffith men had indulged in many things, but no one has fallen so low as to become an actor."

Nickelodeons became all the rage, and Gus Salter, an old actor acquaintance, advised Griffith, who was going nowhere with his acting career, to try writing scenarios for the fledgling industry.

"I haven't reached the point," Griffith objected indignantly, "where I have to work in films."

But times were hard and Griffith decided to give it a try. When he told his wife he intended to write scripts, she remarked:

"What an awful way to make a living. But I suppose it will have to do until something better comes along."

Now We Have Television

One of the reasons trained actors for a long time looked down on acting in movies was the primitive direction they were given. Pioneer James Morrison recalled to Kevin Brownlow the early days at the Vitagraph Corporation, where a young director from England, Albert E. Smith, simply called out: "Number five!" and the leading actor would pull expression number five. Not to confuse matters, there were only five expressions in the known repertoire of acting.

Madge Bellamy was working on *Summer Bachelors* (1926), when director Allan Dwan asked her what she had been thinking about during the shooting of a sad scene. The actress replied that she had recalled some melancholy experiences in her own life.

"Well," said Dwan, "you should have been thinking about the muscles of your face."

Sleight of Hand

At the start of his career Burt Reynolds was doing the television series *Riverboat* at Universal. Whenever he could, the young actor would sneak out to watch in another part of the lot two of the greats—Spencer Tracy and Frederic March—working in *Inherit the Wind* (1960). He was particularly struck by Tracy's non-acting, which was in marked contrast with March's histrionic style. After a while, the older actor noticed the pudgy Burt Reynolds in his riverboat outfit, and said to him during a break:

"Are you an actor, kid?"

"Yessir, Mr. Tracy."

Then Spencer Tracy uttered the words that helped guide the young actor during his career:

"It's a great profession," he said, "so long as nobody ever catches you at it."

Less Is More

"Don't sell it," Charlie Chaplin used to direct actors who exaggerated everything. "Remember, they are peeking at you."

George Cukor was directing *It Should Happen to You* (1953) with Judy Holliday and a little-known actor by the name of Jack Lemmon. Used to the stage and being terribly eager to make a good impression, Lemmon was wildly overacting, and after each rehearsal, Cukor would ask him:

"Less, less, less!" Totally frustrated, Jack Lemmon finally asked:

"Mr. Cukor, don't you want me to act at all?"

"Dear boy," replied the urbane director, "you're beginning to understand."

Nothing Doing

Peter Ustinov's early film career included the role of playing a Dutch priest in a British war movie, *One of Our Aircraft Is Missing* (1942). He had been warned that screen acting, as distinct from the stage, mainly consisted of doing nothing. After he had rehearsed a scene with Hugh Williams, the veteran actor asked him with elaborate politeness:

"Excuse me, young man, what exactly are you going to do in this scene?"

"I don't really know, Mr. Williams," Ustinov shrugged, "I thought I'd do nothing."

"Oh no, you don't," Williams replied with just sufficient emphasis, "*I'm* doing nothing."

The Big Picture

In turning from the stage to the screen, Eli Wallach had been warned by fellow-actors to keep his mouth shut as much as possible, because the camera might pick up his tonsils and gold inlays, magnifying them on the screen. His first role was in *Baby Doll* (1956), which Elia Kazan directed from a Tennessee Williams script. In his first appearance Wallach was greeted by Carroll Baker:

"Hi-ah Silver." Through his clenched teeth, Wallach tried to return the greeting. Kazan ordered the camera to cut.

"What are you doing?" he asked the actor. "We don't want the Japanese version."

Training

Toshiro Mifune, the greatest Japanese film actor of his generation, never had any formal training. He failed the entrance examinations to drama school, being told that he had no talent. When he became famous and was asked about his training, Mifune would reply that his drama school was Akira Kurosawa.

A Star Is Not an Actor

Erroll Flynn was having difficulties with a one-word line during the filming of *The Sea Hawk* (1940). His character, loosely based on the Elizabethan privateer Sir Francis Drake, first glimpsed the white cliffs of Dover upon his return home, and he was supposed to murmur with deep emotion:

"England . . ." Instead, Flynn went up to the screenwriter, Howard Koch, who happened to be on the set, and asked for an elaboration:

"Can't you give me something more—like, 'England, my home, it's been so long,' or whatever . . ."

"But Errol," Koch explained, "instead of all those words, I gave you those dots after 'England . . .' "

"Three dots . . ." the star looked at the script with genuine puzzlement. "You want to me say, 'dot, dot, dot'?"

"No, I want you to say just 'England.' You can act out the rest with your feelings."

"I can't," Flynn flashed his smile, "you see, I'm not an actor."

Self-Knowledge

William Powell had a very clear conception of his own limitations as an actor. Rosalind Russell remembers him during a story conference when he terminated the discussion by stating in a tone that brooked no argument:

"It's beyond my histrionic ability to do this."

Chew Gum, Perhaps

Leo McCarey was making *Going My Way* (1944), and the director asked Bing Crosby to speak his lines while playing the piano. Crosby folded his arms and said:

"If you want someone to do that, you'll have to get an actor."

Phoning It In

William S. Hart, one of the early stars of Hollywood, became so lazy in turning out Westerns that he asked his stand-in to play his role as the masked hero. According to legend, Hart put in an appearance only at the end, when the hero removed the mask.

Preferably a Caesarean

Charles Laughton was notoriously difficult to film because he had to be in the mood before he would act. Watching Laughton treating each scene as an act of childbirth, Alexander Korda once told him:

"What you need is not a director but a midwife."

Custard Pie

Katharine Hepburn believes that "a lot of hogwash is talked about acting. It's not all that fancy," she once told Charles Higham. "When Nijinsky visited Chaplin on a set, Charlie was about to have a custard pie in his face, and Nijinsky said, *'The nuances! The miraculous timing!'* And it's a lot of bunk. You laugh, you cry, you pick up a little bit, and then you're a working actor . . . Life's what's important. Walking, houses, family. Birth and pain and joy—and then death. Acting's just waiting for a custard pie. That's all."

Cross My Heart and Hope to Die

"Move into a scene," James Cagney once described acting, "plant yourself, and then open your face. And when you do, look the other guy straight in the eye and tell the truth." Although producer Darryl Zanuck and director William Wellman have both claimed credit for the famous moment in *The Public Enemy* (1931) when Cagney pushed a grapefruit into Mae Clarke's face, the actor said that he had thought of it on the spur of the moment.

"It seemed a good way of telling the truth in the scene."

The grapefruit scene became so notorious—Bosley Crowther described it later in the *New York Times* as "one of the cruelest, most startling acts ever committed on film"—that for years, whenever James Cagney ate out at a restaurant, he would be presented with a tray of grapefruit.

Scene-stealer

Sometimes movie stars are tempted to go on stage where they fall flat on their faces, and often the greatest stage actors fail to project on the screen. Gary Cooper was a film actor. Newspaperman James Bacon would watch him on the set "do a scene with a noted actor and you would wince. He often sounded like a high school junior delivering lines for the annual school play. Then you would see the same scene on the screen and Cooper would dominate it with a look of reaction and steal it, often from some of the best stage actors in the business."

The urbane John Barrymore once said in admiration that he would never want to act against the taciturn cowboy.

"I could eat up the scenery," he said, "and Coop, with one look or a hand wiping his face, would steal the whole goddamn scene from me."

The Serious Actor

Harpo Marx, an occasional habitué of the Algonquin Round Table, was being trumpeted by the critic Alexander Woollcott as the greatest pantomimist in the world since Chaplin. Some of this praise began to go to his head. Harpo came to believe that he should take acting more seriously, study his motivation, and go through all the other inner processes that "real actors" explored.

Herman Mankiewicz was supervising the production of the Marx Brothers' *Monkey Business* (1931). As soon as Harpo arrived in Hollywood, he went to ask Mankiewicz for an early peek at the script.

"I want to find out what my character is," he announced sententiously. The producer looked dolefully at his old friend from New York and said:

"You're a middle-aged Jew who picks up spit because he thinks it's a quarter."

Harpo decided on the spot to give up his ambitions to become a serious actor.

Listening to Cattle

Alfred Hitchcock's celebrated comment, "Actors are cattle," stirred up a great deal of protest. So the master issued a correction.

"I have been misquoted. What I really said is: Actors should be treated as cattle."

Immediately after the Second World War, Hitchcock directed Ingrid Bergman in *Spellbound* (1945) and in *Notorious* (1946). The Swedish actress was having difficulty with one of the scenes.

"I don't think I can do this naturally," she said and explained her reasons. The director seemed to be nodding sympathetically and listening to her ideas about how else she might act the part. Bergman thought she had finally convinced him when Hitchcock said:

"All right, if you can't do it naturally, then fake it."

(Ingrid Bergman later admitted that this was the best bit of advice she had ever received about acting.)

Reason Not the Need

Orson Welles was directing a night sequence in *Touch of Evil* (1958), but the night was quickly running out. He desperately needed to get one last shot of Charlton Heston running across one of the canals in Venice, California. Welles yelled to him from one end of the bridge:

"Quick, Chuck, run across the bridge!"

"Orson, I will," said Heston thoughtfully, "but can you tell me why?"

"Just do it," begged the director, "and I'll tell you why when you get here."

The Real Thing

Marilyn Monroe went to London to make *The Prince and the Showgirl* (1957) at the time when she was studying at the Actors Studio. She arrived with Lee Strasberg's wife, Paula, as her personal dramatic coach. After Laurence Olivier gave her direction for each scene, Monroe consulted Paula Strasberg for a translation into Method. According to cinematographer Jack Cardiff, before one big scene Paula Strasberg was overheard telling Marilyn Monroe to relax:

"Think of soothing things. Think of Coca-Cola and Frank Sinatra."

Marathon

Almost twenty years later Laurence Olivier was acting the part of an old Nazi in *Marathon Man* (1976), which starred Dustin Hoffman. One of the crucial scenes required Hoffman to appear as if he had been awake for 72 hours. The American actor, known for his complete dedication to realism, actually stayed up for three days and seemed to be disoriented on the set. After the scene had been shot, Olivier put a friendly arm around the exhausted Hoffman and was supposed to have said:

"Next time, Dustin, why don't you try *acting?*"

Tears

There were several difficulties involved with the making of *Birdman of Alcatraz* (1962). Burt Lancaster spent two weeks just working with the sparrows and canaries. Hundreds of the latter had been flown in from Japan, and hundreds died. A bird trainer pulled some feathers from the survivors which prevented them from flying. Confined in a very small cage, the actor finally managed to get the canaries to hop on to his hand. Later the feathers grew back.

But the greatest problem Lancaster encountered in *Birdman of Alcatraz* was fighting his own tears. He became so emotionally involved in his part that the smallest setback the Robert Stroud character suffered would make him break down. Director John Frankenheimer loved it, thinking it was acting, but Lancaster would respond with one of the oldest axioms about performing:

"Oh, no, let the audience cry—not me."

Technique

Henry Koster was directing *Music for Millions* (1944) at MGM, with June Allyson and Margaret O'Brien, then the child star of the studio. There was a musical sequence when Larry Adler was playing "Clair de Lune" on the mouth organ, which was supposed to make Miss Allyson weep. The director thought it a good idea if Margaret O'Brien could weep too, so he carefully explained to the child what he needed. She nodded and asked:

"When I cry, do you want the tears to run all the way, or should I stop them halfway down?"

Points of View

Asked what he looked for in a script, Spencer Tracy replied: "Days off."

Anthony Quinn, who rose to stardom from the barrio of East Los Angeles, said that "in Europe an actor is an artist. In Hollywood, if he isn't working, he's a bum."

Michael Caine, who comes from a Cockney family, explained: "With an American actor becoming an actor is rather like a lady becoming a nun. Whereas with an English actor, it's like becoming a plumber."

Henry Fonda was called upon to sum up the most important thing any young actor must learn. He thought for a moment and replied:

"How to become an old actor."

Acting Sometimes Means Having To Say Sorry

Veteran Hollywood columnist Bonnie Churchill tells this story about Carol Burnett on a transcontinental flight that happened to be showing *The Front Page* (1974). The comedienne hated herself in the film and, having squirmed her way through it, afterwards asked the steward for the mike.

"I'm so sorry you had to sit through this as a captive audience," Burnett said earnestly, "and I must really apologize to you for my performance."

Her speech received a sitting ovation.

CHAPTER 6

Stardust

A Star Is Manufactured

The first stars were made by the public, but soon the studios got into the act of creating their own stars. William Fox, one of the founding fathers of Hollywood, related in 1933 to Upton Sinclair the origins of the star system.

Before making *A Fool There Was* (1916), I consulted Robert Hilliard, who had produced it on the stage and played the leading role for years. He said, "In my experience, I have had to change my leading lady six times. As soon as one scored a tremendous hit in the part, she believed herself to be a Sarah Bernhardt and became unmanageable, and I had to let her go. My advice would be to put the girl you choose under contract, as the part will make her."

We made a test of a girl called Theodosia Goodman, who had no theatrical experience, and decided she would do. She was the daughter of a tailor in Cincinnati. Miss Goodman gave a very remarkable performance in this picture; and then came our problem. If we were going to continue her services, the name didn't have quite the theatrical feeling, and we must find a stage name for her.

One day it was conceived in our publicity department that we had had every type of woman on the screen except an Arabian; our publicity director felt that the public would like an Arabian. He conceived the story that this Miss Goodman was born in Arabia—her father was an Arab and her mother a French woman who had played the theatres in Paris. So we took 'Arab,' and spelling it backwards, made it 'Bara,' and shortened the first name 'Theodosia' to 'Theda' and thus the name 'Theda Bara.' Then the director said, "Now let's not settle on this until we see if it will go over. Let me invite the newspapers to an interview and see if they will swallow this."

He dressed her in the regular Arabian costume, and surrounded her with the proper atmosphere, and then the newspaper boys all came in. He said, 'I want you to meet Miss Bara,' and gave them her history. He said she didn't speak a word of English. The newspaper men left that day and said that the Fox Film Corporation had discovered the greatest living actress in the world. At first when we would want to attract the attenion of Miss Goodman, we would call her 'Miss Bara,' and she would not pay any attention. But after a short time she became used to it, and took to the name perfectly, and she still retains it. Miss Bara got $75 a week for her first picture, and when her contract expired, we were paying her $4,000 a week.

Star Quality

When they were not in front of motion-picture cameras, stars in the studio era spent much of their time posing for publicity photographs. László Willinger found Joan Crawford a tireless subject. Even though her dressing room was a few hundred yards across the street from Willinger's studio at MGM, Crawford would always arrive in a limousine. After one time when she failed to show up because she couldn't find her driver, the photographer asked her whether she could not have crossed the street on foot.

"It's in my contract that I have a limousine," the star explained.

Although she could be a pain to those she perceived as a threat or more powerful, Joan Crawford went out of her way to be nice to others. According to Herman Cohen, who produced the horror film *Trog* (1970) with Crawford in London, she got up every morning at 4 a.m. to get to Shepperton Studios in time to make a huge breakfast for the entire crew. Afterwards, the Hollywood star insisted on washing the dishes.

Joan Crawford on an impulse offered to take a friend to the theatre.

"But you've already seen that play," said the friend.

"Yes, but not in this dress," replied the star.

Madame Defarge

Joan Crawford was well known for bringing her own bottle of 100-proof vodka to any restaurant or private home where she had been invited to dine. Making her first visit to Hollywood, Tallulah Bankhead had invited Joan Crawford to a housewarming party, and the latter brought this time not only a bottle but also her knitting. According to gossip columnist Radie Harris, she clicked her needles like Madame Defarge all through Tallulah's non-stop conversation, until the aggrieved Miss Bankhead exploded:

"No one brings her own entertainment into my home!"

Joan Crawford and Bette Davis had some legendary fights on the set of *Whatever Happened to Baby Jane?* (1962). When asked about their relationship, La Crawford said:

"Bette and I work differently. Bette screams, and I knit. While she screamed, I knitted a scarf that stretched clear to Malibu!"

Bette Noire

Soon after the release of *All About Eve* (1950) everybody was talking about Bette Davis's rather obvious impersonation of Tallulah Bankhead. Asked what she thought of the whole thing, Tallulah replied with measured sweetness:

"Bette and I are very good friends. There's nothing I wouldn't say to her face—both of them."

Love That Passeth All Understanding

Jerry Lewis and Dean Martin's partnership, one of the most successful in show business, ended in bitterness.

"Ours was a love relationship," Lewis explained to Charles Higham, and the relationship ended. "I still love him as a performer. If anyone criticized him in my presence, I'd kill them. But see him personally? No."

Catfight

Columnist Hedda Hopper was once watching Mae West and Alison Skipworth on the set. There was palpable tension and competition between the two stars, each trying to steal the scene from the other. Annoyed at her partner's attitude, Miss Skipworth turned between takes to Miss West and said with considerable dignity:

"I'll have you know—I'm an actress."

"It's all right, dearie," Mae West smiled sweetly, "your secret is safe with me."

Malice in Wonderland

Ross Hunter's remake of *Lost Horizon* (1973) as a musical was an unmitigated disaster. The critics had a field day with the dancers, the sets, and everything else. Vincent Canby wrote that "the High Lama's Palace looks like Pickfair remodeled as a motel," but the most malicious comment, not surprisingly, came from Bette Midler, who entertained her concert fans by referring to the picture as "Lost Her Reason." And to drive it home, La Midler would add:

"I never miss a Liv Ullman musical."

Unkosher Remarks

Joan Fontaine, known for her sharp tongue, was visiting a set of a picture where Orson Welles was just about to be burned to death. With flames dancing around his funeral pyre, Welles called out to the actress:

"I now know what Joan of Arc endured!"

"Keep your spirits up," said Fontaine, "we'll let you know if we get the odor of burning ham."

As one of his affectations in his glory days in the film colony, Orson Welles grew a beard. Errol Flynn sent him as a present a large hunk of ham with a beard glued to it.

After Will Rogers starred in *State Fair* (1933) with a championship hog called Blue Boy from Iowa, the prop man approached the cowboy comedian that Twentieth Century-Fox would like to sell him the hog. Maybe he could use him on the ranch he had in the Santa Monica Mountains and eventually turn him into some good chops and ribs. Will thought about it for a while and then said in his slow drawl:

"Shucks, I just wouldn't feel right, eating a fellow actor."

More Hams

In the late forties a well-known star entered Chasen's restaurant and strode purposefully to his table, fully conscious that he was the cynosure of all eyes. Agent Irving Lazar observed to his dinner companion:

"The fellow is such a ham I bet he wears a clove in his button hole."

During the filming of *Romeo and Juliet* (1936), John Barrymore, who played Mercutio, became irritated with the theatrical acting of Basil Rathbone, in the role of Tybalt. Rehearsing the fight scene, the two actors did their energetic parry and thrusts, protected by almost invisible rubber tips. Director George Cukor was about to put the scene on film, when he noticed that Barrymore had secretly removed the tip from his sword, rather like the dirty trick Claudius makes Laertes play on Hamlet. Cukor stopped and called Barrymore a "dangerous son-of-a-bitch." Pressed what made him do it, John Barrymore confessed:

"I have to be honest. I took off the rubber tip because I can't stand hams."

Verbal Duel

Katharine Hepburn's first starring role in a movie was in *Bill of Divorcement* (1932), where she played literally opposite John Barrymore. The filming was fraught with tension and at the end an exasperated Hepburn said to Barrymore:

"Thank God, I don't have to act with you any more!"

"Oh," replied the famous Profile suavely, "I didn't realize you ever had, darling."

Starstruck

Katharine Hepburn was apprehensive when she was first cast opposite Spencer Tracy, who was already an established star with two Oscars to his credit. On the first day of the set, she decided to break the ice by going up to Tracy and introducing herself. But her nerves in the physical presence of the star made her blurt out:

"Oh, Mr. Tracy, I'm really too tall for you."

The actor looked at the brash young woman for a moment and then said coolly:

"That's all right, dear. I'll soon cut you down to size."

Top Billing

Garson Kanin asked Spencer Tracy why he insisted on having his name appear first on the billing even in his movies with Katharine Hepburn.

"Why not?" asked the irascible star.

"How about ladies first?"

"This is a movie, not a lifeboat," said Tracy.

In one of the classic Hollywood stories about credits, Richard Ney had been cast in a major picture at Twentieth Century-Fox, when he told his agent that he wanted top billing.

"I'll try," said the agent, "but you know that Ronald Colman is also in the picture . . ."

"Makes no difference," said the client. "I want top billing or nothing."

A few days later the agent called Ney and said:

"Well, I got you what you wanted."

"You got me the top billing?" asked the relieved actor.

"No," said the agent, "we got the nothing."

Your Name in Watercolor

Ben Lyon was hired by Howard Hughes, who was just starting out as a producer, and was guaranteed by contract to have top billing in *Hell's Angels* (1930). By the time Hughes had decided to remake the whole picture in sound, Lyon had introduced to him a starlet named Jean Harlow, and Hughes cast her. By the time the movie was finished, he decided to give her top billing: "Jean Harlow in *Hell's Angels*, with Ben Lyon and James Hall."

Lyon walked into Hughes's tiny office, the door of which used to be more or less always open in those days, and the two men started arguing. Hughes finally sent for his lawyer, Neal McCarthy, which increased the decibel level by a third. Gradually, the lawyer took over most of the yelling:

"All right, Lyon!" he shouted in frustration, "you want first billing and damn it, we'll give you first billing. We'll put your name in letters six feet high on twenty-four sheets from here to New York and back again—but we'll paint it in watercolor, and the first time it rains, your name will wash off!"

"Well, at least I'll be safe in California," Lyon shot back. Fortunately this exchange made the disputants laugh so hard that the actor agreed to abide by the producer's decision. And Hughes, being a Southern gentleman, agreed then to abide by the contract he made—to put Ben Lyon's name first.

Anybody Listening?

Irving Thalberg, during his abbreviated career the most powerful producer in Hollywood, never put his name on any of his films. (He did get a screen credit for an early scenario he wrote under the pseudonym I. R. Irving.)

"Credit you give yourself isn't worth having," he once said.

Charlie MacArthur, who worked for Thalberg and was close friends with the producer, remarked about his modesty:

"Entertainment is his God. He's satisfied to serve Him without billing, like a priest at an altar, or a rabbi under the Scrolls."

Mystique

"Garbo is every man's harmless fantasy mistress," Alistair Cooke once wrote. "She gave you the feeling that if your imagination has to sin it can at least congratulate itself on its impeccable taste." But being every man's mistress means also that one cannot truly belong to one man. An ingredient of stardom is intense self-involvement sometimes leading to a life-long love affair with oneself.

Columnist Sidney Skolsky remembers a visit to the MGM lot one day, and talking with Robert Taylor, when Garbo walked by on the way to her dressing room. She plucked a fig from a nearby fig tree and proceeded without a word to her dressing room. The journalist asked the actor why he hadn't said hello. "I don't think she'd remember me," Taylor said, despite the fact that he had just played Armand to her Camille two weeks before.

Take Your Pick

Marlon Brando was considered at first to play the title role in *Lawrence of Arabia*, but Sam Spiegel wanted a fresh face and so he made a star out of Peter O'Toole. Afterwards he made the general comment:

"You make a star, you make a monster." ·

Next Tango in Paris

Joanne Woodward had such a difficult time acting opposite Marlon Brando in *The Fugitive Kind* (1959)—"He was not there," she once told a Tarrytown seminar, "he was somewhere else"—that she said she'd only work with him again if he were in rear projection.

Showdown

In 1946 Errol Flynn published *Showdown*, a thinly disguised satire on life at the Warner studios. The studio retaliated by placing under contract an actor by the name of Paul Brinkman, who looked a dead ringer for Flynn. Brinkman played small roles, but his main function was to hang out in the green room during lunch hour and irritate Errol Flynn.

Showdown became a bestseller and most people believed it had been ghostwritten.

"I'm flattered," Errol Flynn declared. "If the book weren't any good they'd certainly insist that I must have written it."

Journalist Gene Fowler sent a dedicated copy of his latest book to fellow author Errol Flynn. The inscription to the celebrated womanizer read: "Try taking this to bed with you sometimes."

Pain in the Ass

Errol Flynn, according to publicist Jerry Asher at Warner, "had a perverse, sardonic, degenerate sense of humor and he hated that studio." He always tried to get sick at a time when it would cost the studio money. Once he was told by his doctor to get a hemorrhoidectomy. He endured the pain for weeks, so that he could go into the hospital just when his next picture started.

Time Is Money

An MGM contract actress, Pat Dane, arrived late to the set one day and was bawled out by producer Harry Rapf.

"Do you know how much you are costing the studio by being late?"

"Do you know," the starlet shot back, "how much you're costing the studio by being on time?"

On the Horns of the Dilemma

Marilyn Monroe was driving Billy Wilder still wilder during the making of *Some Like It Hot* (1959). She was always late, refused to speak to Tony Curtis, generally behaving like a star. After the completion of the film, the director was asked if he would ever work with Marilyn Monroe again.

"She's impossible," said Wilder. "I have an aunt Minnie whom I love and who's always on time. But who would buy tickets to see her?"

A Thief of Time

After working with her, Billy Wilder thought Marilyn Monroe was a great natural actress. "She would be the greatest," he told a reporter, "if she ran like a watch. Not necessarily a Patek-Philippe; I'd settle for a Mickey Mouse."

Hearing that she was studying with Lee Strasberg at the Actors Studio, Wilder opined that she did not need acting lessons.

"What she needs is to go to Omega College in Switzerland where they give courses in advanced punctuality."

One of the few events at which Marilyn Monroe was known to have showed up on time was the famous luncheon, in September 1959, on the lot of Twentieth Century-Fox where Hollywood hosted Nikita Khrushchev. After lunch, Billy Wilder was overheard telling someone:

"Obviously, the only way to get Marilyn on the set of a picture on time will be to hire Khrushchev as the director."

Some Like It Tight

Tony Curtis was upset during the filming of *Some Like It Hot* over his billing in an ad campaign planned by the publicity department. The star, who was known for his very tight pants during this period, went to complain to Billy Wilder. The director heard him out, and then said:

"The trouble with you, Tony, is that you're interested only in tight pants and wide billing."

According to Tom Wood, who wrote one of Wilder's biographies, "Curtis never brought up the subject again."

Silent Coop

Though the son of an English barrister, Gary Cooper was a Westerner from Helena, Montana, who had spent a couple of years as a cowboy on his uncle's ranch.

"I learned one thing," he used to reminisce without a trace of nostalgia. "I wanted a job in town."

Coop's image as a strong, taciturn type did not go back to his cowboy days. He was doing a guest spot one day on Edgar Bergen's radio show. While

Charlie McCarthy, the ventriloquist's dummy, was chattering away, Cooper was given only monosyllabic grunts, like "yep" and "nope." Audience reaction was so favorable that the actor adapted it as part of his public personality. His taciturnity became particularly useful when pestered by nosy columnists.

Good Move

Although he had been playing in the television series *Rawhide* and doing small parts in several movies, Clint Eastwood became an international star in a rather inauspicious manner. Sergio Leone, an Italian director in love with Westerns, wanted to cast James Coburn in *A Fistful of Dollars* (1964), but could not afford him. Leone screened an episode of *Rawhide* and was struck by Eastwood's indolent way of moving about which he likened to a cat. Soon Eastwood got a call from his agent at William Morris who asked:

"Clint, would you like to go to Europe and make an Italian-German-Spanish co-production of a remake of a Japanese film in the plains of Spain?"

"Not particularly," said the taciturn actor. Eastwood's business manager advised against what he considered a bad career move, but the actor decided in favor because he had never been to Europe and his wife wanted to go.

Nobody thought much of the cheap B Western which could not find a distributor in the United States, and Eastwood returned to another season of *Rawhide*. Meanwhile *A Fistful of Dollars* became a huge success in Europe, and Eastwood was being hailed as the new Gary Cooper. When Sophia Loren came to Hollywood in 1965 she asked to meet the greatest star in town.

"Clint Eastwood?" her hosts looked puzzled. "You mean that guy in that failing television series?"

(Later, when Clint Eastwood formed his own production company, he called it Malpaso, which means "bad move" in Spanish.)

Definition

Clint Eastwood was being interviewed on television in New York while shooting *Bronco Billy* (1980). The reporter was trying to define the actor's image as a ruthless outlaw, and then asked him to define the quintessential Clint Eastwood picture.

"To me," said Eastwood quietly, "a Clint Eastwood picture is one that I'm in."

American Legend

John Wayne was roasted by the Harvard *Lampoon* in 1974. The Duke drove through Cambridge on an armored personnel carrier and faced a press conference with a firm, manly, anti-intellectual defiance. When, in Mark O'Donnell's words, "one of those whey-faced *cinéastes*" asked him, "Mr. Wayne, do you look at yourself as an American legend?" the Duke immediately riposted:

"Well, not being a *Harvard* man, I don't look at myself any more than necessary."

CHAPTER 7

Idolatry

My European Vacation

In the early decades of motion pictures, the most famous character on earth was Charlie Chaplin's "little fellow," known by different names around the world. Its creator found out just how famous he was on a visit to Paris. The inimitable Gene Fowler tells the story in Father Goose, *his biography of Mack Sennett.*

After he [Chaplin] had made his first million dollars, he went to Europe for a vacation. He slipped away from a Parisian hotel to wander incognito in an obscure district on the Left Bank. No one recognized him. He was happy. After all, there *was* some privacy, if one had the patience to seek it.

As he strolled along, Mr. Chaplin suffered an abdominal cramp. He inquired of an angelic porter where one might find a W.C. Mr. Chaplin knew no French and the porter knew no English. After some ineffectual parley in two languages, Chaplin became apprehensive. The stomach ache was now almost beyond control. He did some pantomime. He postured, grunted, wriggled and rolled his eyes to heaven.

The porter was aghast. A madman loose in the Latin Quarter! Probably the third son of a dissipated earl. The porter fled.

Chaplin hastily tried all the resources of his art on a cab driver. This fellow was highly amused. He called to several of his confrères. They, too, watched the Chaplin contortions. Occasionally they applauded, as only the French can when reference is made to bedroom or bath. Several cocottes joined the throng. Chaplin was dismayed. Everyone believed his pantomime to be in the best traditions of the art.

Finally, and after Chaplin was ready to yield to the mercies of nature, a godsend, in the shape of a cheese vendor came from his shop doorway to ask Chaplin in English: "Do you want a job? You could draw in the customers, my amiable citizen."

Chaplin held his abdomen and gasped: "Not a job. A toilet."

The cheese vendor began to consider this problem. At this moment Chaplin unwittingly did a few desperate steps of his famous walk. The cheese vendor's eyes popped as he pointed at Chaplin and shouted: "Charlot! Charlot!"

It was a magic name. That and the walk enlightened everyone. The audience began to mob Chaplin. The cheese vendor, however, helped him to the backyard of his own store, where there stood a building fully as ornamental and useful as any of its Missouri cousins. Chaplin dashed for its hospitable seclusion, the mob at his heels. He barely succeeded in slamming the door and fastening it from the inside with an ancient wrought-iron hook.

By now he was unmindful of the great tumult outside, the hammering at the door and the shouts of "Charlot! Charlot!" But soon he was amazed to see the walls of the building fall. The front wall was first to go, what with a contingent of Latin Quarter admirers using a long wooden bench as a ram against the door. Then the wall on the port side collapsed. The starboard wall yielded next. Then the after-bulkhead went by the board with Chaplin barely escaping the fate of the brave captain who goes down with his ship. The mob now began fighting and screaming among themselves. They wanted portions of the blessed ruins as souvenirs of the unprecedented occasion. A wine peddler with a great red beard gripped the door, but released it when struck by one of his own bottles. The hinges were pried off by a concierge, who consented, after a loud bargaining, to part with one hinge for fifty-three francs. The toilet seat had disappeared mysteriously. Amid cries of robbery, scandal, double-dealing, there were threats to lynch a suspect, a grape-louse exterminator from Gascony.

Two urchins were having a tug-of-war with the wrought-iron hook. Their grandfather claimed they had stolen it from his pocket. He began to cane them.

During this fierce mêlée, Chaplin's stomach ache vanished. He managed to flee, just as a group of grisettes and their tough-looking escorts set upon him, presumably to confiscate his pants.

Meeting Charlie

When Wilson Mizner first met Charlie Chaplin, he congratulated the great little clown on being "one of the few people on earth who had managed to make a living from his hips down."

Comedian Jackie Vernon in his youth had idolized Charlie Chaplin to such an extent that he would write him a long fan letter every week. Although he never got back a reply, Vernon kept up his end of the correspondence for ten years. Then he grew up, became a professional and gave up. Several decades later, he finally met his idol at the Connaught Hotel in London. When he was introduced, Chaplin thought for a moment, and said warmly:

"Of course, Jackie Vernon! Tell me: why did you stop writing?"

Catnip

Film is a mass medium and stars are capable of causing mass hysteria. Mary Pickford was taking a taxicab from the railroad station of a New England town, when the roof of the automobile was torn off by fans.

Rudolph Valentino became a phenomenon—especially in death at the early age of thirty-one. H. L. Mencken described him as "catnip to women," who thronged by the tens of thousands to view his body at Campbell's Funeral Home in New York; several of them committed suicide. His funeral was attended by a crowd of 100,000—mainly women—and caused the worst riot in the city since the one at Astor Place in 1849, which was touched off by demonstrations against the British actor William Macready. A cult developed around Valentino's grave around the anniversary of his death on 23 August 1926; one or several mysterious women still show up, all heavily veiled, in imitation of the actress Pola Negri, who rushed across the country to Valentino's funeral.

Rodolpho himself was a rather simple, ordinary young man, who reached an identity crisis with his stardom. Once he mused:

"What is Valentino? I don't know. In the *Four Horsemen* [*of the Apocalypse*], I played the role of Julio; in *Camille* I was Armand. In *The Sheik* or those other pictures, I didn't know who I was. In *Blood and Sand* I played Gallardo. But what is the role of Valentino? Perhaps a Valentino is simply Jesse Lasky's nightmare."

Early Riser

Joan Crawford could be notoriously hard on those around her, including her children. But she also drove herself very hard. With iron discipline she lowered her voice range, took off excess weight and even when she did not have to be at the studio, she would be at her desk at 6 a.m. The novelist Jacqueline Susann, who started her career as an actress and was a friend of Joan Crawford, asked the star what would happen if once she failed to deal with her fan mail.

"It wouldn't be answered," said the compulsive perfectionist, "and I could never be that rude."

Encore

Joan Crawford told her second husband Franchot Tone to get packing after she caught him in the act with a starlet in his dressing room. Then she caught the train to New York to seek solace in the only love that would last her lifetime: the adoration of her fans. They mobbed her as she emerged from Grand Central Station, and despite a protective cordon by MGM's press agents and New York's finest, the star arrived at her hotel with her dress torn to shreds. Finally safe in her suite, Joan Crawford smiled dreamily at her entourage, who still reeled from the ordeal, and said:

"Let's go back and do it all over again!"

If at First You Don't Succeed

Joan Crawford had her dressing room at MGM off the same corridor as Greta Garbo. Like everybody else on the lot, she was awestruck by the Swedish superstar. As she passed Garbo's door every day for three years, Crawford would call out a cheery "Hello," and for three years there was no response. One morning she was in a great hurry, and Crawford rushed past the closed door without her customary greeting. She was astonished to hear the door open behind her, and a soft voice with the famous lilt ring out:

"Alloo . . . ?"

Garbo Talks

In *Grand Hotel* (1932), Joan Crawford got to work on the same set as Greta Garbo, yet she was still not acting *with* the star. After several days they had not even met. Though explicitly forbidden to do so, Crawford managed to arrange that by seeming accident one day she bumped into the Swedish sphinx, who touched Crawford's face and murmured:

"Our first picture together, and we don't work with each other. I am so sorry. You have a marvelous face."

More than forty years later, toward the end of her life, Joan Crawford confided to biographer Jane Ellen Wayne:

"If there was ever a time in my life when I might have become a lesbian, that was it."

Short Relationship

Columnist Radie Harris was having lunch at Tony's in New York when she saw Greta Garbo at a table with press agent Bernard Simon: they shared a passionate interest in astrology. Harris's luncheon companion, a writer by the name of Thyra Sampter Winslow, was desperate to be introduced to the most famous unknown in the world. The columnist, though she knew Simon well and Garbo slightly, refused to help, so Winslow rushed over to the corner table and gushed:

"Oh, Miss Garbo, I always wanted to meet you, and now at last, I can tell all my friends I finally met the great Garbo!"

"You can also tell all your friends," Garbo gave her an icy stare, "that it was an accident."

Artie Shaw invited the very quiet Greta Garbo and the very verbose Oscar Levant to lunch. After listening to a dozen wisecracks in quick succession, Garbo finally got in a word:

"Better you should stay a legend," she told Levant.

Size Eight and a Half

Marcello Mastroianni is a shy and modest man, unaffected by decades of adulation and an unceasing flow of fan mail from female admirers. He told an interviewer that the only letter that had upset him once was filled with the usual vacuous and suggestive superlatives, until the ending:

"I've never found you so marvelous or so irresistible! Could you please send me by return post a color photograph or a pattern of the cardigan you wore in that film, because I want to knit one just like that for my fiancé . . ."

The Eye of the Beholder

Federico Fellini's films, especially *La Dolce Vita* (1960), had a great impact on Burt Reynolds. Finally, the American actor was in Rome and met Fellini. He told his idol everything that the film had meant to him. After an hour's exposition, Reynolds asked the maestro:

"That's what the film is about—isn't it?"

"If that's what you saw," Fellini replied, "then that's what it's about."

Mistaken Identities

Early in his film career Burt Reynolds was frequently mistaken for Marlon Brando. A little old lady came up to him at an airport once and insisted that he was Brando.

"Lady, I am not," Reynolds protested. She went away to confer with her husband, then came back and said:

"My husband and I are both convinced that you are Marlon Brando." Reynolds began to lose his temper:

"Damn it to hell, lady," he yelled at her, "I am not Brando!" The woman's face lit up with satisfaction:

"Ah, now I know for sure that you are Brando!"

Barry Fitzgerald, in his later years, stopped at a small cafe in Pecos, Texas, during a cross-country drive. A young lad began staring at him, then suddenly exclaimed:

"I'll be a son-of-a-gun if you ain't a dead-ringer for Barry Fitzgerald— that fella that's in the movies. Yes, sir! Y'all look as much alike as twin heifers."

"My friend," said the actor, "I *am* Barry Fitzgerald."

"Don't hand me that stuff, doc," the youth protested. "You don't look like no movie star. But you sure do look like that fella Barry Fitzgerald."

Much as the star tried to insist upon his identity, the lad refused to believe him, equally insistent that the stranger only looked like Barry Fitzgerald. Finally, he left, muttering his conviction. After a minute he poked his head through the cafe doorway:

"You know, you talk a lot like him, too."

Can't Win

Fred Astaire was dining with some friends at Romanoff's, when a stranger came up and said:

"Well, my, Jimmy Smith, how you've changed? You used to be fat, and now you're skinny."

The actor rose to his feet to tell the man politely that he had made a mistake, but he interrupted:

"You used to be taller, too."

"I'm afraid you've made a mistake. I'm not Jimmy Smith, but Fred Astaire."

"So," said the man, "you've changed your name, too!"

The Famous Count

Béla Lugosi (he was born Béla Blaskó in the Hungarian town of Lugos, and only later adopted his birthplace for a surname), first created Count Dracula on the New York stage in 1927, and he would return to the theatre often later in life, when he could not get roles in pictures. Perhaps because he was basically a shy man, Lugosi's ego emerged mainly through his screen persona. Once he was touring in a mid-sized town, which had been plastered with Lugosi's picture on every wall and telephone pole. The actor was going for a walk with his manager, Don Marlowe, when they saw a boy of about ten approach them.

"Just watch, he'll recognize me in a moment," said Lugosi, and then greeted the boy with a gracious smile.

The boy smiled back, and timidly asked for his autograph.

"Certainly," said Lugosi with a triumphant glance at his manager. The actor was about to sign when he asked his fan with mock severity:

"And young man, what is my name?"

"Boris Karloff," said the boy.

Public Places

Jane Powell once remarked that "a celebrity is one who works all his life to become well-known and then goes through back streets wearing dark glasses so he won't be recognized."

Sophia Loren likes to tell a story about the time she was in Paris making *Houseboat* (1958) with Cary Grant, who suggested one free afternoon that they go walking in the city. Then he got worried and said that they'd better disguise themselves so as not to be troubled by autograph seekers and paparazzi. Loren, who was barely known outside Italy at the time, said that she certainly did not have that problem and turned up to the rendez-vous in her usual dress. She could hardly recognize her co-star, wearing a cap, dark glasses, and a shawl obscuring most of his face.

The two began walking, and within minutes Sophia was surrounded by fans, wanting her autograph, to talk to her or just to be near her. Nobody was paying any attention to Cary Grant, who gradually began to loosen the shawl, then the cap came off, and finally the glasses . . . until only a flashing arrow in neon pointing with his name was missing to make sure that he, too, would be recognized.

Even after becoming as famous as Cary Grant, Sophia Loren has retained her natural down-to-earth style. Recently in Los Angeles, where she often lives now, Sophia announced to friends that she was going to the beach with her younger son. Everyone assumed that the star must have been invited to a private waterfront in the Malibu colony, and were horrified to learn that she meant the public sand at Zuma.

"But you can't just go to a public beach," one of her friends protested, "they will simply mob you."

"It will be all right," Sophia Loren replied calmly. "Nobody expects me to go there, so when they see me, they'll assume it must be someone else who looks like me."

Take Me to the Casbah

The three male stars of *Ishtar* (1987)—Warren Beatty, Dustin Hoffman, and Charles Grodin—decided during a break from shooting to explore a nearby Moroccan town. Dustin Hoffman was astonished that Charles Grodin, the least known of the trio, was recognized everywhere and the one most sought out for his autograph. He was puzzled enough to ask his co-star whether he had an explanation for it. Grodin looked up from signing his name for yet another fan, and said:

"I do a lot of community theatre, Dustin."

Role Model

In preparing to play the two investigative reporters in *All the President's Men* (1976), Robert Redford and Dustin Hoffman visited the offices of the *Washington Post* where the real Bob Woodward and Carl Bernstein worked. A group of high school students were being guided about the newsroom at the same time, and as soon as they spotted Robert Redford, they rushed towards him with their cameras at the ready.

"Wait," said a reporter who acted as their guide, "here's the real Bob Woodward. Don't you want a picture of him?"

"No," said one youngster, as he joined the others in the rush.

Urbane Cowboy

Stars of the human variety sometimes have strange effects on other people, making them embarrassed or tongue-tied. I remember one such incident in the summer of 1982, when Robert Redford was launching the Sundance Institute. Sundance is a ski resort in the mountains near Salt Lake City which he bought and began developing after the success of *Butch Cassidy and the Sundance Kid* (1969). Redford had invited a number of film-makers, writers, actors, industry people, and academics to spend a month experimenting with ways of making films away from the pressures of Hollywood. Later the Institute grew to include workshops for playwrights, composers, and choreographers, modeled somewhat on the Eugene O'Neill Theatre Centre in Connecticut.

I was visiting Sundance that first summer as a consultant, and found the hills alive with passionate discussion; forest clearings rang out with scenes being acted out. Redford was very much involved with each project; he was so much one of the guys, that the conference participants referred to him as "Ordinary Bob," in jestful reference to *Ordinary People* (1980) which had recently won him a directing Oscar.

On the weekend, Redford suggested an outing to the nearby town of Lehi, which was having its annual rodeo. Some ten of us, including his daughter Amy, piled into a van which he drove. The actor was decked out in full Western gear, in an upbeat version of the beat-up character he had played in *The Electric Horseman* (1979). He was absolutely stunning, looking like, well, like Robert Redford.

On the way to the rodeo, the movie star was in high spirits, switching with ease from topics that ranged from local water problems—he was chairman of the Regional Sewage District—to raising horses. He stopped by several rural stores to pick up beer, pop, ice cream. Finally he pulled into a gas station, behind a small pickup, where he watched two girls in their late teens who were having some trouble pumping gas. Finally, the actor stuck his head out the window of the van, cocked back his cowboy hat, and called to one of the girls in his most polite, put-on, country accent:

"Maybe, miss, I could help you with that?"

The teenagers looked up at this gorgeous vision and then at each other. There was a split second before it sank in, and then they ran squealing from the scene, as if they had seen the devil.

Redford laughed.

Make My Day

Clint Eastwood was walking once on the Warner lot at Burbank Studios when a young woman confronted him.

"I've wanted to tell you this for a long time," she said angrily. "You're a no-good sonofabitch always making Mexicans the bad guys in your films and killing them."

"Don't be angry," Eastwood tried to comfort her, "I kill lots of other people, too."

When Our Hearts Are Old and Gay

Judy Garland enjoyed her cult among homosexuals. "When I die," she once said, "I have visions of all my gay friends singing 'Somewhere Over the Rainbow' and the flag at Fire Island being flown at half-mast!"

Naïve Fan

Edna Ferber received a request for an autograph from a Hollywood starlet. "It doesn't matter whether you write it or print it," the actress wrote, "because I copy all my autographs alphabetically into my scrapbook."

Sorry I Asked

Browsing in Martindale's, a bookstore long gone from Beverly Hills, F. Scott Fitzgerald noticed a girl at the cashier with two books: *Bartlett's Familiar Quotations* and a copy of his own latest novel, *Tender Is the Night*. Immensely pleased, as every author is when catching a potential reader in the act of actually paying money for one of his books, Fitzgerald asked:

"Would you like me to autograph it?" The young woman looked un-comprehending, so the author said:

"I wrote that book."

"Which one?" asked the girl.

Chinese Fan

Theda Bara received this appeal from a fan in Shanghai:

"Honorable Missie Bara: please mail me your honorable photograph as soon as possible and as honorably naked as possible."

(Also told of Jayne Mansfield with Japanese fan.)

Young Fan

A tribute was held at New York's Town Hall, titled "Bette Davis in Person and on Film," and an eight-year-old black boy delivered perhaps the greatest tribute to a great actress:

"Miss Davis," he said solemnly, "when I grow up, I want to be you!"

Faith, Hope and Charity

During the Second World War, Bette Davis was paying a visit to the Hollywood Canteen, of which she was president. A handsome soldier came up to her and asked bashfully if he could kiss her. Questioned, he confessed that he had accepted a bet for five dollars that he couldn't get the star to kiss him. Miss Davis asked to meet his pal and then in front of him kissed the first soldier, who thereby collected his $5. Then Bette Davis gave $10 of her own to the loser:

"It's for the faith you had in my morals," she explained.

Free at Last

Having retired from acting, Norma Talmadge was still pursued by flocks of fans. Once when she was mobbed leaving a Beverly Hills restaurant, the star fled into her limousine, admonishing the crowd:

"Go away! I don't need you any more!"

Ex-Fan

Dorothy Lamour was dining out when a young man came to her table.

"Miss Lamour, I've seen four of your pictures . . ."

"Thank you!" the actress beamed at her fan.

". . . And they were awful. I'd like to get my dollar sixty back."

Dorothy Lamour went into her handbag and handed him two dollars. "And I'd like forty cents change, please."

CHAPTER 8

Oh, Have It My Way!

Tough Directing

D. W. Griffith once slapped Mabel Normand hard to make her crying-mad for a scene in *The Mender of Nets* (1912). After shooting, Griffith put his arms around her and said:
"There, darling, that's what I wanted. I knew you could do it."

Lillian and Dorothy Gish recalled that when they first came to be interviewed by Griffith at the old Biograph studio in New York, "he chased them all over the studio with a pistol to get their emotional reaction."

Extras

The Civil War battle scenes in *The Birth of a Nation* (1915) involved tens of thousands of extras, and D. W. Griffith spent more than a hundred days shooting them. When people later marveled how he could afford such extravagance, Griffith was fond of saying:
"I worked out an infallible system. Our soldiers used real bullets."

The Five-Letter Word

Being in movies—as opposed to dreaming about acting in them—is a tire-
some and boring affair, especially for extras in a large epic. Cecil B. De
Mille did not merely depict slave-drivers on the screen, he was good at it
himself, and when crossed he could be as capricious as Pharaoh. In his
memoirs, Victor Varconi gives a front-row account of an incident during
the filming of King of Kings *(1927).*

It was a very hot July day and I, as Pilate, was going to offer a choice
to the crowd. Christ or Barabbas. Since it was a De Mille crowd, it was
a very, very big mob.

De Mille was perched high on his usual boom directing them. There
was retake after retake. Always something; perhaps a movement in the
crowd displeased him. He forgot about time and we continued to
make shots past noon without any break. I was completely busy with
my part as was Rudolph Schildkraut with his as Caiaphas. Suddenly
we were both taken up short when De Mille stopped everything and
stepped quietly into the mob of extras.

"I want the lady who made that last remark to come up here next
to me and repeat it," he said.

There was deathly quiet. No movement. De Mille looked into the
sea of faces and once again spoke in that deadly soft but hard voice he
used when angry.

"I repeat, I want that woman to come up here. No one is going anywhere until she does."

None of us had heard anything. We were just tired of doing the
same scene over and over and hoped for a break. The whole crowd
quieted and De Mille repeated his demand but no one stirred. He
then said:

"Every minute we waste on this film costs me $10,000. The woman
who made that last remark has cost me at least one minute. That can't
be tolerated."

He then proceeded to give a fifteen-minute lecture on the wasteful-
ness of squandering valuable film time. According to his figures, it cost
$150,000 for his speech. Most expensive. But he would often do that:
spend precious time lecturing on wasted time. As long as he was doing
the wasting, it didn't seem to bother him.

The extras were getting more and more restless standing there in the
heat. They knew who had spoken and began encouraging her to go up.

Not to be afraid. We finally spotted her near the front of the crowd but she was pulling back very much afraid.

They eventually got her on the platform next to De Mille and he shook his finger at her and told her to repeat exactly what she had said. She was crying and begging him not to make her say it. He insisted and she finally resigned herself.

"I didn't mean it, Mr. De Mille," she pleaded.

"Never mind. Just repeat it so everyone can hear." She took a deep breath, summoned her courage and spoke.

"I said, I wonder when that bald-headed, old son-of-a-bitch is going to break for lunch."

There was utter silence while De Mille studied her intently. Then he said:

"Thank you. LUNCH!"

Ham for Lunch

The shooting was going well past lunch hour, when Ann Sheridan complained to Mike Curtiz:

"It's one-thirty, and I'm hungry. Can't we break?"

"Miss Sheridan," said the director in all seriousness, "we are photographing your face, not your stomach."

Mike Curtiz lost his temper more than once with Cary Grant, who wanted things to go his way.

"Okay, I resign," the director yelled at his star on one occasion. "You can be your own director! your own producer! your own writer! your own musical director—and you'll be the damnedest ham sandwich you ever saw!"

Patience

Soon after sound came to Hollywood, Lionel Barrymore was given a chance to direct at MGM. He worked hard to control the famous Barrymore temper and was so nice to everyone in making his first picture that he came to be known as "Lovable Lionel" on the lot. His next movie, *The Rogue Song* (1930), caused him many more headaches. The actors were blowing their lines, there were endless retakes. Barrymore was still in charge of his temper, but he felt the boiling point not far off, so he called for a break.

"I rushed to a small sound-control booth," he later recounted. "Hardly had I closed the door behind me when the explosion occurred. Words long unused and even forgotten gushed forth in violence. I vigorously and thoroughly cursed everybody and everything. Greatly relieved, I returned to the director's chair and softly announced, 'Places.'

"Later I remarked with a bit of pride to an assistant, 'Patience will always triumph.'

" 'Yeah,' he came back, 'but that broadcast you made from the control booth didn't hurt any.' "

Dr. Jekyll & Mel Hyde

Making movies is made up of innumerable 'Maalox moments,' especially when the director is new to the craft, feels insecure, and happens to be a comedian. Editor Ralph Rosenblum describes in his entertaining and instructive book, When the Shooting Stops, *the tensions surrounding* The Producers (1968), *the first film directed by Mel Brooks.*

"He came to my office, a small guy who looked very nervous, and started to tell jokes, some of which weren't too funny, and I was a little uncomfortable," remembers producer Sidney Glazier. "But finally he told me he had an idea, and I subsequently learned that he had been trying to get it sold for three years and nobody would give him an opportunity to direct. It was called *Springtime for Hitler*—and if it had remained *Springtime for Hitler*, it would have made several million dollars—but we had a Jewish distributor by the name of Joseph Levine who insisted that the Jews would be up in arms, so we reluctantly changed the title to a banal thing called *The Producers*. In any case, Mel stood in front of my desk and did the movie. I was drinking coffee in a paper cup and I began to laugh. I began to choke. He did the movie from beginning to end. He acted every part—he did the fag, everything—and my sides hurt when he finished. You know how Mel is when he's really on. And I said, *I'll do it*. I didn't know where the hell I was going to get the money, but I said I'll do it, I'll do it, and that's how it began."

. . . By the end of the first morning on the set, Mel was already becoming jittery. His only previous production experience had been in live television where everything proceeded at a much faster, more hectic pace. Each installment started on Tuesday; the writers, directors, producers, and stars polished, rehearsed, rewrote, and rearranged as they went along; and the whole thing climaxed on Saturday with a dress rehearsal and then The Air. Was Mel prepared for the differences between TV and film? Did he know that in movies you can only shoot about five minutes of usable film a day? That most of the time on the set is spent waiting and preparing? That, as the director, he would be faced with an avalanche of demands from subordinates responsible for all the intricate aspects of production?

The film director is like a general advancing an army along a broad front. There are ten to fifteen people working on a scene that will be shot tomorrow, or perhaps next Thursday, when production will move outside for location work. The director has to approve their plans so they can proceed. The set director comes in with a sample of wallpaper or a piece of drapery for Friday's scene. The production manager has a money problem that needs immediate attention. Someone else has a logistical question of some kind, perhaps regarding a city regulation on shooting at a certain location. Whatever his expectations, these time-consuming demands weighed heavily on Mel. He couldn't stand the pestering and he couldn't stand the waiting. And because he resisted delegating authority, the demands increased and the delays lengthened.

His inclination was to spend most of his time working with the actors. He would rehearse [Zero] Mostel and [Gene] Wilder to the point where he had them doing exactly what he wanted, and then he would turn around, ready to shoot. [Cameraman] Joe Coffey, who'd been standing by doing nothing all this time, would say, "Mel, where do you want the camera?" Suddenly Mel realized that he should have conferred with Coffey an hour and a half ago, before he began rehearsing. Now he will have to watch the clock while the electricians slowly arrange all the lights, his actors get cold, and an inner voice whispers that he's falling rapidly behind schedule, that people are resisting him, and that Levine is going to take away his "points" in the picture, or maybe even the picture itself.

. . . Mel's impatience quickly extended to the cast, and he soon found himself in a head-on conflict with the mountainous Mostel. The first time Zero couldn't perform with just the inflection Mel wanted, Mel saw the entire project slipping from his grasp. After several faulty takes, he started to shout, "*Goddam it,* why can't you . . ." but Mostel turned his head like a roving artillery gun and barked, "One more tone like that and I'm leaving."

By the end of the first week, Brooks and Mostel headed two enemy camps. On one side was the enormous booming actor with a presence, a range, and an inclination to go overboard with semicomic ad-lib insult that could wither an innocent repicient to his ankles. On the other, a short, sinewy, panther-eyed director whose operating temperature was each day rising closer and closer to his flash point. "Is that fat pig ready yet?" Mel would sputter. "The director?" said Zero. "What director? There's a director here? *That's* a director?"

. . . By the second week we had become aware of two Mels. There was the Mel who did five minutes of ad-lib routines in the morning for the grips and electricians until fifteen people had put their coffees down for fear of spilling them. The Mel who would jump out of the car in the middle of a traffic jam on the way to a location shoot, run over to a stranger's car, knock on the window, point to himself and say, *"Mel Brooks. The Two-Thousand-Year-Old Man. Recognize Me?"* The Mel who on the way to the studio in the morning with a carful of technicians, cameramen, and assistants would take everybody's order with a pencil and paper, and then, with the car double-parked outside the Chock Full O' Nuts at Eighth Avenue and Fifty-seventh Street, run inside, say good morning to the last person on line—"Do you recognize me? I'm Mel Brooks. The Two-Thousand-Year-Old Man, famous comedian, Hollywood director"—and, as the crew watched in hysteria, make his way, one by one, to the front of the line, telling the secretaries, the Con Ed men, the store clerks about his schedule and his budget, his distributor and his points, his men waiting outside, and emerge with a giant bagful of breakfast. And then there was the other Mel, the Mel who seemed to feel he was being ganged up on by the pros, who felt exposed and isolated, who with barely a transition would become angry and tyrannical, whose neck would stretch and tighten and eyes bulge until, as Sidney Glazier remembers, you were sure he would attack you.

The Secret of Directing Actors

Robert Parrish, before he became a director, worked as a cutter on John Ford's films. After seeing *Stagecoach* (1939) he wanted to know why John Wayne turned in a far better performance there than working for other directors.

"Why do you want to know?" Ford glowered at Parrish.

"Someday, I'd like to be a director," the young man said.

"Then why the hell don't you go back to your cutting room and learn how to cut first!" Ford snapped at him.

However, several years later both of them were in the Navy during the war, and Ford invited Parrish to see some of his films he was screening that evening to entertain his fellow officers. Just before the lights went down, Ford turned to Parrish and said:

"Take a piece of paper and a pencil and count the number of times Duke Wayne talks in *Stagecoach* and in *The Long Voyage Home* (1940)."

Parrish sat in the darkened room and did as he was told. When the lights came up, Ford turned to Parrish:

"How many times?" he asked. Parish counted the check marks. They added up to fourteen speeches in both films.

"That's how you make 'em good actors," said Ford. "Don't let any of 'em talk!"

By Dawn's Early Light

Chaplin was a perfectionist, and he was once shooting a night scene with Henry Bergman. After about eighty takes, when dawn first began to break in the eastern sky, Chaplin said that he'd like to try it one more time.

"Oh my God," moaned the exhausted Bergman.

"Henry," said Chaplin with some astonishment, "it's not like you to lose interest this way. We still have a chance for a couple of tries and I think we can get it quite perfect."

"Charlie," said Bergman, suppressing another yawn. "I'm sorry to say this—but to Hell with it."

And he got up, went home, and stayed in bed for the next two weeks.

Know It All

Pioneer director Lambert Hillyer jumped out from the second story of a New York street set while rehearsing a scene in *The Shock* (1923), and broke his arm. Irving Thalberg, who was supervising the film when he was still with Universal Pictures, bawled him out:

"I told you to hire a double for this stunt."

"I did," said the director, "but I had to show him how to do it!"

Read My Mind

After trying to direct Linda Darnell and Cornel Wilde in a scene, a frustrated Otto Preminger finally acted it out for them. But he didn't like the way they copied him:

"Wrong!" he said with Teutonic emphasis. "Don't do it the way I did it. Do it the way I meant it."

Directing Jeff Corey in *True Grit* (1969), Henry Hathaway did not like what he was doing in a particular scene. So he walked the character actor through the action, demonstrating to the last detail how he wanted it done. Hathaway ordered the next take cut, still dissatisfied.

"But I acted it just the way you did it, sir," Corey tried to explain without upsetting the director further.

"Hell," said Hathaway, "I'm no actor."

Hard Work

Director Henry Koster was working on a picture in the forties and sweating blood with one particular starlet. During lunch break, a friend visiting the set remarked:

"You seem to be working awfully hard with that girl."

"That's because I'm making two pictures with her at the same time," Koster replied. "Her first and last."

Comic Rule

W. C. Fields was famous for his gags with bent billiard cues and golf clubs that had pewter handles. In order to sustain a comic sequence, the director was trying to get Fields to break his billiard cue. The old vaudevillian fixed him with his cold stare and ruled:

"It is funny to bend things, not to break them."

The Nightmare

After Marlon Brando agreed to play in *Last Tango in Paris* (1972), he invited Bernardo Bertolucci to come to Hollywood to spend two weeks talking about his character. The director went to Brando's house the first day and ran out of things to say about the character in the first half-hour. They spent the rest of the two weeks exchanging reminiscences about their love life.

During shooting, just before the scene when Marlon Brando has to cry in the picture, the actor stopped and drew Bertolucci aside.

"I don't know how to do it." The director remembered how during one of their talks Brando had told him about a nightmare he had about his children.

"Think of the nightmare," he told the actor, who gave him a look which made Bertolucci fear for his life. He was about to offer to change the whole scene, when Brando said:

"Okay, I'll do it."

Impossible Task

Filming *The Discreet Charm of the Bourgeoisie* (1972), Luis Buñuel tried, in order to get a certain effect, to forbid his leading ladies—Stephane Audran, Delphine Seyrig, and Bulle Ogier—to use makeup in certain key scenes. Still, the actresses managed somehow secretly to fix their hairdos and makeup.

"Buñuel had a strange contraption like a periscope," Stephane Audran told a journalist, "with which he used to spy on us and catch us out."

In Other Words: Shut Up!

Because he worked with them over years both on stage and in films, Ingmar Bergman enjoyed a very close relationship with his repertory of actors. He developed an intuitive way of communicating with them, which was articulated once in a paradox that Ingrid Thulin told Bergman:

"When you begin talking to me, I don't understand a thing you mean. But when you don't talk to me, then I understand exactly what you're saying."

Bergman the Unobscure

One associates Ingmar Bergman with films of the most uncompromising artistic character. It is difficult to imagine that, during the 1951 strike that paralyzed the Swedish film industry, Bergman needed money and made nine one-minute commercials for a product called "Bris" by Sunlight Soap. His biggest challenge, Bergman reminisced, was trying to make nine variations on the poetic theme:

"*Bris* kills bacteria! No bacteria—no smell!"

Yes, Mr. Huston

Eli Wallach was cast in *The Misfits* (1961) because of his close friendship with Marilyn Monroe. With Clark Gable and Montgomery Clift also in the movie, young Wallach knew that he wasn't the top star. Still, he was put out when John Huston took a shot of him and Monroe in a truck which showed only her face. Wallach expected Huston to place the camera on the other side and shoot his face. When the young actor protested mildly, Huston snapped:

"Listen, kid, never tell me where to put my camera or how to shoot."

But after watching the rushes, Huston admitted his mistake. "Okay, we're reshooting that scene, and I'm putting the camera over there," he told Wallach, quickly adding: "And you shut up!"

Next Question?

An actor, worrying about the best way to deliver his next speech, asked John Huston:

"Do I sit down, when I say this line?"

"I don't care," shrugged the director. "Are you tired?"

Kicking and Screaming

In making *Twentieth Century* (1934), Howard Hawks's main challenge was to get comic performances out of actors who had been mainly known for dramatic roles. Carole Lombard was petrified and kept overacting on the first day of shooting a scene with John Barrymore, who looked worried. During lunch Hawks suggested to Lombard that they go for a walk.

"How much are you getting for making this picture?" he asked her. She was surprised and told him.

"What would you say," the director asked, "if I told you that you had already earned all that money this morning—and you didn't have to act any more?"

"You're kidding," the actress said, more surprised still.

"And what would you do," Hawks went on, "if somebody called you a no-good bitch?"

"I'd kick him in the balls," said Lombard, not known for mincing words.

"Well, that's what Barrymore's been calling you."

"You're kidding?" the star looked at him.

"I'm not," said the director, "and you should go ahead and kick him."

When the scene was shot again, Lombard went kicking and screaming at Barrymore.

"Cut! Print!" Hawks yelled, delighted with his strategy. And before Barrymore could find out what brought on the attack, Lombard had burst into tears and ran off the set.

Hawks never had any problem with Miss Lombard from that moment on, and whenever she started another film, Hawks would receive a telegram from her: I AM GOING TO START KICKING HIM.

(When Peter Bogdanovich was filming *Paper Moon* (1973), he spent a great deal of his energy coaxing performances out of nine-year-old Tatum

O'Neal and P. J. Johnson, then fifteen. He ended up telling them this Howard Hawks story, which helped. "When you're directing children," reflected Bogdanovich, "you have to treat them as if they're forty.")

Stage Mother

Filming the screen version of *Life with Father* (1947), based on the Broadway hit by Howard Lindsay and Russel Crouse, director Michael Curtiz was trying to get a six-year-old boy, Derek Scott, to slide quickly down a bannister. After several takes, which were not to his liking, Curtiz asked the boy why he couldn't do it faster.

"Because of my mother," said the child actor. "She says if I slide any faster, I'll slide out of the picture and it won't show."

On another day, Derek Scott kept muffing his lines, despite constant coaching from his worried mother. At the end of the shooting, the six-year-old confided to Curtiz:

"After this picture, I'll have to give up acting. It's too hard on my mother."

Child Actors

Barbara Whiting, a child actress in the forties, told Darryl Zanuck once that she wanted to cancel her contract with Twentieth Century-Fox.

"I'm not getting younger," she said, "and I see no future here." Her contract was canceled.

Like most of the child actors, Barbara attended school on the studio lot between scenes. One day she was slow to appear when called and was still puzzling out something from her geometry textbook when she walked on the set.

"You must like geometry," Otto Preminger said to her.

"Yes," replied the young actress, "it's just like the movies—one triangle after another."

Getting His Goat

John Barrymore was cast as a mountain man in full Tyrolean costume in *Eternal Love* (1929). As an authentic touch, Ernst Lubitsch thought that Barrymore's character, returning from a hunt, should be carrying a dead mountain goat around his neck. After about five takes, the actor spoke up.

"I beg your pardon, Mr. Lu-*bitch*," he enunciated the last syllable, perhaps a touch too clearly. "I know that you're working to make this a truly masterful scene. However, I do have one request."

"Yes, John," said Lubitsch.

"It's about this goat. You see, his as-s-ssssss has been dangling under my nose for the past half hour. Either pour some perfume in the goat's rectum or aim him the other way."

Taming of the Shrew

During the filming of Ferenc Molnár's play, *The Good Fairy* (1935), William Wyler lost his temper on the set and fell out with Margaret Sullavan in front of everybody. He was upset with her interpretation of her role, while she found his directing unbearably slow.

"He's one of those painstaking fellows," she complained, "who will spend a whole day to get a scene that lasts about a minute just right."

After such disagreements it was inevitable that, finishing the film, he proposed and married her. She told an interviewer that his growing passion was manifested in his yet taking more and more close-ups of her face, until costs mounted and he had to be taken off the picture, though Carl Laemmle put him back when he had heard of the reason.

Postscript

Rivalry between directors for good scripts and the services of the best available actors can be at times intense. King Vidor was directing Miriam Hopkins in *The Stranger's Return* (1933), when Ernst Lubitsch also wanted her for his screen version of *Design for Living* (1933). Knowing that the relationship between Vidor and his leading lady was deepening beyond the professional, Lubitsch sent her a script, asking for a reply by the next day. That evening Miriam Hopkins read the whole screenplay aloud to Vidor. They were both elated by the humor and style of the play. On the last page of the manuscript there was a note in Lubitsch's handwriting:

"King—any little changes *you* would like, I will be happy to make them— Ernst."

Exacting Tribute

Directors frequently pay tribute to each other, usually with subtle visual references, which are equated by Jean-Luc Godard to quotations in a book.

Billy Wilder chose a less subtle and more perilous course, by featuring two of his colleagues, both known for their enormous egos, in *Sunset Boulevard* (1950). Erich von Stroheim, cast as the European director who had become a butler in his former wife's household (played by Gloria Swanson), came up with many generous suggestions, and offered Wilder clips from *Queen Kelly* (1928), his own unreleased film with Swanson.

In asking the formidable Cecil B. De Mille to play himself, Billy Wilder took special precautions.

"We made an agreement: he wouldn't tell me how to direct *Sunset Boulevard* and I wouldn't tell him how to direct *Samson and Delilah*."

Auteur! Auteur!

Directors ideally like to write their own scripts, less ideally tell their ideas to a writer, or at least rework the screenplays that writers bring them. Steven Spielberg, though no improvisational director in the Robert Altman mode, still said once:

"If a day goes by when I don't think of something that wasn't in the script I feel I've let that day down, and I haven't contributed as a director."

On the first day of shooting the British spy movie *The Ipcress File* (1965), director Sidney Furie placed the script on the ground and set fire to it.

"That's what I think of that," he told the actors, including Michael Caine who remembers standing in the rain "coughing from the smoke of this rather damp script." He was just beginning to wonder how they were going to shoot the first scene, when the director came up to him and asked:

"Can I borrow your script?"

Unconstructive Criticism

Though rich in imagination, the plot of *Star Wars* (1977) was hard to follow. George Lucas spent two and a half years struggling to simplify it, but even then the script was greeted with something less than constructive criticism by the actors.

"You can type this shit, George," Harrison Ford told Lucas, "but you sure can't say it."

And Mark Hamill, who made his debut in the movie, said afterwards:

"It was not Noel Coward, let's face it."

Conversation Piece

During the final editing, Francis Ford Coppola was having problems with the second half of *The Conversation* (1974); he could not find the proper denouement for the plot. So he was showing a roughcut to small groups of people, soliciting their opinion. Composer David Shire recalls being invited to one such screening with Fred Roos and Walter Murch, who were editing and doing the sound montage.

"Francis, being Francis, first took us all to the best Italian restaurant in San Francisco, and after we were wined and dined sumptuously, we went back to his house which had a screening room, with the most comfortable, stuffed sofas and armchairs."

Coppola then ran the film. After two hours, he turned the lights back on, and saw three pairs of blinking eyes.

"What did you think, Walter?" he asked.

"Well, to tell you the truth, Francis," Murch confessed, "towards the end I was fading out."

The director then turned to Roos who made a similar confession, as did David Shire.

"Well, I must say," said Coppola, "but I could not keep awake to the end either."

So everybody missed the crucial last part of *The Conversation* which had the problems, and another screening was scheduled, this time without an Italian dinner.

No Joy

Ralph Rosenblum, who edited many of Woody Allen's films, recalls in When the Shooting Stops *the struggle to find the right ending and title for* Annie Hall (1977), *which Allen wanted to call* Anhedonia, *a medical term from the Greek meaning 'an inability to experience pleasure.'*

As usual, Woody was in a terrible quandary about how to end the film. On three separate outings in October, November, and December of 1976 he shot additional material for the last segment, much of it an attempt to show the process by which Alvy comes to miss Annie. He shot scenes in which he's calling Annie on the West Coast over and over again, scenes in which he's doing public-service commercials for educational TV, scenes with a new girl friend with whom he seems to be living while still unable to overcome his longing for Annie. He would audition this material for me in the cutting room and we would try to insert it in the movie. But finally I urged him to forget all of these dramatic transitions and have Alvy say "I miss Annie—I made a terrible mistake," on a flat cut from the scene in which Annie and Alvy are sorting out their things in his apartment—which is finally how the last segment gets under way.

The final moments gave Woody the biggest problems. Several conclusions were shot. One of them, true to Woody's inclinations, was a real downer. He meets Annie, repatriated in New York, dragging her new boy friend to see *The Sorrow and the Pity*. The former lovers achieve "maximum awkwardness," and then, the awkwardness serving as the tear-jerker, they say good-bye. As I had done on *Take the Money and Run* and *Bananas*, I suggested he return to the beginning of the film for a clue about how to end.

. . . At one point during the editing of those last few minutes, after it was decided to have Alvy and Annie meet for the Lincoln Center lunch, Woody said something to me like, "What about memory—shouldn't we have them discuss old times?" It was an incident I had forgotten about until, during the writing of this book, I asked my assistant, Sandy Morse, what had struck her most about the cutting of that picture. As soon as the subject of memory arose, I knew what we needed to do. Sandy, who was relatively new to the cutting room then (she has since edited Woody's *Manhattan*), was startled by what followed. I rattled off descriptions of pieces of film I wanted her to get for me—a shot of Annie and Alvy driving uptown from the tennis courts, a shot of Woody squeamishly putting a wild lobster in the pot, a shot of them at the beach, a shot of them in bed (Annie reading and Alvy reaching over to kiss her), shots of Annie arriving at Alvy's apartment with her luggage, Annie holding up the porno negligee Alvy bought her for her birthday, and perhaps a dozen others—many more than we finally used. Sandy quickly fetched me the reels, and I held them up to the light, showing her which frames I wanted—twenty feet of this, three feet of that, eight feet of this . . . make this number one, this number two, and so on. She spliced them all together on a single reel, and I edited them down to a reprise of Keaton singing her nightclub number, "Seems Like Old Times" (all the memory moments are silent). One of my favorite cuts in that montage was Woody and Diane on a pier. He points, and we cut to what they "see," which turns out to be another memory cut of them kissing. That little transition helped augment the power of the reprise, although I put it together so intuitively I was hardly aware of its existence until Woody and I screened the film some time later. The creation of that sequence was an insignificant moment for me, because after years in the cutting room, manufacturing similar sequences for *The Pawnbroker*, *A Thousand Clowns*, and *Goodbye Columbus*, it was as natural an option for me as an old vaudeville joke was for Woody.

"I'll never forget," says [co-writer] Marshall Brickman, describing the moment he first saw the film with this new conclusion, "suddenly there was an ending there—not only that, but an ending that was cinematic, that was moving, with that simple recapitulation of some of the previous scenes, with that music. . . . The whole film could have gone into the toilet if there hadn't been that last beat on it. I think every writer of comedy wants to send them out with something like that, to keep them laughing, extremely hysterical, for an hour and twenty-eight minutes, and then for the last two minutes turn it around and let them walk away with something they can chew on."

There remained, however, the problem of the title. Brickman came up to the cutting room, and he and Woody engaged in one of their title sessions. Marshall spewing forth proposals—"Rollercoaster Named Desire," "Me and My Goy," "It Had to Be Jew"—with manic glee. This seemed to have little impact on Woody, though, for he remained committed to "Anhedonia" until the very end. "He first sprung it on me at an early title session," remembers Brickman. "Arthur Krim, who was the head of United Artists then, walked over to the window and threatened to jump." Nevertheless, with the release date approaching, UA hired an advertising firm and asked them to make a presentation for a campaign based on that title. Their proposal, which was ingenious but which would have added several million dollars to the release budget, was to take out advertisements in newspapers across the country, ads that would include a definition of the obscure word and look like the front page of a tabloid newspaper. Banner headlines would scream: "ANHEDONIA STRIKES CLEVELAND!" or "ANHEDONIA STRIKES TUCSON!"

Woody, meanwhile, was adjusting his own thinking, and during the last five screenings, he had me try out a different title each night in my rough-cut speech. The first night it was "Anhedonia," and a hundred faces looked at me blankly. The second night it was "Anxiety," which roused a few chuckles from devoted Allen fans. Then "Anhedonia" again. Then "Annie and Alvy." And finally "Annie Hall," which, thanks to a final burst of good sense, held. It's now hard to suppose it could ever have been called anything else.

Symposium

A group of American film directors were visiting Rome at the height of the neo-realistic wave and attended a symposium where they questioned their Italian colleagues about their techniques. One of the famous exponents of the new school explained:

"I get up very early every morning. I am absorbed by the sounds of the waking city in the grey dawn. I am drawn to the hubbub of the crowd of people going to work or to the market. I then try to re-create these profound impressions and experiences on paper and later on film."

The American visitors, used to sets and sound stages, listened in respectful silence. Then another Italian, the actor-director Pietro Germi, spoke up:

"I live on the same street as my distinguished colleague. But I am lazy, and by the time I get up, eat breakfast and stagger into the street, I find to my great sadness that he has already observed everything, ingested everything and digested everything. There is nothing left for me. So I am forced to go back to my apartment, where I sit down and start to think up a story that would make a good movie."

What's Wrong with That?

Federico Fellini was once asked to speak at a symposium devoted to the art of the director. He declined and when some of his colleagues tried to pressure him to change his mind, Fellini explained:

"Most of these conferences consist of two kinds of people: those who talk about things they don't understand, and other people who don't understand what they are talking about."

Foreign Films

During the vogue for Italian realism, Billy Wilder asked his cameraman to shoot a few scenes of their current picture out of focus.

"I want us to win the foreign picture award," he explained.

During a discussion comparing European and American films, Wilder remarked:

"What seems to make them more adult than ours is that we don't understand the dialogue."

Passion Play

Following the surrender of Germany in the spring of 1945, Billy Wilder was brought to Berlin by the U.S. Army to help restore the German film industry and other forms of entertainment in the devastated country. He was asked for permission to revive the famous Passion Play performed every ten years by the villagers of Oberammergau since 1634. Although the production has always been controversial because of its anti-Semitic slant, Colonel Wilder gave it the go-ahead. But when he was further approached about whether Anton Lang, a notorious Nazi sympathizer, could also resume playing the role of Christ in the cycle of biblical plays, Billy Wilder replied:

"Certainly—if you use real nails."

Immunity

Shortly after the end of World War II, a delegation of high-level studio executives toured Europe. Some people in Hollywood wondered how they could leave their shops for such a lengthy period.

"Why shouldn't they?" commented columnist Hedda Hopper. "They got so many tetanus shots that they needn't worry of the odd knife in the back."

Freudian Slip

During the war and the occupation of France, Jean Renoir was happy to be invited to Hollywood, where he signed a multi-picture deal at Twentieth Century-Fox. By the time he finished the first film, he let some of his friends know that he was unhappy with the American studio system. Word of this reached Darryl Zanuck, who told the great director that he had no objection to canceling the rest of their contract.

"Thank you," Renoir shook Zanuck's hand gratefully. "I'm so happy to be released from Sixteenth Century-Fox."

Mortal Coil

The Russian director Grigori Kozintsev was attending a discussion of his film of *Hamlet* (1964) at the Institute of Theatre and Music in Leningrad. Several people criticized the hens heard cackling around the castle of Elsinore during some of Hamlet's most intimate soliloquies; they felt that this lowered the tone of the tragedy. Kozintsev refused to recant.

"Long live hens," he said, "and down with pathos!"

All the King's Horses

Dmitri Shostakovich was frustrated scoring Grigori Kozintsev's *Hamlet* (1964), because the sound effects on the rough sound-track were too loud.

"If it is a question of choosing between music and text," said the composer, "I agree that Shakespeare's words should drown out the music. But I'm not prepared to agree to horses' hooves drowning the music."

Four years later, when Kozintsev was trying to get a reluctant Shostakovich to score his proposed film of *King Lear*, he promised that "there will be less music in this film than there was in *Hamlet* and there won't be any noise of horses' hooves."

Duel

David O. Selznick was disappointed with the score Dmitri Tiomkin had turned in for the love scene in *Duel in the Sun* (1946).

"This isn't love music," said the producer.

"Sorry," Tiomkin replied, "but that's the way I make love." However, he went and rewrote the score. After Selznick heard it, he congratulated Tiomkin:

"This is so much better! Where did you get that fire and passion?"

"Vitamin pills," said the composer.

Clash of the Titans

Republic Studios signed Arthur Rubinstein to play the part of a concert pianist. In the script one of the turning points was a scene in which the soloist would be maliciously drowned out by the conductor. Rubinstein objected that no musician would ever do such a thing to another, and walked out, leaving the studio in a state of panic about the project.

Meanwhile, the pianist went off to fulfill a recording engagement with Leopold Stokowski. The two giants were not on the best of terms, and while Rubinstein tried to play a passage slowly and with great feeling, he noticed that Stokowski was speeding up the orchestra, until the piano could barely be heard. After the session, Rubinstein drove back to Republic and apologized to director Frank Borzage:

"No need to change the script. I was wrong."

Mythmaker

"When you directed *The Blue Angel* (1930)," an interviewer once asked Josef von Sternberg, "were you conscious that you were transforming the actress you discovered [Marlene Dietrich] into a myth?"

"I am always conscious when I direct," Sternberg replied with a straight face.

Biblical

During the filming of *The Scarlet Empress* (1934), Sam Jaffe kept asking so many questions of his director that Josef von Sternberg, who liked to have things done his own way, completely lost his temper.

"Mr. Jaffe," he thundered, "I am Josef von Sternberg and I have thousands of followers."

"You're very fortunate," said Jaffe, "Jesus Christ had only 12."

CHAPTER 9

At the Court
of the Grand Mogul

Fatal Mistake

In 1931 Sergei Eisenstein came to Hollywood at the invitation of Jesse Lasky, then head of Paramount. The connection had been made by the English writer and man about film, Ivor Montagu, who captured the moment when things went wrong for Eisenstein. Lasky had invited the Russian director and his party to dinner at his house. After dinner, the women and men went their separate ways.

We four men, in our other room, leaned back in the depths of our impossibly padded, doze-inducing, deep armchairs.

It was then that we made our first and, I firmly believe, fatal mistake. Lasky spoke:

"Mr. Eisenstein, Mr. Montagu, now that we are alone together— what *do* you think of our pictures?"

Neither Sergei Mikhailovich nor I was foolish enough for either to look at the other. But we both hesitated a fraction too long. A fraction of a second was enough. It did not matter what we said after that.

In the Land of Nod

There is the story of Jack Warner turning in frustration to one of his publicity men:

"If there's anything I can't stand," he declared, "it's yes-men. When I say no, I want you to say no, too."

When Fred de Cordova first arrived in Hollywood, he sought out his friend Mark Hellinger, the Broadway columnist turned movie producer, who gave him some advice:

"Executives here will tell you they don't like yes-men. But there are very few no-men working."

Walter Pidgeon was walking on the MGM lot in the company of fellow actor Hugo Haas when they met a producer. Haas made a deep bow as he passed.

"You know," said Pidgeon, "you don't have to do that."

"You can never tell," Haas replied. "Tomorrow that same guy may be the doorman around here and refuse to let me in."

Frank Freeman, one of the top executives at Paramount during the golden 1940s, brought his boxer puppies to the studio one day. A writer, Bob Welch, observed a producer bending down to pet them. And then straightening up, the producer muttered:

"What am I petting them for? They already took up my option."

Producer Joe Pasternak was embarrassed that people had been sending him Christmas gifts without an accompanying note so that he could thank them. He mentioned this to Edith Gwynn, who printed in her column that the producer wanted to know who were the six people who had sent him ties. In the next few days 150 people contacted Pasternak.

Darryl Zanuck declared once that he didn't want to vacation in the Rockies because the climate disagreed with him. Alan Young, the comic actor, heard him and said:

"It wouldn't dare."

The humorist Irvin Cobb recalled a script conference in the 1930s during which the head of the studio—either Samuel Goldwyn or an ardent follower—found unexpected disagreement from one of his staff.

"From now on, whenever you talk to me," said the boss, "keep your mouth shut."

Credibility Gap

Don Hartman, assistant to Sam Goldwyn, drove the boss home one night. Backing out of the driveway, he grazed Goldwyn badly enough that he stayed home the following day. Hartman called to apologize.

"It's all right," said the injured mogul, "you didn't do it on purpose."

"But how can I make anyone believe it?" said Hartman.

Lèse Majesté

An oft-repeated incident had Gene Fowler (or John Barrymore, or Dorothy Parker) tell Sam Goldwyn in the heat of a story conference:

"Don't you point that finger at me: I knew it when it had a thimble on it!"

Another time Gene Fowler was having a difficult time coping with Hollywood and the bottle, when he heard that his agent was on the RKO lot negotiating a new contract for him. The writer burst into the room and startled the proceedings, having taken his pants off, which he now tossed on to the table:

"I want these cleaned and pressed in ten minutes."

A chill came over the negotiations.

(A similar story has been set with Jack Warner as the recipient of Fowler's nether-garments, but the former newspaperman had never worked for Warner.)

Audience Research

An even more famous story is from the mid-forties, when Herman Mankiewicz no longer had the security at Paramount under his friend B. P. Schulberg, and was living from one odd-job contract to another, like a Scott Fitzgerald character. (Being known as Orson Welles's collaborator on *Citizen Kane* in a town where emperor Hearst wielded enormous power did not help.) Mank was fast sinking into debt and booze, when his friends—whom he had helped in the past—managed to get him a writing job at Columbia Pictures. To make sure that nothing untoward happened to jeopardize his employment, the friends begged him to avoid the execu-

tive dining room, where Harry Cohn lorded it over a high table, taking
sadistic pleasure in humiliating underlings and needling writers.

Mankiewicz managed to stay out of sight for three weeks, when he was
summoned to a screening by Harry Cohn, to be followed by a discussion
over lunch. The meal got under way and the boss, ready to bait a new vic-
tim, asked Mankiewicz from the head of the table what he thought of the
movie.

"I think it will make money," said the writer diplomatically.

"I think you're full of horseshit," the president of Columbia Pictures
replied.

"I'm sure I am," Mankiewicz muttered, still anxious to avoid a confron-
tation.

"The picture stinks!" Cohn began shouting. "And I think the audience
will think it stinks! In fact, I know it!"

"And how do you know when a picture stinks?" asked Mank quietly,
putting out his bait.

"If a picture is great," Cohn went for it, "I sit still. If a picture is good,
I move just a little. But if a picture stinks, my ass wiggles all over the
place."

All the minions and writers nodded vigorously to this revealed truth—
except Mankiewicz. He had an audience and he had his fill of this coarse
bully.

"Just imagine," Mank said, ignoring his friends' frantic signals to keep
quiet, "the whole world wired to Harry Cohn's ass!"

Everybody around the table burst out laughing, while Harry Cohn
screamed:

"Get this sonofabitch outta here!"

23 Varieties

With all the money and ego tied up in the film industry, it is a wonder
that lawsuits are not more common. In 1946 director Charles Vidor took
Harry Cohn to court, trying to break his contract. He also claimed $78,000
in damages for the abusive language that the chief of Columbia Pictures
had used against him. Since Cohn, along with practically everybody else
in Hollywood, always indulged in colorful language, the lawsuit raised a
lot of eyebrows.

"Oh, I called him a Hungarian sonofabitch quite often," Cohn admitted
in court, and then explained to the judge: "But I didn't call him anything
bad. We were friends."

Vidor's lawyers introduced evidence that Harry Cohn used the word "sonofabitch" in twenty-three different variations. Called to the witness stand, B. B. Kahane, who was Cohn's vice-president, explained that the exact meaning depended on the way his boss said the word:

"When he says, 'Well, I'm a sonofabitch,' that means he is surprised. When he says, 'That's a sonofabitch of a scene,' he means it was a perfect scene. When he says 'You're a son of a bitch,' it all depends on how he says it."

The suit was dismissed, the court finding that obscene language was "part of Mr. Cohn's speaking vocabulary . . . used by him as superlative adjectives, and not intended by him as insulting or for the purpose of humiliating the plaintiff."

(The Hungarian-born director might have had better luck if he had focused on the other part of the epithet, which Shakespeare employs in *The Merry Wives of Windsor* as an unmistakable insult: "O base Hungarian wight!" says Pistol to Bardolph, "wilt thou the spigot wield?")

S.O.B.

Columnist Sidney Skolsky was having a meeting with Harry Cohn in the latter's office, when one of Columbia's vice presidents, Benjamin ("B.B.") Kahane came in to ask about something. On leaving, Kahane forgot to close the door.

"You see that stupid son-of-a-bitch?" Cohn said of his trusted lieutenant. "He doesn't know enough to close the door. That's why I'm sitting here and he's sitting in the outer office."

Bible Lesson

Harry Cohn was always having arguments with his brother Jack, who suggested one day that Columbia should produce one of those popular biblical epics.

"What do you know about the Bible?" Harry asked scornfully. "I'll bet you fifty dollars you don't even know the Lord's Prayer."

Jack thought for a moment and began reciting:

"Now I lay me down to sleep . . ."

"Well, I'll be damned," Harry Cohn interrupted, and pulled a fifty-dollar bill from his pocket. "I honestly didn't think you knew it."

We All Make Mistakes

Being a bully, Harry Cohn respected only people who would stand up to him. One day writer Jo Swerling found his boss screaming at him in various expletives surrounding the fact that Swerling's wife had just collided with Cohn's Rolls Royce. Swerling listened calmly to the outburst and then explained:

"She must have thought that you were in it."

From the Mouth of Babes

Jo Swerling, originally a Hearst reporter, also worked at the Goldwyn studio. One day he was summoned by the boss to see a rough cut of the last picture he had worked on. Swerling was seated in the projection room between Goldwyn and his 12-year-old son, Samuel Goldwyn, Jr. During the screening, the writer became aware of his employer fidgeting and groaning.

"I don't understand it," he heard the senior Goldwyn mutter, "I don't understand it."

Swerling became apprehensive, but decided to seek a second opinion. He turned to the boy on his other flank, who seemed absorbed in the picture, and asked:

"Don't you understand it, kid?"

"Yes, Mr. Swerling," said Sam Jr., "I understand it all right."

When Swerling turned triumphantly back to the father, the senior Goldwyn was ready for him:

"Are we making pictures for children?" he scorned.

Hail the Conquering Hero

Samuel Goldwyn arranged a big reception for David Niven's return from the Second World War. A limousine brought him to the studio where all the employees turned out to cheer and lined the streets, decorated with banners, which read: "Welcome Home, David Niven." The actor, a bit embarrassed by all this, was finally accompanied to the executive building. There, flanked by all the top brass, stood a beaming Sam Goldwyn, who shook his hand warmly and said:

"Welcome home, David. I've just loaned you to Paramount."

Carl Laemmle arrived back to his studio from a trip east. At the entrance to Universal he was greeted by a lineup of performers in full Western garb, shouting hail to the returning conqueror. Uncle Carl looked at the clear sky, which made it ideal shooting weather, and then at the welcoming delegation, and said ungraciously:

"Look at all the sunshine! Why ain't you people working?"

Vaudevillian

George Jessel went from vaudeville to Twentieth Century-Fox where he became an executive under Darryl Zanuck. The comedian was genuinely grateful to the mogul's largesse and became the archetypal "yes-man" in Hollywood. He became so well-known for singing the praises of his boss that he began to make fun of himself for doing so.

As master of ceremonies at a White House photographers' dinner, attended by all of official Washington, Jessel raised his glass to the President:

"This is one place where I don't have to raise my glass and ask that we drink to the greatest living American—Darryl F. Zanuck."

Valet Parking

Being a vaudevillian, George Jessel's self-abasement act was bound to get broader. The most famous story found Jessel lying in the gutter in front of the Mocambo Club. A small crowd began to gather, so the doorman went up to him and asked whether he was sick or needed assistance.

"Run along, my man," Jessel waved his hand. "I'm just saving Mr. Zanuck a parking place."

Cross My Heart and Hope To Write

"Don't say yes until I finished talking!" is perhaps the most famous line attached to Darryl Zanuck; Mel Gussow used it as the title of his biography of the longtime boss of Twentieth Century-Fox. In fact, Zanuck liked people who would tell him the truth—up to a point. The mogul had just gone to a resort in Caliente to relax after the release of *Noah's Ark* (1928). Despite his dictum that "when you get a sex story in biblical garb, you can open your own mint," this particular turkey was laying eggs all over America. Nursing his wounds and a drink at the bar, Zanuck felt a sharp kick on his shins. Trying to turn round, he found himself facing Arthur Caesar.

"What was that for?" asked the producer.

"For taking a book," said the writer, "that's been a smash hit for 5000 years and making a flop out of it." According to legend, Zanuck immediately offered a long-term contract to Caesar, who became one of several people to whom another immortal epigram is attributed. "From Poland to polo in one generation," he said of Zanuck, one of the few Hollywood moguls who was actually born in America.

He Moved Himself

Hugh Walpole, a fashionable British novelist between the two world wars, was invited by Darryl Zanuck to watch the rushes of his latest production. Walpole despised the average Hollywood movie, but fortunately it was the time of year when he was disabled by hay fever. During the most sentimental scenes, while Zanuck was visibly moved by his creation, Walpole was overcome with successive waves of sneezing which lasted until the end of the rushes. As the lights snapped back on again, Zanuck noticed the novelist's puffy eyes and patted him on the shoulder:

"No need to be ashamed, Hugh, I was just as affected. But somehow I never cry."

There Is a Difference

Zanuck was famous for making a fool of himself over foreign women whom he tried to make over into Hollywood stars.

"Any of my indiscretions were with people," he once said, "not actresses."

A New Toy

Though a man of simple personal tastes, Howard Hughes's eccentricities caused tremendous waste even by Hollywood standards. The millionaire bought RKO studios without ever having set foot there, and the entire studio waited nervously for his unannounced visit. When finally the new owner showed up several months later, he took one look at his acquisition and gave the order:

"Paint it!"

James Kern was directing a musical, *Two for Tonight* (1935), on the old Pathé lot owned by RKO in Culver City. He was ready to shoot a scene with Tony Martin and a large group of extras, when a call came through from Howard Hughes's office in Hollywood, less than ten miles away. Hughes wanted to see a rehearsal before it was put on film. Kern said respectfully that all was ready to go, and he would wait for the boss to come and watch. But the boss had another idea.

"I want you to dismantle the sets," Hughes ordered, "and bring them with the props, the cast and costumes, to the Goldwyn lot." The Goldwyn studio in the heart of Hollywood, where RKO sometimes rented space, was within easy walking distance of Howard Hughes's own office.

Without further discussion, the stagehands worked overtime late into the night to take apart the elaborate sets and shipped them across town, where the director and the cast reassembled them the following afternoon. Hughes came to watch the rehearsal for a few minutes, gave a perfunctory nod and left the set. Nobody said a word and Kern proceeded with filming *Two for Tonight* without further interference from Hughes. This whim was reputed to have cost $30,000 at a time when European film-makers made entire movies for that amount.

Magic Kingdom

Walt Disney, unlike Howard Hughes, was an artist who created his own studio. His problem was that he wanted to exert too much control over every aspect of his empire. Charles Shows worked for many years with Disney as a writer-producer, and published a collection of anecdotes about the master of the Magic Kingdom, these among them.

Since Walt Disney personally examined every foot of film produced at his studio, he was quite adept at spotting even the smallest mistakes.

One day a few of us studio staffers were arguing about how quick Walt's eye really was. One director, who had seen Walt spot mistakes that no one else could see, even contended that Walt could catch a mistake on a single frame of film as it was run full speed in the projection room.

Since a single frame of film is about one inch wide and runs at the rate of 24 frames per second, that means a single frame is on the screen only 1/24 second. Most of us found it hard to believe that anyone, including Walt Disney, could spot a mistake that was visible for only 1/24 second!

We finally decided that the best way to find out whether Walt could perform this incredible feat was to test him. Thus we had a film editor cut one tiny frame in a strip of film and in its place cut in another frame—a picture of a woman, stark naked.

When the time of the screening arrived, we all sat nervously quiet in the sweatbox watching Walt. He stared at the screen as the film was shown, not saying a word.

All of a sudden Walt yelled, "Hold it!" The film projector stopped. Walt raised his hand. "Back the film up a few feet." Then, "Hold it!"

And sure enough, right there on the screen was the single frame of the nakedest woman we'd ever seen.

Walt registered surprise. He asked what the hell a picture of a naked woman was doing in the middle of a Mickey Mouse cartoon. Since nobody could think of a more inventive answer, we just told Walt the truth—that we wanted to see if he could really spot a mistake on a single frame of running film.

Walt looked pleased. He had succeeded in catching the mistake, and he was proud of his keen eye. So instead of firing all of us, Walt laughed off the incident by remarking, "If that gal had had any clothes on, I wouldn't have paid any attention to her."

· · ·

Since critics had often called Walt Disney's art "old-fashioned," he decided to try to improve his artistic image. One of America's top artists, Eyvind Earle, was brought in to develop a new, more modern visual style for the art backgrounds for Walt's new feature-length animated cartoon classic, *Sleeping Beauty*.

Every day Eyvind spent eight to ten hours painting, lulled by the strains of taped classical music. He created exquisitely beautiful backgrounds, about three feet in width and one foot high. Day in and day out, week after week, Eyvind painted the bright, colorful, inspired backgrounds. As he completed each painting, he hung it on the studio wall like a valuable art treasure. With the taped background music inspiring him to ever greater heights of expression, Eyvind soon covered the walls with his paintings and started hanging the priceless works in the halls.

Though Walt had commissioned Eyvind to create a more modern art style for *Sleeping Beauty*, he never came by to see how the famed artist was progressing. I began to wonder if Walt had completely forgotten about the backgrounds. I didn't know how much the artist was being paid, but I knew Eyvind Earle didn't work cheap. It must have cost the studio a fortune as he sat, month after month, painting backgrounds that Walt never looked at.

At last the day arrived when Walt appeared. He walked into Eyvind's room to see how the new, modern backgrounds were coming along. Walt examined them carefully, one by one, not saying a word. He inspected every tree, every flower, every cloud, every raindrop, for what seemed like an eternity—especially to the silent Eyvind Earle, who watched him anxiously, waiting for the final appraisal of his hundreds of hours of work.

Finally Walt turned to the nervous artist and gave his verdict in four words.

"Not quite that modern," was all he said.

Eyvind Earle defeatedly sank into his chair, muttering angrily to himself. But even his quiet retorts didn't console him, for he knew that Walt couldn't possibly shove all those paintings where Eyvind had *suggested* he shove them!

Napoleon Complex

"One could have swung a scythe five and a half feet off the ground at a gathering of movie moguls," wrote Philip French in his book about them, "without endangering any lives; several would scarcely have heard the swish."

Emmanuel Cohn, general manager of Paramount Pictures, was drafted during World War II, and put in charge of making army films. One day a general's wife came to inspect the operations at Fort Lee, New Jersey. After chatting with Cohn, she was about to take her leave, and said:

"It's obvious that you are not a regular army man, sir, or you would stand up when a lady entered your office."

"Hell, ma'am," the mogul replied, "I am standing up."

His Big Break

When news reached America about the 1917 revolution in Russia, Lewis J. Selznick, who was born on a *shtetl* near Kiev, cabled the deposed Czar Nicholas II:

WHEN I WAS A BOY IN RUSSIA YOUR POLICE TREATED MY PEOPLE VERY BADLY. HOWEVER NO HARD FEELINGS. HEARD YOU ARE NOW OUT OF WORK. IF YOU WILL COME TO NEW YORK CAN GIVE YOU FINE POSITION ACTING IN PICTURES. SALARY NO OBJECT. REPLY MY EXPENSE. REGARDS TO YOU AND FAMILY, LEWIS J. SELZNICK.

The enterprising showman did not get a reply, even at his own expense. And soon thereafter the czar lost his life, as well his chance to break into pictures, a novelty he had always despised.

Ultimatum

Louis B. Mayer was called by one wag "the czar of rushes," but in fact he reported to a boss in New York. Nicholas M. Schenck was president of

Loew's, which owned MGM in those days, yet he earned a lower salary than his employee. L.B. enjoyed being the highest paid executive in America during the Depression. When Schenck was asked how he could permit his employee to earn more than him, he waved his hand tolerantly:

"Oh, Louie likes that sort of thing."

During the war, Louis B. Mayer took up horse racing and breeding, and soon he owned one of the finest stables in the United States. He announced that he would run his stable the same way as MGM—built on stars. But he got so involved with this hobby that Nicholas Schenck issued Mayer an ultimatum:

"Either you produce horses or produce pictures."

Chicken Soup with Everything

After L. B. Mayer sold his racing stables, he became interested in breeding chickens. At one point he invested several thousand dollars in two hundred hens, which through a mix-up were sent to the MGM lot, instead of Mayer's ranch. At around lunchtime, the chef of the commissary spied L.B. coming in and rushed up to him:

"We have some *real* chicken soup today, Mr. Mayer," he beamed. "Those hens you sent are the best I've ever seen."
(Some sources make Jerry Mayer, his brother, the poultry breeder.)

In fact, every day the MGM commissary served homemade chicken soup with matzoh-ball as a specialty of the house. It cost only 35 cents, and, according to legend, as a young man L.B. had promised his dear mother that if he became rich, he would always have chicken soup with real chicken.

There is another story from Mayer's youth, when he was courting a girl, and one day he arrived at her house with hands behind his back.

"Guess what I've got!" he was bursting with excitement. The young lady might have been expecting jewels, or at least flowers, but Mayer triumphantly displayed a plucked, uncooked chicken in each hand.

Behind the Bushel

Louis B. Mayer was so histrionic that he was sometimes called Lionel Barrymore Mayer. "He was known to plead," wrote journalist Ezra Goodman, "importune, threaten, advise and otherwise register every possible emotion during a business conference and, after achieving what he was after, to register still another emotion—crass contentment."

Many Hollywood observers commented on Louis B. Mayer's powers of persuasion. According to Sidney Skolsky he gave an Oscar-winning performance at least once a week in his office, and the columnist reproduced what the mogul might have said to Joan Crawford:

"I look on upon you as my daughter. I treat you, I feel for you, as if you were my own daughter. You didn't have to come to me to complain about the script. I was ready to spank the director and producer. Do you think I'd let my daughter play in such a terrible script? No!"

Then Mayer would fall on his knees, look at the American flag in the far corner of his large office and make his voice quiver:

"As true as I'm a good American, Joan, I wouldn't let anyone harm you any more than I'd allow anyone to harm that flag."

Can't Get Good Help

Despite his self-image as the paterfamilias of a vast and contented family, Louis B. Mayer was more feared than liked. A writer in his longtime employ once cracked:

"I'd rather have TB than L.B." George S. Kaufman apparently was so taken by these words that he hummed them to a tune.

One time L.B. was looking to hire a prominent New York agent to be his assistant. The prospect wired back:

NOT ONLY DO I NOT WANT TO BE MAYER'S ASSISTANT · I DON'T EVEN WANT TO BE MAYER.

Billy Rose, the flamboyant Broadway showman, was often wooed by the studios. "I wouldn't live in Hollywood," he once declared, "if they elected me Mayer."

Revelations

The British producer J. Arthur Rank relied on guidance from above. He once told an interviewer:

"I can never understand how anyone can take on the responsibility for planning any big show without guidance from God. . . . I am in films because of the Holy Spirit."

Time magazine once wrote about Jules Stein, the founder of the Music Corporation of America which bought Universal Studios, as one of America's richest men.

"Aren't you surprised to learn that you are one of the richest men in the country?" asked a friend.

"No," said Stein, "I was only surprised how poor the others were."

Redundancy

Lew Wasserman, generally considered the most powerful man in today's Hollywood, was once offered the job to head up MGM. Wasserman, who was already head of MCA, then the most powerful agency in the film business, declined:

"Why would I want to become head of MGM?" he asked. "I'm the head of every studio in town."

How Films Get Made

Frank Capra was working for Columbia Pictures when he wanted to make *It Happened One Night* (1934), but he could not find two stars to play in a comedy. After the female lead was turned down by Miriam Hopkins, Myrna Loy, Constance Bennett, and Margaret Sullavan, finally Claudette Colbert agreed to do it on her four-week vacation from Paramount at twice her usual salary. Capra wanted Robert Montgomery for the male lead, but he was not interested. The project was about to die for lack of interest, when Louis B. Mayer called from MGM and asked Harry Cohn for a favor:

"We've got a bad boy down here I'd like to punish," he said. (In those days, banishment from MGM to Columbia was the equivalent distance from St. Petersburg to Siberia.) So Harry Cohn summoned Frank Capra:

"We've got to make the picture now," he told him, "Louis Mayer wants to punish Clark Gable."

It Happened One Night earned everybody an Oscar, and as extra punishment, it made Clarke Gable into a star.

CHAPTER 10

Where Ignorance Is Bliss

Nature of the Beast

L. B. Mayer wanted to hire Joseph Mankiewicz to work as a producer at MGM, but the latter wanted to write and to direct.

"No, you have to produce first," Mayer insisted, "you have to crawl before you walk."

Mankiewicz always thought that this was the best definition of producing he had heard.

Producer Lamarr Trotti gave this definition of his profession:

"A producer is a man who asks you a question, gives you the answer, and then tells you what's wrong with it."

Upon being told that two of Hollywood's most unpopular producers in the forties were close friends, the writer Robert Hopkins remarked:

"No wonder they get along so well. Each is the other's idea of a gentleman."

Biting the Hand

As a stock character, the film producer seems to be the epitome of crassness, insensitivity, ignorance, cheating, and lying. During the golden age of Hollywood, these same producers, moguls, executives, or supervisors hired writers at the highest salaries in the history of Grub Street. The same writers, in their spare time or after leaving the business, gave rise to some of the most biting definitions of their employers:

—The playwright Sidney Howard once said that there were only two kinds of producers: "those who produce pictures that the writers and directors create for them, and those who try to be directors and writers without competence as either."

—And another writer, Eddie Welch, defined the producer as "a man who knows exactly what he wants but can't spell it."

—Harry Ruskin, a writer in the forties, described a certain producer as "so cautious that he has worn the back of his head bald from bending over backwards."

—Commenting on a typical Hollywood producer who was long on words and short on action, Ben Hecht observed:
   "He can compress the most words into the smallest ideas of any man I ever met."

I'd Rather Be Vice President

Hollywood wags defined the producer as an executive who wears a worried look on his assistant's face, and an associate producer as the only one who would associate with the producer.

In the tradition of anti-lawyer jokes, an assistant producer has been called a mouse studying to be a rat.

More realistically it has been said that the assistant producer is the man who gets fired when the producer makes a bad picture.

Fred Allen said that the toughest job in the industry falls to the assistant producer. "When he arrives in his office in the morning, there's a molehill on his desk, and by nightfall he has to make a mountain out of it."

Why I Want To Be a Producer

Someone asked Michael Caine at one of the film weekends organized by Judith Crist in Tarrytown whether he ever felt the bug that infects most stars sooner or later—the desire to direct. The actor replied that he would rather be a producer:

"Directors have to be on the set all the time, and the one thing I've noticed as an actor in fifty-two pictures is that every time it starts to rain the producer goes back to the hotel and you all sit there and get soaked. And he also has more Monets and Picassos on his wall; and he always has a bigger house than everybody. In Hollywood anyway. I noticed that very early on, and I thought, that's what I want to be. I want all the paintings; I want to be back in the hotel when it's raining."

One Prodigy After Another

A producer once brought to Samuel Goldwyn a new book to be considered for a screen adaptation. Its title was: *The Making of Yesterday: The Diaries of Raoul de Roussy de Sales, 1938–1942.* While listening to the pitch, Goldwyn kept staring at the book.

"How do you like that?" he was astounded. "Four years old and the kid keeps a diary."

The Same Only New

Samuel Goldwyn one morning came into his office and said to his longtime assistant Miriam Howell:

"We've got to get some new blood around here. I want to sign up a young writer, talented but completely unknown, who'll bring us new ideas and a fresh viewpoint."

"I know just the man for you, Mr. Goldwyn," said Miss Howell.

"What's his name?" asked the mogul.

"He's a young playwright by the name of John Patrick."

"Never heard of him," said Goldwyn. "Who else can you come up with?"

The Same Only Different

Toward the end of his unsuccessful visit to Hollywood, Sergei Eisenstein was finally summoned to a meeting with Samuel Goldwyn, known for having the most artistic taste among Hollywood producers. Ivor Montagu went along.

The scene is indelibly engraved upon my memory. When we went around to do business it was Eisenstein's custom to leave the formalities to me. We sat down around the office and I introduced everybody. Then Sam addressed us—he spoke to me, seeming to be under the misapprehension that Eisenstein needed an interpreter.

"Please tell Mr. Eisenstein," he said, "that I have seen his film *Potemkin* and admire it very much. What we should like would be for him to do something of the same kind, but rather cheaper, for Ronald Colman."

Today He'd Fax It

An agent for a writer known for his social conscience tried to sell one of his client's ideas to Samuel Goldwyn.

"If I want to send a message," said the mogul, "I will use Western Union."

Lesbians

In one of the most famous stories about Samuel Goldwyn, which has been told in many variants, the mogul had bought the rights to a novel called *The Well of Loneliness* (1928) by Radclyffe Hall. One of his executives, who knew the book, reacted immediately:

"We can't make that as a picture, Mr. Goldwyn, the book deals with lesbians."

"So all right," said Goldwyn, "where they got lesbians, we'll use Austrians."

(Arthur Mayer, who worked for Goldwyn, found this story credible "not so much for Sam's unfamiliarity with the vagaries of Eros but as an indication of his grasshopper agility as a story editor." Mayer also quotes "Americans" instead of "Austrians" in the punchline, and tells the anecdote in connection with *The Captive*, which Gilbert Miller produced on Broadway in 1926. The play was among the first to deal with homosexuality, though very delicately—using violets as a symbol of the third sex. One unfortunate result was, according to *Variety*, that the show "kayoed the violet business at florists.")

At about the time that *The Well of Loneliness* first came out in print, Michael Arlen asked Dorothy Gish for advice about casting a certain role in his new play *The Green Hat*. The actress suggested a name.

"Thanks," said Arlen, "but isn't she a lesbian?"

"A lesbian?" gushed Miss Gish. "My dear—she's the wooden bucket itself from *The Well of Loneliness!*"

Happy End

During the filming of *Some Like It Hot* (1959), an elderly Sam Goldwyn asked Billy Wilder about his next project. The writer-director replied that he had always been fascinated by Nijinsky. Goldwyn wanted to know more, so Wilder sketched for him the tragic life of the Russian ballet-dancer who died after spending forty years in an insane asylum.

"How can you make such a picture," asked the horrified mogul, "about a madman believing that he was a horse?"

"It will have a happy ending," Wilder reassured him with a straight face. "He will wind up winning the Kentucky Derby."

High Concept

Once in a script conference, Darryl Zanuck got carried away with his own enthusiasm:

"I want to remake *Air Force* in a submarine," he said.

Sturm und Drang

Arnold Schoenberg's reputation for being difficult both as a man and as a composer had preceded him to Los Angeles, where he fled the Nazis in the mid-thirties. Nevertheless, Irving Thalberg asked Schoenberg to write the score for *The Good Earth* (1937), the picture he was producing from Pearl Buck's novel.

"Imagine, Professor," said Thalberg with a sweeping gesture: "China, earthquakes, plagues of locusts, floods, human passions clashing, and in the midst of all this, a young woman is giving birth to a baby during a thunderstorm! Isn't that a wonderful opportunity for a composer?"

"I'm afraid not, Mr. Thalberg," Schoenberg is supposed to have replied: "You see, with all these things going on, why do you need music?"

Stolen Goods

Arthur Rubinstein visited one of the top Hollywood film composers at home. Spread out on every available table and chair were the scores of well-known classical compositions.

"Tell me," asked Rubinstein looking around, "don't you ever compose anything by heart?"

Miklós Rózsa, known for his many memorable film scores, was fond of telling about a Hollywood colleague who had been given the task of doing the full score for a picture within a week:

"How terrible," Rózsa sympathized. "It will take so much out of you."

"Not out of me," replied the composer cheerfully, "but out of Brahms, Tchaikovsky, and Dvořák!"

While working on *Humoresque* (1946), Oscar Levant was asked by producer Jerry Wald whether he could cut six minutes out of a Brahms concerto to fit the editing of a scene.

"Sure I can do it," Levant replied, "but you'll be hearing from Brahms in the morning!"

And I'd Also Like To Conduct

During the scoring of one of his pictures on a recording stage, an impatient Josef von Sternberg decided to take over the conducting of the orchestra.

"Stop!" the director shouted after a few moments, "where are the saxophones?"

"We have 'tacit' here," the first saxophonist explained that the score indicated silence.

"Well," said the director, "I want to hear it."

But Can She Type?

A producer by the name of James Gardiner was having lunch at a Hollywood eatery in the forties when the head of his studio came to his table. The producer introduced the woman he was having lunch with, explaining:

"She is my amaneuensis."

"I'm no such thing," the lady protested furiously, "I'm only his secretary!"

Public Domain

Producers are usually a secretive and tight-lipped breed. A classic piece of Hollywood advice about making it in the business is "to go out and build a better mouth trap."

A producer in the forties, Edward Small, was well known for his preference to make movies out of stories that were in the public domain, which meant he did not have to pay for them. He was having lunch one day at the Brown Derby with a stunning-looking starlet, when a friend came up and whispered to him:

"You'd be better be careful. She's not in the public domain."

When Alfred Hitchcock confessed to a Hollywood executive that he didn't see many pictures, the man turned to him in astonishment:

"Then where do you get your ideas?"

Something To Declare

A French customs official, looking at Alfred Hitchcock's passport, asked what was meant by his stated occupation as "Producer."

"What exactly do you produce?"

"Gooseflesh," Hitchcock replied.

Hello, He Lied

David Niven ran into an independent producer, and asked how his current picture was doing at the box office.

"I'll be perfectly honest with you," the producer said with a confidential air: "I won't answer."

De Gustibus Non Disputandum

A producer once suggested to Jack Warner that he would like to do a film with a Mexican setting.

"I don't like Mexican pictures," Warner replied. "All the actors in them look too goddam Mexican."

During World War II, Jack Warner held the rank of colonel in the army. Unable to read the whole of the U.S. Army manual, he got his story department to prepare a synopsis so that he could understand it.

Point Counterpoint

Word got out that the Marx Brothers were planning a film to be called *A Night in Casablanca* (1945). Being told that Warner Brothers might sue because the title was too close to their *Casablanca*, Groucho Marx replied:

"I'll sue them for using the word Brothers."

It's a Puzzlement

H. G. Wells visited Hollywood during Mussolini's invasion of Ethiopia in 1936. The celebrated writer was invited to a star-studded reception at Pickfair where a producer asked him:

"Mr. Wells, you wrote *The Outline of History*, and you know all about history. There's one thing about this war that's puzzling me. Can you explain why the Italians are fighting Utopia?"

Thesaurus

Early in his career, agent Irving "Swifty" Lazar was on a transatlantic call to Moss Hart when he slipped the word "egregious" into the conversation.

"Don't use words you can't define," Hart told him.

"I can define 'egregious' perfectly," said the agent, "I came across it when I was looking up the meaning of 'eclectic.'"

"What were you doing looking up 'eclectic?'" the playwright wanted to know.

"Why, I look up 'eclectic' all the time!" Lazar concluded the topic huffily.

The Fake Writer

Charlie MacArthur was another one of the Hollywood screenwriters more remembered for his practical jokes and drunken exploits than any great scripts. Irving Thalberg's early death robbed MacArthur of a patron and a genuine friend; their two families vacationed together in Europe just before the producer died. Looking for ways to cheer himself up, MacArthur one day introduced to the new production chief, Bernie Hyman, a pleasant young Englishman, whom he described as one of the brightest new writers in London, being hailed as a worthy rival of George Bernard Shaw. The only problem, said MacArthur, was Kenneth Woollcott being dead set against writing for the movies, but perhaps Bernie might be able to persuade him otherwise. Impressed, Hyman managed to talk the young man to accept a year's contract at a thousand dollars a week.

A year went by without MGM finding out that Woollcott was not a writer, but someone who had pumped gas into MacArthur's car at a Beverly Hills gas station where the presentable young man was working for forty dollars a week.

"Kenneth Woollcott flourished as a Metro writer for the full year," wrote Ben Hecht in *Charlie*, his affectionate portrait of his friend, "writing nothing and, coached by MacArthur, making the properly superior faces in conference. Neither Bernie nor any of the dozen directors and producers with whom he 'conferred' ever found out that Kenneth was a fake, incapable of composing a postal card."

Believe It or Not

An Australian writer visiting Universal Studios was introduced to Carl Laemmle, who asked how long he had been in America.

"Two weeks," said the visitor.

"It's amazing," said the mogul, "how well you speak English after only two weeks."

Horror Film

Roger Corman produced a number of horror pictures capitalizing on the success of Steven Spielberg's *Jaws* (1975). He conceived one such project, which he wanted to build around a monstrous-looking prehistoric shark that somehow survived in the ocean depths. In vain did the people working for him try to point out that normal sharks were already a prehistoric species, Corman went ahead and designed his shark, which had two fins instead of one. He called the project *Up from the Depths* (1979), and assigned it to Charles Griffith, who went off to the Philippines—which doubled for Hawaii—to write and direct it almost at the same time. It soon became clear from the pages that came back from Manila, that the script was evolving from the horror genre into a comedy. When Griffith had proposed to change the title to "Something Fishy," Corman decided to act. He dispatched his assistant Steve Kovacs as a plenipotentiary who would either make the wayward director come to his senses, or could fire him and take over the project.

"Make sure Chuck has this above his typewriter." Corman gave Kovacs a single sheet of paper. It contained instructions about the essential ingredients for a horror film. Kovacs read through it on the plane and his eyes fell upon the signature at the bottom. It read: "Hitler."

CHAPTER 11

Cunning Linguists

Can't Believe My Ears

King Vidor was having problems in *The Wedding Night* (1934) with Gary Cooper's mumbling and Anna Sten's heavy Russian accent. She had a particularly hard time in the middle of a love scene with pronouncing "Earth's return"—a phrase quoted from Walt Whitman. Vidor was all for cutting the text, but Sam Goldwyn, who was watching the filming of the scene, wanted it kept. Finally, after several takes, even Goldwyn was losing patience and he went up to the two stars. He told them about the sorry state of box office receipts during the Depression, and that he was staking his entire career and reputation on this picture.

"And I tell you," the mogul concluded, "that if this scene isn't the greatest love scene ever put on film the whole goddamned picture will go right up out of the sewer!"

Goldwyn then marched out, and Gary Cooper turned to King Vidor and asked incredulously:

"Did he say it, or didn't he?"

"He said it," Vidor concurred.

(*The Wedding Night* was nicknamed by insiders as "Goldwyn's Last Sten.")

The Goldwyn Canon

Samuel Goldwyn, along with Mrs. Malaprop and Dr. Spooner, is one of the few fictional or historical characters who have given their names to a form of linguistic deformity. By the 1940s, Goldwyn's peculiar usage became a minor industry among Hollywood writers and press agents, both as a way of ridiculing the archetypal, uneducated, and foreign-born mogul and as the sincerest form of flattery. It is very difficult to distinguish between these imitations and the genuine article, especially since Goldwyn himself grew tired of quotes attributed to him and late in life tended to disclaim all of them. "They never print that twinkle in my eye," he once said.

Samuel Goldwyn's various obituaries in February 1974 listed the following half-dozen as genuine:
- Our comedies are not to be laughed at.
- I've been laid up with intentional flu.
- I love the ground I walk on.
- For this part I want a lady, somebody that's couth.
- I want to make a picture about the Russian secret police: the GOP.
- Any man who goes to a psychiatrist should have his head examined.

Arthur Mayer considers authentic Goldwyn's resignation from the Will Hays organization—"Gentlemen, include me out"—which became a favorite quote with Averell Harriman, a close friend of Sam Goldwyn.

"A verbal contract isn't worth the paper it's written on," is disputed by Garson Kanin, who had also worked for the mogul. Another favorite: "I can answer you in two words—im-possible," is traced back to Chaplin and an old music-hall gag by A. Scott Berg, in his recent biography of Goldwyn.

Berg, who spends only a paragraph on Goldwynisms, cites also the famous reminiscence about the old days of film-making:

"We've passed a lot of water since then," and,

"I would be sticking my head in a moose," and,

"Anything that man says you've got to take with a dose of salts."

Maybe Bacon Wrote Them

The following sound apocryphal, and worth repeating.

"I ran into George Kaufman the other night," Sam Goldwyn was telling a friend. "He was at my house for dinner."

Another time it was Goldwyn asked to a dinner.

"I can't make it," he said regretfully, "but I hope you'll give me a raincoat."

Invited to the Mardi Gras celebration in New Orleans, Goldwyn declined:
"Even if they had it in the streets, I wouldn't go."

Making some ambitious travel plans, the mogul declared:
"I want to go where the hand of man has never set foot."

Returning from England during the war, he concluded a political argument about the international situation:
"I've just come from 10 Drowning Street, so I know what I'm talking about."

Science

During one of his trips to England, Goldwyn was shown a medieval sundial.
"How does it work?" asked the mogul.
"With the shadow moving with the progress of the sun," he was told.
"What will they think of next?" Goldwyn marveled.

During the height of the nuclear scare in the late 1940s, Samuel Goldwyn was giving a speech.
"Gentlemen, do not underestimate the danger of the atom bomb," he intoned solemnly. "It's dynamite!"

In the Office

After an argument with one of his associates, Goldwyn tried to be conciliatory: "You are partly one hundred percent right."

He patted another on the back and congratulated him for "always taking the bull between the teeth."

Getting tired of a debate, the anglophile mogul excused himself:
"I'm going out for some tea and trumpets."

A secretary asked Samuel Goldwyn whether she could destroy some very old "dead" files.
"Go ahead," her boss said. "But make copies of them first."

Art

A sculptor once raved to Sam Goldwyn about the expressive beauty of Mrs. Goldwyn's hands.

"Go ahead," Goldwyn told him, "make a bust of them."

A producer invited his friend Sam Goldwyn to a preview of his latest picture.

"Isn't that a real, old-fashioned swashbuckler for you?" he asked afterwards.

"The trouble is," said Goldwyn, "it buckles where it should swash."

After *The Best Years of Our Lives* (1946) won the Academy Award for best picture, Goldwyn said:

"I don't care if it don't make a nickel, so long as everyone in the United States sees it."

Of another of his productions, he declared:

"It will create an excitement that will sweep the country like wildflowers."

And Goldwyn enthused about yet another:

"This will start with a bang in Hollywood and degenerate throughout the whole world."

With Creative Talent

Recommended the name of a director who was known in Hollywood for his artistic temperament, Goldwyn declared:

"No, I would rather deal with a smart idiot than with a stupid genius."

Directors were one of Sam Goldwyn's pet peeves.

"They always bite the hand that lays the golden egg," he once complained.

Goldwyn had set his mind on hiring a director.

"He's too caustic," one of his executives warned him.

"To hell with the cost," replied Goldwyn, "pay him what he wants."

Engaged in a dispute with Ben Kahane about hiring an actor on loan-out, Goldwyn agreed to arbitration "with the understanding that I get the man."

Discussing another actor he had under contract, Samuel Goldwyn told an assistant:

"He's living beyond his means, but he can afford it."

Sam Goldwyn promised an actor he had just signed:

"You stick with me and in one year you'll have your foot in Grauman's chow mein."

The Play's the Thing

The Gershwin brothers and George Balanchine came to see Samuel Goldwyn for a story conference.

"Hold on, fellas," Goldwyn shouted at them from his second-floor office, "I'll be right there. And then we'll get into a cuddle."

"Sex," Sam Goldwyn once told a writer, "will outlive us all."

Samuel Goldwyn wanted to congratulate Joseph L. Mankiewicz for a script he had recently turned in.

"You write with great warmth," he dropped him a personal note, "and charmth."

On That Happy Note

A writer who had just complained that during his contract at the Goldwyn studio he had never heard a single Goldwynism, went to see the boss before leaving.

"It always makes me very unhappy," Sam Goldwyn told him, "to say goodbye to a clog in my machine."

The Curtiz File

Though not as widely imitated, the sayings of the Hungarian-born director Mike Curtiz enjoyed a long vogue inside Hollywood. David Niven was instrumental in spreading Curtizisms beyond the industry, when he borrowed one for the title of his first book of memoirs: "Bring on the empty horses!"

On another famous occasion, Curtiz told Gary Cooper, who was waiting on a horse for his scene to begin:

"Now ride off in all directions."

"This scene has a lot of activity," Curtiz explained to some extras: "it is busy like a bee-dive." Another time he bellowed at a large crowd through his bullhorn:

"Separate together in a bunch," and then instructed the extras not to "stand around so much in little bundles."

Setting up a scene, he gave the order:

"Everybody move helter . . . !" Then he looked through the camera, and dashed back to the microphone: ". . . and skelter!"

You Know What I Mean

Often teased about his heavy accent and original use of the language, Curtiz once confessed:

"I don't speak the King's English. I speak director's English."

In discussing a shooting script, he once said to an assistant:

"Don't talk to me while I'm interrupting."

"Keep quiet," he told another, "you're always interrupting me in the middle of my mistakes."

On one of those days when nothing seemed to go right on the set, Curtiz complained to his assistant:

"Everyone wants to jump into my throat!"

He was arguing with a writer about how to rewrite a scene.

"You can't do it that way," said Curtiz. "You spoil the anticlimax."

Talking over a set design, Curtiz instructed the art department:

"I want this house overfurnished in perfect taste."

And dispatching an assistant for a prop, who came back with the wrong one:

"The next time I send a dope," Curtiz yelled, "I'll go myself."

To Tell You the Truth

"Tell me honestly what you think of the man," an executive asked Curtiz about a certain producer on the lot.

"If I told you the truth," said the Hungarian, "I'd be a hypocrite."

Curtiz was asked his opinion about a musical by a rival director.

"It's dull from beginning to end," he said, and then added thoughtfully: "But it's loaded with entertainment."

He told Olivia de Havilland:

"Don't fix your hair—it's nice if it's loosey."

Trying to compliment a perfumed actress whom he was interviewing for a role, Curtiz said with an exaggerated dose of Central European charm:

"Darlink, you stink so beautiful!"

Just Another Day

A man greeted Curtiz on the Warner lot with a friendly "Howdy, stranger."

"What do you mean—stranger?" Curtiz asked him. "I don't even know you."

Mike Curtiz was late for an appointment. He finally came in running, excusing himself:

"I'm very sorry, but I ran like a fire hydrant."

In the middle of a conference in his office, Curtiz was continually harassed by telephone calls, which he could not resist answering. Finally he told a caller:

"I'm out, but call me back in an hour."

Arriving sleepless on the set one morning, Curtiz explained:

"I got a phone call from Jack Warner at one in the morning. He pulled me out of bed. It's a lucky thing I was playing gin rummy."

Curtiz was negotiating a new contract with Warner Brothers. Asked by a friend how the negotiations were progressing, the director said: "It's just fine. I gave them two choices: take it or leave it."

Bring on the Empty Poodle

Mike Curtiz was preparing to shoot one of the street scenes in *Casablanca* (1942), a carefully arranged bedlam of extras, donkeys, and local Moroccan color.

"Wery nice," Curtiz told the prop man after surveying the scene, "but I vant a poodle."

"Mike, you never asked for one," said the prop-master. "We don't have one."

"Vell, get vun," the director demanded.

"What size?"

"A big vun, of course!"

"What color?" the prop man asked timorously.

"Dark, you idiot!" Curtiz exploded. "We're photographing in black and white."

The prop man said that it might take half an hour, so Curtiz retired to play chess with actor Paul Henreid (who tells this story in his memoirs), while Humphrey Bogart looked on. Half an hour later the prop man returned and said:

"Mr. Curtiz, we've got one. Will you come and look?"

Curtiz went outside and beheld a splendid standard poodle.

"Vat do I vant with this goddam dog?" the director asked with obvious astonishment.

"You said you wanted a poodle, Mr. Curtiz."

"I vanted a poodle in the street!" Curtiz began yelling. "A poodle! A poodle of water!"

Not Boris

Another Hungarian, producer Joe Pasternak, exploded in the middle of a heated script conference:

"You call this a script? Give me a couple of $5,000-a-week writers and I'll write it myself!"

Joe Pasternak was ecstatic about discovering a new singing talent.

"You should hear her sing," he enthused to a fellow producer. "She's a female Lena Horne."

Droppings

Just before shooting a scene, Gregory Ratoff, the Russian-born director working in Hollywood, ordered quiet on the set. When it had no effect, he yelled:

"And if you can't keep quiet—shut up!"

On another occasion, Ratoff instructed his actors and the crew:

"I vant to hear it so quiet we can hear a mouse dropping." An assistant pointed out that people might be more familiar with this expression in connection with a pin.

"Eggzactly," Ratoff stood corrected, "like a mouse peen dropping."

Paradox

Gregory Ratoff began to work on a musical. After reading the script he summoned writer Jack Henley.

"This is the greatest musical yet I have directed. It is sensational."

"Then why did you want to know whether I'd have time to work on the script?" asked Henley.

"I want you to work on it," said Ratoff, "because it stinks!"

Lapses

Harry Rapf, executive at MGM during its golden era, was also known for his *lapsus linguae*. He was explaining to Herman Mankiewicz how a script needed a more climactic ending:

"It should have a big exciting finish—like an earthquake: a catechism of nature!"

Listening to a pitch about Marie, Queen of Roumania, then at the height of her celebrity, Harry Rapf said:

"I don't like mythical-kingdom stories." But when somebody suggested filming the life of the Virgin Mary, he asked:

"Can it be done in modern dress?"

And MGM's answer to Samuel Goldwyn once told Irving Thalberg:

"I woke up last night with a terrific idea for a picture—but I didn't like it!"

(This last one is often told about Goldwyn himself.)

Period Piece

Harry Cohn was reading through the final script of *The Bandit of Sherwood Forest* (1946) which was about to go into production at Columbia. The dialogue was full of old English expressions such as "Yes, sire," or "No, sire," when addressing the king. Cohn pushed the intercom button and asked for the writer, who was quickly fetched.

"The story is great," said Cohn, "but this is a medieval drama, see? What's all this modern slang, 'Yes, sirree, no sirree?' "

The Deaf Aide and the Hearing Aid

During his long tenure at the helm of Twentieth Century-Fox, Spyros Skouras had a faithful old assistant, Ulric Bell. Bell's hearing deteriorated over the years, and Skouras tried for a long time to persuade him to buy a hearing aid. Finally he succeeded, and the first day Bell came into the office wearing the device Skouras asked in his impenetrable Greek accent:

"Now can you hear me, Ulric?"

"Yes, I can, Mr. Skouras," Bell replied, "but now I don't understand you."

CHAPTER 12

Strictly Business

The Movie Business

Soon after starting to work at Universal, Carl Laemmle, Jr., asked his father how much profit the studio had made since he had founded it.

"I tell you a story," said the senior Laemmle, "about another young man like you, who upon graduation from college, went into his father's clothing business. 'Dad,' he asked one day, 'when are we going to take inventory and find out how much profit you have made during the past forty years?' The father thought for a moment and then pointed to an upper shelf: 'Take that bolt of calico, son, and measure it and figure out what it's worth. That's what I started with. All the rest you see in this place is profit.'"

Ethics

For many years Paul Kohner ran a small talent agency on Sunset Boulevard with a distinguished client list that included Ingmar Bergman as well as Yul Brynner and Charles Bronson. In the 1960s Richard Kahlenberg, fresh from government service under the Kennedy Administration, went to work at the Kohner Agency, and at one of his first meetings with Kohner dropped a remark about the ethics of the business.

"When I was a schoolboy back in Europe," Kohner replied, "we were assigned to write an essay on the subject of Ethics. And I had a friend in school who did not know what the word meant, and he went home to ask his father, who ran a small tailoring business, 'What is ethics?' And his father said, 'Well, the other day a man came in to have a pair of pants cuffed. I did it and the man paid me with a new crisp bill. As he was leaving the shop, I noticed that there were actually two banknotes stuck together. Here comes the ethical dilemma: should I tell *my* partner?"

Laughing 'Till It Hurts

One of the great financial scandals to hit Hollywood was the so-called Begelman affair. David Begelman was first suspended and then fired as president of Columbia Pictures, after admitting that he had been forging signatures on checks, including one by actor-director Cliff Robertson. The incredible twists and turns of this story, chronicled in David McClintick's best-selling *Indecent Exposure*, had some lighter moments. During one of these twists, in December 1977, when Begelman had just been reinstated at Columbia Pictures, he made his reappearance at the company Christmas party. Because in Hollywood everything is a joke and everything is deadly serious at the same time, senior executives began to tell Begelman jokes to Begelman as a way of breaking the tension.

"Well, it looks like Columbia will be forging ahead with David Begelman," one of them said.

"I hear, David," ventured another, "that they're going to make a movie of your life, with Cliff Robertson in the lead."

Begelman laughed and joined in the fun.

"How would the Polish government have handled the David Begelman problem?" he asked.

"Just like Columbia Pictures," came the answer.

A few weeks later, when the magazine *New West* published additional damaging material about David Begelman's past, the joke went around the corridors of Columbia suggesting that the company ought to buy the film rights to the article.

"It would make a great movie," someone quipped, "but no one would believe it."

Act of Kindness

With the growing isolation of Britain as the Second World War began, the film industry suffered a sharp decline. Alexander Korda, who was head of Denham Studios, saw an opportunity beyond the current misfortune to get rid of his stockholders. He called a meeting of the principals, many of whom were wealthy aristocrats, and explained that the war and lack of access to American stars made it likely that they would be losing more and more money. At first the stockholders protested that they were there to help the British film industry for patriotic reasons.

"Taking money from you," Korda persisted, "is like stealing. That's why I have prepared a document here for your signature, which will disband the company and you won't be losing any more of your money." After they signed, overwhelmed by his forthrightness and decency, Korda asked:

"And what shall I do with the old negatives of the films that we have made?" The stockholders were at a loss to answer: they certainly had no use for old negatives.

"Well, you made those films, Alex," said one of them, "so they are yours to keep."

"How kind of you," said the producer, seemingly choked with emotion. "My life's work . . ."

"No, you must keep them!" they all insisted now in a chorus.

"Well, then . . ." said Korda, with tears in his eyes, "I will send you a release to sign in the post."

And that is how Alexander Korda ended up sole owner of all the films he produced, and which made him millions immediately after the war.

The Time for Quality

There is an adage in the stock market dating back to 18th-century London that the time to buy stocks is when blood is running in the streets. At the onset of the Depression Wilson Mizner was being offered a writing contract by a Hollywood studio that was having financial trouble. Mizner asked his agent if he should take the risk and whether the studio would go for his kind of quality material.

"Good as gold," replied the agent without hesitation, "they're in a swell position. They owe a big New York bank a hundred million dollars. That'll take time to pay back and require the very best pictures."

A Head for Numbers

Lew Grade, one of the titans of Britain's television industry, decided to invest in films. Having seen a fortune disappear with the Dino De Laurentiis epic *Raise the Titanic!* (1980), the mogul observed:

"It might have been cheaper to raise the Atlantic."

In the middle of a heated argument, Lord Grade made reference to something being as obvious as the answer to two plus two.

"What is two and two?" his antagonist insisted.

"Buying or selling?" asked the tycoon.

Apocalyptic Budget

Clint Eastwood was approached but declined to play the role that eventually went to Martin Sheen in *Apocalypse Now!* (1979). Eastwood later heard that the budget for Francis Ford Coppola's epic movie had topped $35 million.

"For that sort of money," he said, "we could have invaded somewhere."

Epic Proportions

When Cecil B. De Mille was pouring all his energies and the studio's money into *The Ten Commandments* (1923), Jesse Lasky tried to reason with him. As his partner explained over dinner that they had already sunk more into the picture than could ever be recouped, De Mille snapped at him indignantly:

"What do they want me to do? Stop now and release it as *The Five Commandments?*"

Toward the end of his career De Mille returned to *The Ten Commandments* (1956). Publicist Leo Guild asked the veteran director about his obsession with biblical themes.

"Why let two thousand years of publicity go to waste?" asked De Mille.

Exception to the Rule

In 1934 publicist Arthur Mayer wrote an article in *Liberty* magazine with the title, *Why Hollywood Loses Money on Good Pictures*. Not long afterwards he bumped into Cecil B. De Mille:

"How can you say good pictures lose money? My pictures are invariably profitable."

"But yours are the run of De Mille pictures," Mayer replied.

(Though in his book of memoirs, Mayer admits *en l'esprit d'escalier* that he came up with the pun only three hours later. Frank S. Nugent, film critic of the *New York Times* in the late thirties also made use of the same play on words:

"A run of De Mille picture—March comes in like a lion and goes out a like a ham.")

Low on the Hog

Soon after the release of Mel Brooks's satire *The Producers* (1968), which was made for under a million dollars, Associated Press columnist James Bacon found himself discussing low-budget movies with a well-known Hollywood producer. The man thought it was simply not kosher to make a successful movie for a million dollars.

"Why not?" asked the newspaperman.

"Because," the producer replied in total seriousness, "you can't steal a million dollars from a million-dollar picture."

Rome Wasn't Burned in a Day

Samuel Goldwyn's production of *They Shall Have Music* (1939), in which he proudly featured the violinist virtuoso Jascha Heifetz, went down in flames at the box office. Word on it was that "Heifetz fiddled while Goldwyn burned."

The Pages Went That a Way

John Ford was directing a film for Samuel Goldwyn when he fell one day behind schedule. Goldwyn visited the set and asked what he would do about catching up.

"Sam, how many script pages do you reckon I should be shooting a day?" the director asked the mogul.

"About five," Goldwyn replied on the spot.

Ford asked for a script and calmly ripped out five pages from the unfilmed portion of it.

"Okay," he said, "we're back on schedule."

Inferno

Sol Wurtzel rose from being William Fox's secretary, taking notes during rushes, to head of B pictures at the studio. His one foray into A pictures was the disastrous version of *Dante's Inferno* (1935) with Spencer Tracy. With unconscious humor, Wurtzel blamed the flop on having a summer release. *Inferno* opened during a heat wave.

Magic Act

Orson Welles had a lifelong fascination with magic. When he was riding high in Hollywood, he was invited to a party at the home of RKO boss Charles Koerner. Welles performed a number of his disappearing magic acts, which were so well received by the assembled company that the host felt compelled to remark:

"You should have seen the way Orson made three million dollars disappear at the studio."

Putting Money Where Your Mouth Is

It had been King Vidor's long-nurtured ambition to make a film with an all-black cast. The coming of sound made it possible to draw on the rich heritage of Negro spirituals, preaching, banjo playing, dancing, and the blues. On a visit to New York, Vidor went to see Nicholas Schenck, chairman of Loew's which owned MGM, about his project: it had already been turned down by the sales department because in those segregated days the film could not be shown in white theatres. Finally, to demonstrate his commitment, Vidor offered to invest his substantial salary in the project. Schenck was impressed and gave the green light:

"If that's the way you feel about it, I'll let you make a picture about whores."

And that's how King Vidor got to make *Hallelujah* in 1929.

Happy End

F. Scott Fitzgerald completed only one screenplay during his sojourn in Hollywood. When producer Joseph L. Mankiewicz read *Three Comrades* (1938) he told the writer to change the ending so that the heroine would not die.

"*Camille* would have brought in twice as much if Garbo had lived," he reasoned.

"What about *Romeo and Juliet*," Fitzgerald countered, "would you have wanted Juliet to live?"

"That's just it," Joe Mankiewicz argued, thinking in typical Hollywood fashion only about the 1936 movie version: "*Romeo and Juliet* didn't make a cent."

Poison

In 1938 the *Independent Film Journal* named the following stars of "unquestioned dramatic ability" as box-office poison:

Mae West, Greta Garbo, Joan Crawford, Katharine Hepburn, Marlene Dietrich, and Fred Astaire.

For some reason Greta Garbo's films always flopped in Ireland, prompting a critic to write:

"If Miss Garbo really wants to be alone, she should come to a performance of one of her films in Dublin."

Alla Nazimova's pictures lost so much money at the box office that one critic called her "a luxury only America could afford."

The Cabinet of Dr. Caligari (1919), now considered one of the great classics of the early cinema, was called by American critics and exhibitors by other epithets, including "an insult to human intelligence." Arthur Mayer, who suggested to Sam Goldwyn that they import the film to America, remembers a couple of theatre owners actually suing for malicious and wanton damage to their reputations, alleged to have been caused by the masterpiece of German Expressionism.

Stix in Revolt

Despite its great success in New York, London, and elsewhere, Alexander Korda's *The Private Life of Henry VIII* (1933), starring Charles Laughton, encountered hostility in the American heartland. Resisting the flood of period costume pictures that followed, one Kansas City, Missouri, theatre owner told a salesman from Hollywood that he would not show any more films "in which men wrote with feathers."

In 1934, when Ben Hecht and Charlie MacArthur were among the highest paid writers in Hollywood, they were offered an unrefusable deal to make their own independent pictures in Astoria, Long Island—one of the pioneering centers of American movie-making. The two former newspapermen turned playwrights turned screenwriters became true hyphenates: they wrote, produced, and directed their own movies. They had a lot of fun, but the pair lacked business sense. One of the rules of the office was to throw all the unopened mail into the blazing fireplace. Hecht recalled writing only one letter during this period, when a theatre owner from Iron Mountain, Michigan, complained in the *Exhibitors' Herald* that *The Scoundrel* (1935) was bad for business, and even annoying to the audience.

"Charlie and I spent a day answering Iron Mountain," Ben Hecht wrote in his memoirs. "We pretended in our letter that its citizens lived in trees, played with cocoanuts, told time with sticks and were otherwise wanting in American initiative."

But the exhibitor had the last word. His reply appeared in the next issue of his trade paper:

"Messers Hecht and MacArthur, I have received your letter, framed it and hung it in the lobby of my theatre, where it is attracting a great deal more attention than did your motion picture."

Muy Cheapo

Even after *Gone with the Wind* (1939) had become the biggest money-maker in Hollywood history up to that time, the accountants were having a field day over who should pay 60 cents for a can of liver to feed the cat in one of the Loew movie houses. The auditors representing producer David O. Selznick felt that this should be paid by MGM as the distributor, whereas Louis B. Mayer's men had charged it against the picture's budget.*

According to legend, David Selznick was about to make a deal to buy a highly desirable piece of land for his new studio. But on his way to finalize the transaction he stopped to get an ice cream at a sidewalk stand. Feeling he had been overcharged for the cone, Selznick argued so long over the penny that he arrived too late to the realtor, who in the meanwhile had sold the lot to Harry Cohn of Columbia Pictures.

Deep Pockets

Amidst much hullabaloo Warner Brothers signed Humphrey Bogart to a fifteen-year contract. He was to be guaranteed a minimum of $5 million. When the long document arrived (68 pages long, which his agent boiled down to 15 pages), Bogart noticed that the breakdown of payments added up only to $4,999,999.25, and he refused to sign. Roy Obringer, the Warner attorney assigned to deal with the star, finally reached into his pocket and put the 75 cents on the table in hard cold cash, which Lauren Bacall allegedly picked up to spend on herself.

The Art of Negotiation

Samuel Goldwyn wanted to conceal just how badly he needed to borrow an actor on loan-out from Darryl Zanuck. The secretary told him that

---

* British director Richard Lester found the following entry on the computer-generated cost sheets for a picture he was directing: "80 cents: Paint for director's name on parking space."

"How does one calculate 80¢ worth of paint?" Lester inquired. "Is it 13.33 cents per letter? Does Steven Spielberg have to pay $1.20?"

Zanuck was in an important meeting and could not be disturbed. Goldwyn kept pestering until Zanuck came to the phone.

"Darryl!" Goldwyn opened the conversation. "What can I do for you today?"

On another occasion, David O. Selznick received a midnight call.

"David, you and I are in terrible trouble," the voice announced ominously at the other end.

"Why, Mr. Goldwyn?" Selznick asked, thinking that at least Hollywood must have burned down.

"You've got Gable, and I want him," Goldwyn explained.

(Also told of Selznick calling Louis B. Mayer, to borrow Clark Gable for *Gone with the Wind.*)

Sam Goldwyn had just finished making a picture with Gary Cooper and wanted him for another project. Hunt Stromberg held a prior option on the star's services and decided to exercise it. Goldwyn heard about it through the rumor mill and got on the phone at once to Stromberg.

"It isn't that I mind you taking Cooper," he said in a hurt tone, "but at least you might have called me and said, 'Sam, I need Cooper right away, and can I have him if it doesn't interfere with your plans?' And then I would have said 'No.' "

Such a Deal

After the success of *The Secret Life of Walter Mitty* (1947), Samuel Goldwyn tried to lure James Thurber to his studio in Hollywood. As an opener, the mogul offered the humorist $500 a week. Thurber was quite content to be working for Harold Ross at the *New Yorker* so he declined by politely explaining that "Mr. Ross has met the increase." Goldwyn raised the offer to $1,000 a week, and when he did not hear back immediately, to $1,500. As Thurber kept declining, Goldwyn kept raising, until he reached $2,500, but met with no success.

Time passed, and after a while Samuel Goldwyn decided to write Thurber again. He may have forgotten his previous offer, or thought better of it, but he now proposed a salary again of $1,500 a week.

"I'm sorry," Thurber wrote back, "but Mr. Ross has met the decrease."

Hell Knows No Fury

Dorothy Parker was approached to write a script, but she did not like the money she was offered.

"You can't take it with you," she told the stingy producer, "and even if you did, it would probably melt."

Science Is Not Golden

In France a film extra who has lines is called a 'silhouette.' A more important difference is in pay-scale: a speaking role gets paid four times as much as a face in the crowd. Simone Signoret tells the story about an extra who claimed at the end of the day 500 francs instead of 120, because he had spoken a line.

"Well, then," replied the producer, "you missed a splendid opportunity to shut up."

A Deal Is a Deal

For a part in his first talkie, called *Black Waters* (1929), British producer Herbert Wilcox needed to borrow Louis Wolheim, who was under contract to Howard Hughes at RKO. Hughes was extremely charming and amenable, and then named his price: he would loan out Wolheim for three days at the exorbitant price of $20,000, or about 10 percent of the total budget. Wilcox had been so captivated by Wolheim's performance in *All Quiet on the Western Front* (1930) that he was willing to go along with the extortion. However, when he called his director with the news, Marshall Neilan refused to use Wolheim in the picture at any price. Since no contract had been signed, Wilcox went back only an hour after his first meeting to Howard Hughes, and explained to him the problem, apologizing for wasting his time.

"You made a deal with me for twenty thousand dollars," Hughes replied quietly. "Wolheim will report on your set on Monday and will be available for three days. And I want that twenty thousand before he starts work."

Wilcox saw that arguing was out of the question, and paid up. In his memoirs he remarked ruefully on the incident, as probably one of the reasons why Hughes was a multimillionaire, and he himself was not.

Something Tells Me

A producer wanted to secure the services of Charles Bronson, but he first had to persuade the actor's agent, Paul Kohner, about the merits of his case. He had given Kohner a copy of the script to read and was trying to anticipate the next question.

"And I do know about Charlie's usual price," the producer said reassuringly, "and believe me, I can double it." Without a beat to draw his breath, Paul Kohner said:

"The script must be *terrible*."

Confusion

Before he became a producer, Leland Hayward was one of the busiest agents in Hollywood in the forties. Like many of the top agents today, he represented so many people that he sometimes got confused. Clifton Fadiman tells the story how Ginger Rogers complained to Hayward that she had been sent a terrible script. The agent stormed into the offending producer's office:

"How can you insult Ginger with such drivel?" he demanded.

"Get out of here before I throw you out," the producer roared back at him. "You sold us that story!"

The End of the Rainbow

During one of his periodic quarrels with his good friend B. P. Schulberg, who was his boss at Paramount, Herman Mankiewicz handed in his resignation as contract writer. He was shocked when it was accepted. Worried at the sudden loss of $1500 a week, Mankiewicz phoned his agent, Myron Selznick, who was positively delighted:

"I always said you were worth twenty-five hundred dollars a week, and now I can get you that. Let me call you back in an hour." The hour passed, then the day, and then two weeks, during which Schulberg had sent Mankiewicz a conciliatory offer to take him back at his old salary. Riddled with gambling debts, Mankiewicz called his agent and told him he wanted to go back to Paramount. Myron Selznick went into a fury.

"Look," he shouted, "I told you that you're going to get twenty-five hundred dollars a week, and that's what you're going to get, even if you don't work for a year!"

Flesh Peddlers

Whenever two or three are gathered together in the movie business, conversation will inevitably turn to the subject of agents. More disliked than even critics, feared or hated by both their own clients and the buyers, the ten-percenters, or flesh-peddlers as they used to be called, are considered a necessary evil in the entertainment industry.

The ambivalence was summed up in a classic quip by a star in the 1940s: "I worship the ground my agent is buried in."

And Basil Rathbone spoke for many when he described an agent:

"He is the Hollywood version of Robin Hood. He steals from the rich and he steals from the poor."

"I came across our agent yesterday," Errol Flynn informed an actor with the same agency. "He was the picture of a guy with nothing to do, and he was doing it."

One of the parties to greet David Niven's return to Hollywood from the war was a big bash at Romanoff's organized by his agent Jules Stein, the founder of MCA. On the day, Niven came down with the flu. Addressing his assembled friends through a speaker phone, the star said:

"I wish Jules Stein could take ten percent off my temperature."

A joke about Paul Small, a well-known agent of the studio era, had him phone the Weather Bureau when a visitor had asked what the temperature was.

"It's exactly ninety degrees," Small reported, "less ten percent."

He was also Jack Haley's agent, who once inscribed a picture:

"To Paul Small. In appreciation of what you have done for Paul Small."

Man Bites Hog

At a dinner honoring and roasting Jack Benny, his agent Sam Lyons gave a very brief speech.

"There are many things I should like to say about Jack Benny," he said. "But I don't believe in biting the ham that feeds you."

Strangers in the Night

Director Paul Aaron dropped by to eat at Musso & Frank's a few years ago, and seeing a man at the bar, went up to him.

"Hello, Phil," he said and proceeded to have a pleasant conversation with him for several minutes.

"I'm very sorry," the man finally said, "but I'm drawing a blank: do I know you?"

"I'm Paul Aaron," the director introduced himself, "and you're Phil Gersh, my agent."

What Agents Do

Like many a hopeful actor, Harvey Korman was told when he arrived in Hollywood that he must have an agent. He did not know how to get one, but was curious how agents went about getting work for their clients. One day he managed to get a pass to a studio lot through a friend, who pointed out a small diminutive man with a huge cigar as one of the most famous Hollywood agents. Having nothing better to do, the would-be actor followed the agent into the Producers' Building, watched him march up to the receptionist outside one of the plush executive suites, take out the cigar from his mouth and heard him address these words to the secretary:

"Anytink for Barbara Stenvick today?"

Then he left.

The Fault, Dear Brutus

George Lucas made his first feature film, *THX 1138* (1972), for American Zoetrope, Francis Ford Coppola's company which Lucas had helped to found. Warner Brothers had no faith in the picture and insisted on a recut version before agreeing to distribute it. For eleven years Lucas refused to speak to Ted Ashley, who ran Warner's film division at the time. Finally, Ashley, in a vain attempt to get distribution rights to *Raiders of the Lost Ark* (1981), produced by Lucas, made a contrite confession of his sins. Tom Pollock, who represented the filmmaker in negotiations with Warner, commented:

"It was right out of the Vatican."

After *American Graffiti* was first shown in January 1973 to a wildly enthusiastic audience at San Francisco's Northpoint Theatre, producer Ned Tannen (who later became head of Paramount Pictures) called the movie unreleasable. Universal Studios took away the picture from George Lucas, and cut some four and a half minutes from it. *American Graffiti*, which cost $775,000, became the most profitable film in Hollywood history, returning fifty dollars for every one invested.

Despite this, neither United Artists nor Universal picked up their option to produce *Star Wars* (1977), George Lucas's next project. Alan Ladd, Jr., finally bought the idea for Twentieth Century-Fox, having to fight his board of directors, some of whom hated *Star Wars* so much that they refused to call it by name, referring only to "that science movie." Lucas was paid only $50,000 as writer and $100,000 for directing, opting instead

to retain a larger percentage of the merchandising and licensing rights—
which the studio's lawyers considered the "garbage" provisions of the contract. The garbage eventually brought Lucas untold sums.

Having made the most successful film in the history of motion pictures,
George Lucas was in the driver's seat. Fox had an option on the sequel,
The Empire Strikes Back (1980), but Lucas drove a hard bargain. His
company ended up with an agreement guaranteeing profits that began with
50 percent of gross rentals and rose to an unheard-of 77 percent. The film-
maker had also instructed Tom Pollock (who later became chairman of
Universal Studios) to negotiate in reverse all the clauses that Fox had
forced on him with *Star Wars*; he was to correct every slight, and to give
Lucas total control. When the final contract for *The Empire Strikes Back*
was drawn up, Tom Pollock presented it on the Jewish holy day of Yom
Kippur to Alan Ladd, Jr., with these words:
"This is your day of atonement."

It Might Have Looked Better

The new trend of merchandising all the props, clothes, and scenery, somewhat in the manner of athletes and sports events, has given cause for critics
to worry. "You get a feeling," wrote Peter Rainier in the Los Angeles
Herald Examiner, "that if *The Wizard of Oz* were made today, the yel-
low brick road would be brought to you courtesy of Carpeteria."

Licensed To Sell

The craze for James Bond films quickly became a merchandising bonanza.
After *From Russia with Love* (1963) there were Rosa Klebb dolls with
deadly spikes coming out of her shoes. Colgate-Palmolive brought out a
line of bathroom products for men in 1966, trumpeting an aftershave lotion
with the advertising message: "007 Gives Any Man the License to Kill . . .
Women." The smaller print beneath read: "Dangerous? Sure, but what a
way to go."

Old Hat

At the height of Chaplin's popularity, one of London's leading hatmakers
displayed a bowler with a notice which read:
"The hats we manufacture are known throughout the world. This is the
hat worn by Charlie Chaplin, the uncrowned king of film comedy."

A rival hatmaker glued a postscript across the display window, which said: "And that's why the whole world laughs at him!"

The Movie Business—Part II

Dawn Steel, one of Hollywood's rare female executives with real power, made her reputation in merchandising. She scored big at Paramount by bringing Coca-Cola and McDonald's on board the first of the Star Trek movies. Before she got into the film business, however, Ms. Steel became notorious by acquiring the rights to the *The Book of Lists*—to be reprinted on bathroom tissue.

With the shakeup that followed in the mid-1980s the abrupt defection of Michael Eisner and Jeff Katzenberg to Disney Studios, the corporate owners of Paramount Pictures looked at Dawn Steel and liked what they saw. In offering her the top job in the film division, one of her bosses argued:

"If you can market toilet paper, Dawn, you can market motion pictures."

CHAPTER 13

In the Money

Inexorable Logic

Ben Hecht and Donald Ogden Stewart were both between writing assignments. Hecht, in his day the highest paid writer in Hollywood, was receiv-
ing $6000 a week, while Stewart drew a measly $2000. He went and complained to his producer.

"I'm willing to concede that Hecht may be worth twice as much as I
am—when he is working. But I can loaf as well as anybody in Hollywood,
including Hecht, and I think it's only fair that I should be paid as much
for loafing as he is."

George S. Kaufman was greatly insulted when Adolph Zukor offered only
$30,000 for the motion-picture rights of one of his Broadway hits. He sent
back a telegram offering $40,000 for his Paramount Pictures studio.

Lynn Fontanne and Alfred Lunt were quintessential stage actors, and did
not like working in Hollywood. They finally agreed in 1932 to re-create on
screen their favorite roles in Ferenc Molnár's comedy, *The Guardsman*
(1931). At a press conference arranged at MGM and attended by many of

the studio's executives, a reporter asked the Lunts whether it was true that they were getting $60,000 for playing their roles. The sum was high for those days of the Depression and especially in relation to what actors received on Broadway.

"Alfred and I would have worked for less," Miss Fontanne admitted sweetly, "but nobody asked us."

It's Only Money

Herman J. Mankiewicz maintained that initially everybody came to Hollywood "in pursuit of a lump sum." And another wit, Charlie MacArthur, declared that "Hollywood money is something you throw off the ends of trains."

Playwright Howard Lindsay was lured to Hollywood after co-authoring the huge Broadway hit, *Life with Father*. One of the Broadway columnists printed a nasty crack about "money going to Lindsay's head."

"Thanks for the information," the writer cabled him. "I always wanted to know where it went."

Fanny Brice said about her time in Hollywood:

"I was out there eight months. I worked five weeks and got three years' pay."

George Raft was among the great spenders: he was reputed to have gone through ten million dollars during his career.

"Part of the loot went for gambling," he once said, "and part for women. The rest I spent foolishly."

Stratagem

Francis X. Bushman, the first of the movie idols, started as a sculptor's model, having won "the most handsome man" contest sponsored by *Ladies World* magazine. He was working in 1915 for the Essanay studio in Chicago for $250 a week, but his agent David Freedman knew that in the gold-rush atmosphere that prevailed among the competing film studios, the sky was the limit for talent with a proven following. How to prove it was the problem, and Freedman conceived of a plan.

The agent instructed Bushman to take the train to New York. Freedman met him at Grand Central, carrying a large sack of pennies. The sack had a small hole, and as the two gold-diggers walked along Forty-second Street they were followed along the trail of pennies by a surging crowd. By the time they arrived at the Broadway offices of the Metro Film Corporation, the movie executives looking out the window beheld such a mass of followers that they felt lucky to sign Bushman on for a mere thousand dollars a week.

Conflict of Interest

The British actor Donald Crisp (1880–1974) grew enormously wealthy in Hollywood; he sat on the board of the Bank of America which financed many of the loans to Hollywood producers. Sometimes as a banker he found himself in the embarrassing position of having to turn down producers who, had they received the financing, might have given him work as an actor.

Sweetheart Deals

While Mary Pickford may have been known to millions of fans as America's sweetheart, inside Hollywood she was considered to have one of the best business heads. In fact, she was sometimes called "the Bank of America's sweetheart." Samuel Goldwyn recalled from the early days of the Famous Players' studio how star salaries were negotiated—not so differently from today.

When Mary Pickford first went with Mr. Zukor he paid her five hundred dollars a week. Her success was so marked that before her contract had expired he voluntarily raised this to a thousand dollars. After this— but I am anticipating.

Whenever I saw Mr. Zukor looking homeless as a small-town man in house-cleaning time I knew what was the matter.

"How much does she want now?" I used to ask him laughingly.

"We're fixing up the contract," he would answer with a significant lift of the eyebrows.

It often took longer to make one of Mary's contracts than it did to make one of Mary's pictures. Yet, strangely enough, the beneficiary herself took no hand in the enterprise. The warfare of clauses was waged entirely by her mother and her lawyer. Indeed, Mr. Zukor has often told me that Mary Pickford had never asked him for a cent.

"Then how do you know she's discontented?" I once inquired of him. "How does she act?"

"Like a perfect lady," responded Mr. Zukor stoically.

I made no comment, but I have always understood that one of the advantages of being a perfect lady is that you can create a certain atmosphere without creating the basis for any definite accusations.

During the time that this contract was being negotiated the newspapers published an item to the effect that Charlie Chaplin had just signed a new contract whereby he was to receive $670,000 a year. Right here was where Mr. Zukor experienced a most acute manifestation of his periodic disorder.

When the Chaplin contract was announced every film-producer knew that Mary Pickford was negotiating a new contract, and I know of one specific offer she received at fifteen thousand dollars a week.

On account of the pleasant relations that had always existed between Mary Pickford and Mr. Zukor, however, she finally accepted the new contract with him, in which Lasky and I joined with Mr. Zukor, as the contract for ten thousand dollars a week, to apply on fifty percent of the profits of the picture, seemed unusually large.

During this period of dissatisfaction she spoke to me one day about the Chaplin contract. "Just think of it," said she, "there he is getting all that money and here I am, after all my hard work, not making one half that much."

This reminds me that, some time after the contract was made, Mary Pickford started working on her first picture, entitled *Less Than Dust*, and I saw more of her than I ever did before. As the enterprise was so large we decided to have a separate unit for her, which meant a separate studio that no one else worked in but Miss Pickford. As there was trouble one day, and Mr. Zukor being away, I went over to see her. Until that time any difficulties were always straightened out with Mr. Zukor. While I was there she made this remark to me: "What do you think? They all seem to be excited around here over my getting this money. As a matter of fact, one of your officials said: 'Watch her *walk* through this set. For ten thousand dollars a week she ought to be running.'"

Keeping Score

Arthur Rubinstein became legendary in Hollywood for his fees, not just his finger technique. For three days of playing odd bits of Rachmaninoff's Second Piano Concerto for the dubbing of *I've Always Loved You* (1946) he loftily demanded $85,000 from producer Frank Borzage. Rubinstein once admitted that asking for unreasonable and arbitrary fees has only helped to convince movie producers that he is, indeed, the world's greatest pianist.

Igor Stravinsky, who lived many years in Los Angeles, was once offered a mere $4,000 to score a film. The composer turned down the job.

"But this is what we paid the previous guy," the producer insisted.

"Ah, but my predecessor had talent," Stravinsky retorted with irony that might have been lost on the money-man, "and I have not, which makes the work for me that much more difficult."

Merit Is Always Recognized

F. Hugh Herbert was a minor writer toiling in the vineyards of Hollywood in its golden age. During one of his frequent periods of unemployment, he had made the studio rounds, and no matter how often he had tried, was unable to get an appointment to see MGM's all-powerful production chief, Irving Thalberg.

Great was his amazement, therefore, when one night he answered his doorbell, and there stood before his door, the great Thalberg himself. Herbert was dumbstruck by this visitation, and after a long, awkward pause, Thalberg spoke:

"You are F. Hugh Herbert, aren't you?" The writer nodded. There was silence again, and then Thalberg said: "Come to see me at the studio tomorrow." And the apparition left as abruptly as he had come, leaving the writer to toss through a sleepless night.

The following morning he went to the MGM executive building and was ushered at once into the sanctum, outside which so many of the powerful had spent so many hours waiting. Thalberg greeted him warmly and promptly handed him a fat, long-term contract. Herbert, still mystified, began working at MGM and found out only by accident the reason for his good fortune. Apparently, Thalberg was seeing a girlfriend in the neighborhood, and went to the wrong house in the dark. When he saw Herbert, he quickly covered up his mistake for which Metro ended up paying a rather expensive bill.*

How Not To Get a Raise

While still in medical school, Robert Taylor was signed by MGM on a long-term contract which started him on $35 a week. The public liked him and he became the studio's latest romantic lead, even though his salary

---

* Samuel Marx recalls that Herbert developed "such a deep love for MGM that, when he married, he asked for and received permission to have the ceremony performed in a churchlike set on the back lot of the studio."

was still only $75 a week. Egged on by his agent, Taylor asked for a private meeting with L. B. Mayer. As the agent waited outside, the actor timidly made his request. Mayer talked glowingly of his paternal feelings and about his two daughters, Edie and Irene.

"If God had given me a son," the mogul continued, "if He had blessed me with such a great and wonderful joy, I can't think of anybody I would rather have wanted than a son exactly like you."

Taylor left the office in a daze.

"Well," asked his agent, "did you get the raise?"

"No," said Taylor, "but I got a father."

How To Get Fired

King Vidor recalled in his young days working for a director on a Western serial, when the sun was fast sinking behind the Hollywood hills and one more shot had to be taken to complete the episode. One of the actors chose this strategic moment to negotiate a substantial raise. The director asked the actor to finish the scene, assuring him that they would discuss the raise later.

"Why should I?" asked the rebellious actor.

"Because I tell you to," commanded the director, pushing the actor in front of the camera, and signaled with his other hand to the cinematographer to start cranking.

"Bang! Bang!" the director yelled, and with the automatic reflex of a natural ham the actor clutched his heart and expired.

"Cut!" the director yelled, and told the actor rising from the dust: "Now you are finished in this story, and you can go try for a raise at another studio!"

We Never Make Mistakes

Early in his brief movie career, Rudolph Valentino was having a hard time making ends meet. His wife, Natasha Rambova, went to see the studio head where he worked about a raise.

"Please remember," said the executive, "that this studio has spent over one hundred thousand dollars trying to fool the American public about your husband. Now don't you get fooled, too."

How Not To Get Hired

In the late 1920s Jed Harris was the sensation of Broadway, directing and producing several consecutive hits. He lost a fortune in the crash of 1929 and inevitably his mind turned to Hollywood, the only place relatively un-affected by the Depression. He arranged to have some mutual friends in-troduce him to Louis B. Mayer as a potential MGM producer.

"How much do you want a week?" L.B. came right to the point.

"First tell me how much you get," said Jed Harris, thus terminating the job interview.

The Wheel of Fortune

Though many in the entertainment business went through years of hard-ship and struggle to make it, getting thrown off the Hollywood gravy train—now mainly driven by television—can cause major trauma. In his Don't Get Me Wrong—I Love Hollywood, *producer and columnist Sidney Skolsky captured the artist's dilemma in the studio era.*

One writer I knew, Lew Lipton, who was under contract to MGM, got caught up in the Beverly Hills trap and stood as a lesson to me. He was living in an absurdly large house in Beverly Hills, and his wife was spending his dough faster than he earned it in Saks and I. Mag-nin on what I call Schlepp Row. Things seemed to be going well; then one day his secretary—in a studio, secretaries always know everything before it happens—told him his option was not being picked up. The news struck like a bolt of lightning; he was frantic with worry. Unable to work, he left the office early and went home to break the news to his wife.

At home he discovered his wife had a monkey on her back. She was addicted to their large house and swimming pool, Saks and I. Magnin. She ranted and raved. Tears streaming down her cheeks, she accused him of betraying her, of being a failure. Finally, he tried to call a halt to the scene by announcing that he had to go out—it was his night to play poker with several executives from the studio.

"How dare you!" she screamed, outraged by what she considered his total irresponsibility. "You're losing your job! We won't be able to pay our bills, won't be able to keep this house, and you want to go out and gamble away what little money we have!"

"I have to go," he explained. "I can't let on I know I'm being fired."

The logic of his argument failed to register on her. Nevertheless, she dried her eyes and regained her composure.

"If you go to that poker game, I won't be here when you get back," she said in a subdued tone.

Her words were a dagger. But he had to go; he had to risk losing her.

He left the house and drove off in their Cadillac, thinking wistfully that it, too, would soon be repossessed by the finance company.

Two players in the poker game, Eddie Mannix and Bennie Thau, were top brass at MGM. Mannix was the general overseer and trouble-shooter at the studio. Thau was the man who handled contract nego-tiations when an agent was involved because Mayer didn't like to see agents. He was a smooth, well-mannered man who would pat you on the back while looking for a nice spot to knife you. The stakes were high to accommodate them.

Lipton didn't have to ask luck to be a lady this evening. She smiled on him from the start. Straight flushes, four of a kind, a full house. Pot after pot fell into his eager hands. He could do no wrong. He soon had a pile of chips stacked up in front of him worth thousands of dollars.

He was riding high. Losing his job no longer mattered. He had won enough dough to buy the time needed to land a job with another studio.

But luck, like all ladies, had reserved the right to change her mind. Lipton began losing. The pile of chips dwindled. Soon he was writing IOU's. Making wild bets, bluffing stupidly, driven by desperation. He sank deeper and deeper into debt.

When the game ended, Lipton owed more than $20,000, most of it to Eddie Mannix and the rest to Bennie Thau. Mannix and Thau conferred with each other, then agreed that they would have to re-new his option in order to collect the dough he'd lost to them. Lipton was elated. He felt like the game's big winner.

He drove home, hoping his wife would be there. When he pulled into the driveway, he saw light shining from the master bedroom. He went inside and raced up the stairs, his heart pounding.

His wife was propped up in bed, smoking. Her eyes were red; she had been crying all evening. He rushed to her and flung his arms about her.

She said, "I couldn't leave you. I guess we'll just give up the house and—"

He interrupted and told her what had happened, what a lucky loser he had been.

"Thank God, thank God." Tears again streamed down her cheeks, but this time they were tears of joy.

Then they both laughed and cried and hugged each other. He went to bed a happy man. Losing $20,000 had made him a winner. It had saved his job, put joy back into his marriage, and made it possible for him to go on living in the Beverly Hills trap.

The Road to Ruin

Clark Gable felt such solidarity with ordinary workers that he often engineered for a scene to break or to be postponed so that extras and non-contract players would get paid another day's wages. In his final years he had ironclad contracts stating that he would work only eight hours a day, 9 to 5. Lilli Palmer, acting with him on *But Not for Me* (1959), was impressed by Gable's total professionalism. The King would appear on the set at the stroke of nine, with all his lines memorized. He took direction without questioning or challenge. Just before the eight hours were up, he would look at his watch and call, "Five more minutes, boys!" At five o'clock exactly, even in the middle of a take, Clark Gable simply got up and left. Lilli Palmer once begged him to stay so that they could finish their scene.

"If I stayed on for a couple of minutes just one single time," he told her, "that would be the thin end of the wedge."

Solidarity Forever

During the 1930s the battle began for unionizing the film industry in Hollywood. Herman Mankiewicz was against organizing writers under the Screen Writers Guild, because he thought the profession was already vastly overpaid.

"If you keep yelling for your rights," he told one fellow-writer, "somebody's likely to give them to you, and we'll all be working for seventy-five dollars a week." Another pro-unionist tried to convince him to join by arguing:

"We're not doing this for the $2500-a-week writer; we're fighting for the $250-a-week writer."

"All the $250-a-week writers I know," Mankiewicz rejoined, "are getting $2500 already."

Silver Lining

Herman Mankiewicz had been living high on the hog in Hollywood, making $2500 a week during the Depression, when he visited back in New York. As he haunted some of his hangouts he grew more and more nostalgic.

"I'd leave Hollywood in a minute," he confided to Bennett Cerf, the founder of Random House, "if I could make a decent living here. But the best I could hope for is $35 a week."

"At what?" asked Cerf.

Around 1950, three writers, including Raymond Chandler, were discussing what a bunch of bastards their Hollywood employers were. Then one of them began to see a silver lining in the fact that at least the studios were mainly run by Jews.

"After all, the Jews know how to pay for what they get. If a bunch of Irish Catholics were running the motion picture business, we'd be working for fifty dollars a week."

Monkey Business

John Barrymore appeared in a picture with a monkey. He grew very fond of the animal, named Clarabelle, and asked her trainer if he could buy her as a pet.

"How much do you make, Mr. Barrymore?" asked the trainer.

"$3000 a week," said the star.

"Well, I think Clarabelle likes you too, and she makes $5000 a week—so she might like to buy you."

Pastime

Walter Slezak was a star in Europe when he was brought to New York by the brothers Shubert. When the Austrian character actor went to Hollywood in the thirties he was first represented by Edington & Vincent, through an arrangement with his New York agency which also took half the commission on everything the actor earned in films. The Hollywood agents apparently found splitting the fees stale and unprofitable, and one day Slezak was informed by the switchboard operator at Edington & Vincent that his contract had been sold to the Swinburn Agency.

Unfamiliar with American business practices, Slezak was puzzled why anybody would want to buy his insignificant contract. "But Mr. Swinburn was honest and told me," wrote the actor in his autobiography *When Does the Next Swan Leave?* "It seemed that he and Mr. Edington were indulging in the great California pastime of golf and got bored playing for money. So they began betting their unimportant clients on each hole. I was lost on a putt on the seventh green."

CHAPTER 14

In the Writers' Building

Door Signs

So many people kept dropping by Gene Fowler's office to exchange jokes and drinks that he couldn't get any work done. The writer changed the sign on his door to read: "Horace Witherspoon, Jr. Famous Polish Impersonator."

After that he found peace.

Dorothy Parker had the opposite problem: nobody ever visited her little cubicle in the Writers' Building. She felt completely isolated and lonely, until one evening she scratched out her name on the door and replaced it with a sign that read: "Men."

From then on she never lacked for company. In fact, when her producer demanded to know why she missed her deadline for delivering a script, the inimitable Dotty dashed off a note:

"Because I've been too fucking busy—and vice versa."

Enough Hungarians

During the 1930s, with the growing menace of Nazism, so many talented Central European playwrights emigrated to Hollywood that an anonymous wag posted a notice at MGM:

"IT'S NOT ENOUGH TO BE HUNGARIAN; YOU HAVE TO HAVE TALENT TOO."

(This line is often attributed to Sir Alexander Korda's door in London; he was supposed to have posted the warning for dozens of émigré countrymen who sought him out for work.)

By the late 1930s there were so many Europeans working at the MGM writing department that Charles Lederer hung out a small sign in his doorway:

"ENGLISH SPOKEN HERE."

Towards the end of the war, a ray of hope appeared in this sign posted at MGM:

"BUDAPEST BOMBED—THREE PLAYWRITING FACTORIES DESTROYED."

Punching In

One of the archetypal Hollywood stories has a studio chief—Harry Cohn, Jack Warner, take your pick—walking past the Writers' Building. Not a sound to be heard, and so the mogul screams to an assistant:

"Why aren't they typing?"

Jack Warner instituted a policy for everybody to punch a time clock and put in a full day's work from 9 to 6. Creative types, especially writers, resented this regimentation, but Warner said:

"If executives can come in at nine, railroad presidents can come in at nine, bank presidents can come in at nine, why can't writers come in at nine?"

Whereupon, the writing twins Julius and Philip Epstein (their credits included *Casablanca*) handed in the first thirty pages of a new script with a note to Jack Warner:

"Dear J.L. Have the bank president finish the script." And when another film made from their script bombed at a suburban preview, the mogul blamed the writers:

"This is absolutely the worst crap you have ever written!"

"I can't understand it," said Julius Epstein sweetly. "We came in every morning at nine."

Let Me Outta Here

Another writer who hated the 9 to 6 rule was Arthur Caesar. While working on contract at Warner's he leaned out of his office window and hailed a passerby, who was heading towards the studio gate.

"Call my mother, will you please," he yelled loud enough for people to hear him. "Tell her I'm okay—they treat you pretty well here, the food's not bad, the guards are pretty decent—but please ask her to mail me a carton of cigarettes!"

(The famous old MGM lot in Culver City looked so much like a correctional facility that it was often used to film prison scenes. Legend has it that long ago, when a certain actor signed with MGM, a friend sent him a cake with a file hidden inside.)

Arthur Caesar had a sign on his desk, which could serve as a motto for many a Hollywood writer:

"I don't want to be right; I just want to keep working."

Yes Dice

When Zoe Akins was working at Fox, her cell in the Writers' Building was next to that of the gregarious Arthur Caesar, who kept open house. After a while, Miss Akins went to complain to Al Lewis that she couldn't work in the office any longer; the walls were too thin and she kept hearing things.

"If there's one thing I cannot stand," she declared in her Missouri accent, "it's mace. And there are definitely mace in those walls." Lewis went with her to look for the mice, and opening Caesar's office next door, they found him with three or four grips shooting craps, tossing the dice against the wall. When Caesar heard what the problem was, he gallantly went next door to enlighten her:

"It's not mace, Miss Akins—it's dace!"

Writer's Block

John Neshi was up for a role in *Silverado* (1985) and was asked by Larry Kasdan to come and talk about it. At the back of the office, the actor wondered why a large cardboard box had hundreds of holes in it.

"Oh that," said the writer-director, and casually pulled out a large gun with which he shot some pellets to make more holes in the box. "I'd rather do anything but write."

Efficiency

During the forties efficiency experts enjoyed a brief fad in the Hollywood studios. Writers, perhaps because they spend so little money in the larger scheme of film-making, became a special target of one particular expert at MGM. He figured out that if the towel racks were placed lower in bathrooms, fewer paper towels would be used. He ordered a stop to the delivery of coffee to individual offices. And as a final economy measure he decided to remove pencil sharpeners from each office, allocating instead just two for each floor of the Writers' Building.

The day after this latest edict, Harry Ruskin—he wrote many of the Dr. Kildare and Andy Hardy scripts—ordered three dozen pencils, and soon he was seen tossing them out his window just after a few minutes' use. An hour later he ordered another three dozen. Word reached the expert, who came running to Ruskin's office to ask what he was doing.

"I don't think it would be economical," Ruskin explained, "for a man making 50 cents a minute to take three minutes to walk down the corridor to sharpen a pencil."

Leaving the office, the expert came upon a group of screenwriters huddled around an open fire they had built on the landing, burning a large hole in the new carpeting. They were making coffee, they explained, in order to save the studio the time it would take them to walk to the commissary. Needless to say, the writers won that round and the expert was fired.

The Writer's Revenge

Despite the money to be made, playwright Philip Barry once remarked that the MGM lot is not a happy one. And F. Scott Fitzgerald chronicled the peculiar humiliations that the old studio system meted out to writers in the Pat Hobby stories he wrote for Esquire *at the end of his life. The following story from the studio era, told by Allen Rifkin and Laura Kerr (in their book* Hello, Hollywood), *have cheered many a contract screenwriter:*

Winfield Sheehan, production chief at Fox, thought he would punish a writer named Samson Raphaelson by not allowing him to write. He gave orders through his story editor, Colonel Jason Joy, that Rafe would have to report to work every morning at nine and stay at the studio until six. He was to be given no writing assignment, and if he broke the slightest clause in his contract, it would be torn up. The punishment was to last six months, but Sheehan was clearly hoping that the writer would give up in frustration.

But the story had a surprise ending. Raphaelson behaved in an exemplary way, collecting and saving every cent of his huge salary. He remained calm even when further humiliation was heaped on him, and he was asked to conduct visitors around the studio lot. He developed a great spiel about the studio, the mystique of its president, William Fox, and the world of movies. His chance for revenge came one day when he was asked to give the guided tour to a group of men in somber suits, who turned out to be from the Chase National Bank in New York, which bankrolled most of the studio's films. The contract writer turned on the charm and the bankers were enchanted with his manners and the wealth of useful information provided about every aspect of the studio's operations. In summing up the tour, Rafe said with an expansive gesture:

"This is all part of the wonderful efficiency with which Mr. Sheehan runs this studio. No ordinary person from publicity conducts tours at Fox; Winnie Sheehan wants the best, and he's willing to pay for it. He pays me $3,500 a week to do this!"

Not long afterward, Darryl Zanuck was named to head the studio.

(*Another version—without names—has the writer making $1,000 a week showing around the lot some stockholders, one of whom offers him a $10 tip. "Thanks very much," the writer refused sweetly, "but I'm very well paid as a messenger," as he pulled out a check stub to prove it.*)

The Way to a Mogul's Head

Many years of experience as a Hollywood writer induced Wilson Mizner to buy into the Brown Derby restaurant with Herb K. Somborn, a former husband of Gloria Swanson. It promptly became the principal rendezvous of the movie stars and magnates.

"It's just a gag," Mizner explained, "I have tried for years to get an idea into the movie moguls' heads but I find it easier to get some gravy into their tum-tums."

When I Say Yes, I Mean No

Wilson Mizner was too much of an individualist to fit into the factory system. Under a writing contract to Twentieth Century-Fox, he was once seen hurrying across the lot, clutching his first paycheck. Another writer asked him where he was heading.

"To the doctor," Mizner answered. "I want him to paralyze the muscles which move my head sideways. From now on I'm determined only to nod up and down."

Mizner called Hollywood "the land where nobody noes." He was working once on the Warner lot, sitting in a booth, watching the parade go by. Jack Warner, head of production, called to him:

"Tomorrow, then?"

Mizner vigorously nodded in the affirmative and then asked:

"Tomorrow what? I didn't hear what you said. I was just giving you the answer you want."

The Proverbial Telephone Book

Frustrated at the kind of ideas and comments he would get, Wilson Mizner went one day into Jack Warner's office and dropped the Los Angeles telephone book on his desk:

"This might have been good for a picture—except it has too many characters in it."

Porcupine

Mizner did not like working at Warner Brothers. He once accused Jack Warner of having "oilcloth pockets so he could steal soup." One of Mizner's celebrated sayings defined working at the studio:

"It's like fucking a porcupine—a hundred pricks against one."

Pound Foolish

Howard Hawks was directing *The Big Sleep* (1946) and got into an argument with Humphrey Bogart about how one particular character in the original novel had died: was he murdered or did he commit suicide? They decided to send a telegram to Raymond Chandler, and the author replied that he couldn't remember either.

Later, Jack Warner was going through the expenses for the film and came across the telegram. He personally telephoned Howard Hawks and asked whether it had been really necessary to waste seventy cents on such a detail.

"That's one way to run a business," Raymond Chandler commented, having been an oil executive himself before becoming a writer.

Raymond Chandler had just finished working on *Strangers on a Train* (1951) for Alfred Hitchcock. The script was delivered to the Warner Brothers studio at 8.30 a.m., and at 9 a.m. he received a telegram from his agent that he had been taken off salary. Thus the studio saved having to pay the writer half a day's wages.

"The bastards," Chandler commented in a letter to his friend, the British publisher Hamish Hamilton, "no wonder nobody ever, or hardly ever, tries to deal ethically with them. One week I got a touch of food poisoning and didn't do much work, so I refused to accept any pay. Nevertheless, to meet a deadline I knew nothing about when I took the job I worked Saturdays and Sundays to clean it up. I could just as easily have held on to the final pages to the end of this week. But I said to myself, 'I'm not dealing with pikers? I was wrong. They're all pikers. . . . They would rather save a thousand bucks by cutting off a writer before he has time to catch his breath than save fifty thousand by using their brains during production."

We Need a Few Good Men

With the coming of talkies, a panicked Hollywood turned to Broadway, not just for actors but also for writers. Suddenly, Herman Mankiewicz found himself in great demand. His boss at Paramount, B. P. Schulberg, sent Mank back to New York with the urgent task of recruiting a staff of dialogue writers. The former drama critic (he was George Kaufman's assistant on the *New York Times*) and failed dramatist headed straight back to his old haunt at the Algonquin, where he said writers were so thick "they get in your hair." Addressing the pallid and huddled masses he announced that he had returned to his native town to set them free under the auspices of "The Herman J. Mankiewicz Fresh Air Fund for Writers."

Pauline Kael has written that Mank's recruits changed the course of Hollywood movies. One of them was Ben Hecht, whom Mankiewicz lured out to the West Coast with the celebrated telegram:

WILL YOU ACCEPT THREE HUNDRED PER WEEK TO WORK FOR PARAMOUNT PICTURES · ALL EXPENSES PAID · THE THREE HUNDRED IS PEANUTS · MILLIONS ARE TO BE

GRABBED OUT HERE AND YOUR COMPETITION IS IDIOTS •
DON'T LET THIS GET AROUND.

The Rules of the Game

*Ben Hecht responded to the invitation. He came, he saw, and he described
the Hollywood writing scene in his autobiography,* A Child of the Century.

I was given an office at Paramount. A bit of cardboard with my name
inked on it was tacked on the door. A soiree started at once in my office and lasted for several days. Men of letters, bearing gin bottles, arrived. Bob Benchley, hallooing with laughter as if he had come on the
land of Punch and Judy, was there; and the owlish-eyed satirist Donald
Ogden Stewart, beaming as at a convention of March Hares. One
night at a flossy party Don appeared on the dance floor in a long overcoat. "That's silly and showing off to dance in an overcoat," said the
great lady of the films in his arms. "Please take it off." Don did. He
had nothing on underneath. F. Scott Fitzgerald was there, already
pensive and inquiring if there were any sense to life, and muttering,
at thirty, about the cruelty of growing aged.

Listening to Mankiewicz, Edwin Justus Mayer, Scott Fitzgerald, Ted
Shayne and other litterateurs roosting in my office, I learned that the
Studio Bosses (circa 1925) still held writers in great contempt and considered them a waste of money. I learned, also, that Manky had gotten
me my job by a desperate coup. The studio chieftain, the mighty B. P.
Schulberg, smarting from experience with literary imports, had vowed
never to hitch another onto the pay roll. Manky had invaded the Front
Office, his own two-year contract in his hand. He had announced that
if his friend Hecht failed to write a successful movie they could tear
up his contract and fire us both.

I was pleased to hear this tale of loyalty and assured Manky the *New
York Times* would be happy to take him back on its staff if things
went awry.

On my fourth day, I was summoned and given an assignment. Producer Bernard Fineman, under Schulberg, presented me with the first
"idea" for a movie to smite my ears.

An important industrialist, said he, was shaving one morning. His
razor slipped and he cut his chin. He thereupon sent out his butler to
buy an alum stick to stop the flow of blood. The butler was slowed up
by a traffic jam and the great industrialist, fuming in his onyx bathroom, had to wait fifteen minutes for the alum stick. The movie I was

to make up was to show all the things that were affected in the world by this fifteen-minute delay. I recall of the details only that something went wrong with the pearl fisheries. The whole thing ended up with the great industrialist's mistress deserting him, his vast enterprises crashing, and his wife returning to his side to help him build a new life.

I relate this plot because my distaste for it started me as a successful scenario writer. I had seen no more than a dozen movies but I had heard in my four days in Hollywood all that was to be known about the flickers.

"I want to point out to you," said Manky, "that in a novel a hero can lay ten girls and marry a virgin for a finish. In a movie this is not allowed. The hero, as well as the heroine, has to be a virgin. The villain can lay anybody he wants, have as much fun as he wants cheating and stealing, getting rich and whipping the servants. But you have to shoot him in the end. When he falls with a bullet in his forehead, it is advisable that he clutch at the Gobelin tapestry on the library wall and bring it down over his head like a symbolic shroud. Also, covered by such a tapestry, the actor does not have to hold his breath while he is being photographed as a dead man."

No Show

At the height of his power at MGM, Irving Thalberg was notoriously difficult to see. The waiting room outside his office had what was known as the "million-dollar bench" for all the high-priced talent that could be found sitting there. George S. Kaufman was once summoned to see the young mogul and he said:

"On a clear day you can see Thalberg."*

Writer Frank Scully had an important lunch date with Louis B. Mayer. The entire Scully household was filled with anticipation about the meeting. Returning home that afternoon, Scully's wife asked how the lunch went.

"Fifty-fifty," responded the writer, "I showed up and Mayer didn't."

The Honor System

"Will you give me your word of honor," Sam Goldwyn once asked a writer, "that you will work for me when you finish your current project?" When

---

* In a celebrated episode, the Marx Brothers lit a pile of papers outside Thalberg's office, and then screamed "Fire!" in a variety of dialects, thus smoking out the elusive producer.

the writer seemed to hesitate, Goldwyn persisted: "If you can't give me your word of honor, will you promise?"

And this brings me to one Goldwyn anecdote which is absolutely guaranteed to be genuine. My old friend Paul Jarrico as a young writer was on a project with Joe Pasternak when he received a call that Samuel Goldwyn would like to see him. He dropped by the studio on Sycamore Street, where the producer told him in outline a story he wanted Jarrico to write. Seeing the writer's evident enjoyment on his face, Goldwyn said:

"You'll do it then?"

"I have a meeting, Mr. Goldwyn, this afternoon with Mr. Pasternak," Jarrico explained, "and I have to discuss his timetable with him."

"Do the decent thing, Paul," Goldwyn said in deadly earnest. "Do this job for me and don't even tell him."

Literacy Volunteer

Harry Cohn announced one day that he was taking the train to New York.

"You'd better take me with you," said Norman Krasna, who was working as a writer at Columbia.

"What the hell do I need you for?" Cohn asked with his usual suaveness.

"You'll need me, Mr. Cohn," said Krasna calmly, "because you'll have to write out your meal orders on the train."

"So what?" asked Cohn.

"You can't write," the screenwriter explained. "If you don't take me, you'll starve to death."

Finally Met a Man He Didn't Like

Will Rogers entertained a low opinion of screenwriters, perhaps the only exception to his universal love of mankind.

"In Hollywood," he once observed, "the woods are full of people that learned to write, but evidently can't read. If they could read their stuff, they'd stop writing."

Rogers also had a disconcerting habit of greeting every scriptwriter he met with a breezy "Hi, boy! What you spoilin' now?"

After seeing the original version of *The Ten Commandments* (1923) Will Rogers remarked:

"It's a fine motion picture up to the point where God finishes and the script writer takes over."

The Hack

One of the Hollywood screenwriters was introduced to Thomas Mann during his exile from the Third Reich. The man immediately began effacing himself in front of the Nobel Prize novelist, saying that he was a mere hack, and that he could not be called a writer in the presence of such a master. Thomas Mann listened with bemused patience, but afterwards he remarked to a friend:

"That man has no right to make himself so small. He is not that big."

CHAPTER 15

Literati

Eminent Authors

Samuel Goldwyn launched Eminent Authors as an answer to Famous Players, Adolph Zukor and Jesse Lasky's ambitious attempt to bring established stars of the stage and opera to the screen. Goldwyn assembled a number of then well-known and now mostly forgotten authors, but he was after bigger fish, and especially the poet and dramatist Maurice Maeterlinck. Even before winning the Nobel Prize in 1911, the Belgian symbolist was known throughout the world and Goldwyn thought he had scored a major triumph in bringing such a respectable author into the gold-rush world of picture-making. A few years later, the budding mogul chronicled their first meeting in New York, in his book Behind the Screen (1923):

As he entered I was struck by the placidity of that rather large face. It was round and calm as a lake on a still August day. All our conversation was conducted through an interpreter, and in this manner I gathered that M. Maeterlinck viewed the cinema with enthusiasm and was confident that he would be able to convert his art to its uses.

"Very well, M. Maeterlinck," responded I, "I am anxious that we should procure exclusive rights to your works, and I am willing to make the same contract with you that I have previously made with Mary Roberts Rinehart."

The Belgian lifted his eyebrows in childlike bewilderment. It was quite evident that the name of our American novelist aroused no slumbering chord of memory.

"The same then as Gertrude Atherton's," I ventured. This effort at impressiveness failed as ignobly as my first. Indeed, mention of all the writers we had assembled called from him only that vacant smile, that politely groping gaze of a man being addressed in Choctaw or Sanskrit.

It is sad but it is true that the eminence of our Eminent Authors had never been detected by M. Maeterlinck. He had not heard of a single name on our list.

"Very well, then," I surrendered at last. "I mean, I'll give you ——— thousand dollars."

And then at last M. Maeterlinck's face beamed with intelligence. The dollar was one contemporary author with the works of which he seemed thoroughly familiar. Indeed, I am compelled to record that invariably in all our subsequent intercourse the utterance of this word dollar acted very much as a pebble thrown upon that lake-like expanse of countenance. It created widening circles of comprehension and cheer.

Stung

The only extra coaxing Goldwyn had to do was to reassure Maeterlinck that lack of experience in motion-picture technique was no handicap. He urged the writer to take his favorite book and adapt it into a scenario. Maeterlinck took the advice and the dollars; a few weeks later he turned in a manuscript based on his bestseller, a semi-mystical, non-fiction treatise called *The Life of the Bee*. Sam Goldwyn locked himself into his office and with joyous anticipation began to read. A few minutes later he came through the door screaming:

"My God, the hero is a bee!"

Hope Springs Eternal

Sam Goldwyn was not a man to brood over his mistakes, and the bee incident is entirely passed over in his memoirs. So is the story which is preserved of his parting with Maurice Maeterlinck. The mogul is supposed to have placed a friendly arm on the shoulder of the world's most eminent author as he ushered him from his office:

"Don't worry, Maurice," Goldwyn said, "I'm sure you'll make good yet."

Personal Attack

In another time and another place, Luis Buñuel once remarked: "I've always found insects exciting." But not enough to make a film about them. His first movie was called *Un Chien Andalou* (1928), and when the poet Garcia Lorca, himself an Andalusian, saw it, he took it as a personal attack on him. Buñuel recalled in his memoirs how Lorca would snap his fingers and say:

"Buñuel's made a little film, just like that! It's called *An Andalusian Dog*, and I'm the dog!"

Brand Name

Samuel Goldwyn had once hired the noted author Louis Bromfield (1896–1956), but gave him no script assignment. Bromfield sat around the studio for several weeks, before going to see the boss.

"Mr. Goldwyn," he said, "you pay me all this money, yet I'm not doing anything to earn it."

Goldwyn counseled patience.

"But why on earth," Bromfield persisted, "did you hire me?"

"For your name, Mr. Bronstein," Goldwyn replied, "for your name."

(Clifton Fadiman, acknowledging that the above might be apocryphal, goes on to mention his own first encounter with Goldwyn, who greeted him warmly: "I'm glad to meet you, Mr. Freedman. I've been reading you in the *Times* for years." Fadiman had never worked for the *Times*. In the case of Louis Bromfield, it is possible, of course, though not at all likely that Goldwyn might have been confusing him with Leon Bronstein, who was an extra in two Vitagraph movies in 1914–15. A couple of years later he became quite eminent as Commissar Leon Trotsky, founder of the Bolshevik Red Army.)

Art Versus Money

George Bernard Shaw, whose celebrated career in the theatre began synchronously with the film age, had resisted the blandishments of movie moguls for several decades. Through his characters and his own public persona, Shaw reveled in verbal pyrotechnics; to him the idea of silent movies was anathema. When one of the Hollywood producers tried to seduce him with a long, flowery pitch, GBS cabled back this critique:

"Your telegram is too literary. It is obvious that your aspirations would conflict with mine. I am the literary man. Besides, the costly and unnecessary length of your cable convinces me that you are a poor businessman and I want a good businessman."

A few years later Samuel Goldwyn (whom Alexander Woollcott once described as "a sensitive, creative artist with a fine sense of double-entry bookkeeping") went on a personal pilgrimage to see Shaw in London and met a similar reception.

"The trouble is, Mr. Goldwyn," the playwright declared upon terminating their interview, "that you are concerned only with art, whereas I am interested in money."

A Hairy Hound from Budapest

Given his hostile and hard-nosed attitude, the film world was set agog by news in the mid-1930s that Shaw had finally entrusted the film adaptation of his plays exclusively to someone who was not even a businessman and barely a film-maker. The mystery man was a penniless Hungarian exile, who might have charmed the pants off GBS, had they not been both naked the first time they met.

"The Apocrypha of the first encounter between Gabriel Pascal and George Bernard Shaw," wrote S. N. Behrman, "are as various as the accounts of other miracles." Most accounts agree, though, that the two men met in 1925 swimming off Cap d'Antibes on the French Riviera in dawn's early light and in the nude. After the barest of introductions, Shaw inquired what nationality accounted for the deep tan. Gabby Pascal confessed he was Hungarian*; GBS opined that he must be gypsy. Pascal then declared himself a "czar of the Italian film industry" (he was married at the time to the Italian star Maria Carmi), and lifelong admirer of Shaw's oeuvre, which he wanted to produce for the screen. But the Irishman was not impressed.

"This is no occupation for a man of talent," he told the flamboyant

---

* Alan Jay Lerner, whom Pascal approached in 1952 about doing a musical version of *Pygmalion*, which was to become *My Fair Lady*, described the producer as "a Rumanian who claimed to be a Hungarian and looked like a Himalayan."

Hungarian. "One day you will be hard up and having nothing left in the world but your imagination. Then come and see me, and maybe I will let you film one of my plays."

Fadeout. Gabriel Pascal went through ten years of peaks and valleys of an independent producer's existence. While working on *The Miracle*, a story about the seven stages of reincarnation, the producer, already possessed of a strong mystical streak, went to India to consult Sri Meher Baba, a famous guru, whom later he would describe as "that sweet charlatan." Pascal landed back in England via the United States on a Dutch cargo ship, totally broke. He borrowed a pound from a Hungarian he knew on Bond Street, spent most of it on a shave and breakfast at the Savoy (his first meal in a day and a half), and with the remaining half a crown in his pocket, he decided that conditions were ripe to look up his old friend GBS. The maid at the Shaws' London residence blocked his entrance.

"You go and tell your master," Pascal said grandly in his broken English, "that the film producer from Rome whom he met in Cap d'Antibes is here." As an afterthought, he added: "Tell him the young man with the brown buttocks."

The Beginning of a Beautiful Friendship

Admitted into his formidable presence, Gabriel Pascal informed GBS that it was his destiny, confirmed recently by his Indian guru, to make Shaw's message more widely known through the medium of film, and finally he felt ready to do so. Amused but also mesmerized by this apparition of what could only be described as a Shavian character, the master remembered his interest in money, and inquired with an ironic smile:

"And may I ask you, young man,"—Pascal was forty, and Shaw nearly eighty—"how are your finances?"

"I have all the money one needs to make a start," the young man replied with a self-possessed smile, "provided one has talent, which I have limitless." And Pascal reached into his pocket, pulling out the half-crown coin with a flourish.

"This is all I have on earth," he said truthfully, "and even this I borrow."

Shaw was, among other things, well-known for his frugality—some called it miserliness. Yet this famous interview ended, according to Pascal, with GBS giving his future producer the cab fare to get back to his hotel.

So began the collaboration that led to the filming of several works in the Shavian canon. What had been denied to Samuel Goldwyn for all the gold in the Hollywood hills was granted practically gratis to a nobody from Central Europe. (Shaw even changed the name and elaborated on the character of Zoltán Kárpáthy in the script he wrote for *Pygmalion*, adapting it to that of his producer.)

Nobody could understand how the hard-headed dramatist, who insisted in drawing up his own contracts with the toughest provisions in the business, would make this deal with the visionary Hungarian. Shaw himself wrote that "Gabriel Pascal is one of those extraordinary men who turns up occasionally—say once in a century. . . . Until he descended on me out of the clouds, I found nobody who wanted to do anything with my plays on the screen but mutilate them. . . ." Beyond the Shavian hyperbole, the explanation may have been as simple as that given by Blanche Patch, Shaw's longtime secretary: "GBS never met a human being who entertained him more." And Pascal explained the bond between the old man and himself even more tersely:

"I spoke his spirit," he once said.

Ham-Ho

Bernard Shaw once said that films bored him: "They show interminably people getting in and out of limousines, trains and buses. I am not interested in how people get to different places, but what they do when they get there."

Yet, despite his long-held contempt for film as a vulgar medium compared with the stage, Shaw threw himself into Gabriel Pascal's productions of his films with his usual zest, overwhelming his disciple with help. A confirmed unbeliever, GBS even played an extra pretending to be carried away by religious fervor at a revival meeting in *Major Barbara* (1940). It was his little joke, and he later wrote to Pascal hoping he had not stolen the scene by dancing too exuberantly or singing too loudly.

"I suddenly felt myself twenty years younger," he excused himself.

Just as Shaw published many of his overflow ideas into prefaces, which were sometimes longer (and more entertaining) than the plays, he tried this approach with a prologue to *Major Barbara*. It was done at Pascal's suggestion, but Shaw did not need much persuasion to play himself. "If I appear," he made his token protest, "it will ruin the regular actors. I can't do that to Rex Harrison." Although *Major Barbara* was not a success, the prologue was much admired, even by the acidulous Dorothy Parker, who said that for sheer sex appeal, Shaw surpassed any leading man.

Shaw was both a shameless ham and a superb actor; GBS would have made the best Saint Joan according to Sybil Thorndike, who created the role in 1924. But there too Shaw faced competition from an unexpected quarter. The Second World War had already broken out by the time

Gabriel Pascal had got around to thinking about filming *St. Joan.* The British government was for postponing the project, remembering that the English had burned the French patriot. Pascal got as far as talking to Charles De Gaulle about the film, and later claimed that the General had given him the green light only on condition that he could play the Maid himself.

Apocalypse

Marc Connelly told the story of William Faulkner's first meeting with Irving Thalberg, who asked the writer whether he had seen any of MGM's famous films.

"Ah don't believe ah know which pictures are yours," Faulkner replied truthfully. "Do you make the Mickey Mouse brand?" Thalberg was not amused:

"No," he said icily, and told Faulkner that he wanted him to familiarize himself with the studio's major films and stars. The writer from Mississippi was set up in a small screening room, where he began to view the latest celluloid masterpieces. After about ten minutes the novelist reeled out into the corridor where a fellow writer became alarmed at the anguish of his face.

"Bill, what's the matter?" The normally phlegmatic and slow Faulkner could only say:

"Jesus Christ, it ain't possible!"

You Can Go Home Again

Perhaps the most famous of the Hollywood writer stories is about the time William Faulkner asked his producer at MGM whether he could work at home. His agent at the time was Leland Hayward, who received a call from Metro asking him where the hell his client was. In the thirties nobody was supposed to go out the studio gates without letting the front office know. Hayward had no idea where Faulkner might have disappeared to, but he started making frantic phone calls all over town. Finally he had an inspiration of trying him at his home in Oxford, Mississippi. Faulkner answered the phone.

"Bill, what the hell are you doing down there?" yelled the agent, and the writer answered in his mild drawl:

"Well, ah asked my producer if ah could work at home, and he said fine, so heah ah am."

Mutual Admiration

William Faulkner was invited by Howard Hawks to a hunting party with Clark Gable. During a lull, Gable asked who were the best contemporary writers.

"Hemingway, Willa Cather, Thomas Mann, John Dos Passos, and myself."

"Do you write for a living?" Gable asked in surprise.

"Yes," Faulkner confessed, "and what do you do?"

Thankless Tasks

When Ernest Lehman did the screenplay of *Who's Afraid of Virginia Woolf?* (1966), he had such respect for the text and fear of the author that he hardly changed a line. In fact, his contribution was supposed to be exactly twenty-seven words, four of which were, "Screenplay by Ernest Lehman." When Edward Albee read the version, he said ungraciously:

"Twenty-seven words, all bad."

Nunnally Johnson, having adapted more than a hundred original books and plays, said that he kept the friendship of fewer than ten of the writers whose works he had transplanted to the screen. After he had already done John Steinbeck's *The Grapes of Wrath* (1940) and thought he had a good working relationship with the author, Nunnally was later assigned to do a film version of *The Moon Is Down* (1943), which was then playing on the New York stage.

"Have you any suggestions?" Johnson called the author.

"Yeah, tamper with it," said Steinbeck.

I Always Knew I'd Been Adapted

Movie scripts feed on plays, novels, and short stories, for which producers often pay extravagant sums. Sometimes only the title is kept for the film version. One of the notorious examples of wholesale adaptation was the screenplay based on Noel Coward's *Design for Living*, which allegedly kept a single immortal line from the original: "Kippers on toast."

Creative Differences

There were ten different endings for the film version of James Thurber's *The Secret Life of Walter Mitty* (1947), but none of them quite satisfied

Sam Goldwyn. He phoned Thurber at the *New Yorker* and explained at great length to him the new ending.

"Look, Mr. Goldwyn," the humorist interrupted him, "I know nothing about moving pictures. I don't know what you've done with the rest of my story, and I don't particularly care. I sold you the book and that's that. How can I say whether or not your new ending is right?"

Sam Goldwyn was stunned for a moment and then said:

"Thank you, Mr. Thurber, thank you. Now, why can't I get criticism like that in my own studio?"

Later Sam Goldwyn brought James Thurber to Hollywood to adapt his own story *The Catbird Seat*. He was given an office and a secretary. As soon as he began dictating, she said:

"I'm sorry, I don't do dialogue. I only take letters." Thurber took this obstacle in his stride. He began each scene with "Dear Sam."

The writer turned in the script and the producer told him to revise it. Thurber told Goldwyn to go and climb a tree. That was unusual enough, but then he committed the unheard-of sin of returning the entire $28,000 advance, including his agent's ten percent.

Touch of Genius

John Huston worked with Tony Veiller on adapting *Night of the Iguana* (1964) by Tennessee Williams to the screen. The scene where Richard Burton, drunk and feverish, is trying to keep away from Sue Lyon, who comes to seduce him, worked well, when Huston showed it to the playwright.

"The only change he wrote," the director told an interviewer in *Action* magazine, "was the thing that made the scene. When the girl opens the door suddenly, a glass falls onto the floor, leaving broken bits of glass scattered about the room. When the scene is played, both of them are barefoot. Burton walks on it and doesn't even feel being shredded. The girl sees this and joins him walking barefoot across the glass. It was the difference between an extraordinary scene and a pedestrian one. It's also an example of Tennessee's extraordinary powers of dramatization."

Means and Ends

John Collier, novelist and short-story writer, was occasionally hired to write screenplays. He found the pressure of deadlines in the film business difficult. Once he had spent almost a year writing the first hundred pages of a script, but tried to assure his producer that he would be finished with the rest in two weeks.

"I've only got twenty pages to do," said Collier.

"But, John," said the exasperated producer, "if it took you twelve months to write a hundred pages, what makes you think you can do twenty in just two weeks?"

"It's not the pages I have to write that are giving me trouble," said Collier with a writer's logic, "but the ones I've already done."

At another time John Collier was engaged to write a screenplay based on a novel he was working on at the same time. His friend, the writer Paul Jarrico, was having lunch with the producer for whom Collier was adapting the script, and being asked how Collier was doing, Jarrico reassured him about the writer's progress. Later that day, Jarrico reported to Collier about the conversation:

"I told him that all was well, and that the end is in sight."

"Which end?" asked Collier.

The Only Good Indian

During his final period in Hollywood, F. Scott Fitzgerald read in the paper that the Pasadena Playhouse was producing an adaptation of his novel, *A Diamond as Big as the Ritz*. Surprised that he had not been informed, the author called up the box office and anonymously reserved two seats near the back. Although broke, Fitzgerald decided to dress up like one of his characters, and persuaded his girlfriend, the columnist Sheilah Graham, to do the same. He ordered a limousine and chauffeur and the two arrived at the Playhouse in style. It looked deserted. After a while, somebody told them that indeed a group of acting students were doing a class exercise in an upstairs rehearsal hall. Fitzgerald and Graham sat on a wooden bench, two ghosts from the Jazz Age, as the students, wearing their street clothes, performed a barebone version of Fitzgerald's extravagant fable.

Afterwards, the author decided he wanted to go backstage and give encouragement to the young actors. He introduced himself and could not help noticing their embarrassment. They were surprised to see him—it was quite obvious that most of them had thought that Fitzgerald was dead. And within a few months he was.

The producer Walter Wanger approached Budd Schulberg with the idea of collaborating with F. Scott Fitzgerald on a script.

"I thought Fitzgerald was dead," said Schulberg.

"I hope not," Wanger replied, "I've been paying him $1,500 a week."

Literary Life

French playwright Henri Bernstein muttered after one of his stints in Hollywood:

"Geniuses, geniuses everywhere I turn! If only there was some talent!"

S. N. Behrman was invited to a small Hollywood dinner party which included Somerset Maugham and Aldous Huxley. Afterwards the urbane playwright told a friend:

"It certainly gives you a thrill to dine with two of the world's greatest writers—and hear Ruth Gordon talk."

Anti-Climax

Graham Greene had finished a draft of *The Third Man* (1949) when he learned that it had to be discussed with David O. Selznick, who held the American rights, despite the fact that Alexander Korda was producing the picture in England. So Greene and director Carol Reed journeyed to Southern California to see Selznick. His first objection was to the title:

"Listen, boys, who the hell is going to a film called *The Third Man?*" He suggested something like *Night in Vienna*, "which will bring them in."

Then Selznick passed on to his biggest problem with the story.

"It won't do, boys," he told Reed and Greene: "It's sheer buggery."

"Buggery?" one of them asked.

"It's what you learn in your English schools," Selznick explained. The Englishmen were practically speechless, while the man who produced *Gone with the Wind* went on:

"This guy comes to Vienna looking for his friend. He finds his friend's dead. Right? Why doesn't he go home then?"

Graham Greene, who had spent months working on the script, tried to explicate the subtler points of the story, pointing out that Joseph Cotten's character does in fact fall in love wih Harry Lime's girl within a day of his friend's death.

"Why doesn't he go home before that?" Selznick persisted.

About ten years later Sam Zimbalist invited Graham Greene for a lunch at the Dorchester Hotel. The producer was having trouble with the remaking of *Ben Hur* (1959), which did in fact cause his untimely death. Would Greene look at the script and solve the central problem? The writer asked what it was.

"You see," Zimbalist explained, "we find a sort of anti-climax after the Crucifixion."

CHAPTER 16

From Pitch to Script

Original Flavor

The writing team of Charles Brackett and Billy Wilder was working on the script of *Midnight* (1939). As was frequently done before the Writers Guild of America prohibited the practice, the supervising producer, Arthur Hornblow, Jr., had assigned a third writer to fix up the pages as they were being turned in. Ken Englund saw little to correct, but rewrote anyway.

"The trouble with this," Hornblow informed Englund regarding the re-written script, "it doesn't sound like Brackett and Wilder. You've lost the flavor of the original."

The writer waited while the producer mused:

"Who do we have under contract who writes like Brackett and Wilder?"

"Well," Englund offered tentatively, "Charlie Brackett and Billy Wilder are sitting in their office with nothing to do. Why don't you send them my script and they'll give it that Brackett and Wilder flavor?"

"That's a hell of an idea," said the grateful producer.

An Idea Is Born

Joe Mankiewicz was having lunch with Norman Krasna, who told him an idea that he thought might make a play. Later L. B. Mayer hired Mankiewicz to be a producer at Metro and Mankiewicz pitched him on the idea. It was about lynching in the South, at a time when MGM was famous for its musicals. L. B. hated the idea, but finally agreed to buy it. Mankiewicz instructed Sam Marx, head of the story department, to buy the story from Krasna. The next day Krasna called Mankiewicz that he had received a call from Metro:

"Listen—could you do me a favor? It's been so long since I told it to you, I've forgotten what I said. Would you put it down for me?"

Mankiewicz dictated ten pages to his secretary, MGM made the film (it was called *Fury* (1936)), which won Krasna an Academy Award.

I Wish I'd Thought of That

A smart writer knows that in Hollywood the best ideas by definition come from the producer or director, whoever has the power. It was already so in the old days of the silent movies, except that Mack Sennett, the master of slapstick, really had all the best ideas himself. He would sit around with his writers and throw out five or six suggestions that he did not like enough. After an hour and a half, one of his top-paid writers would venture out with one of those ideas, as if he had just thought of it, and Sennett, who had forgotten that it was his idea, would jump at it:

"That's it! That's the idea we want!" And he would give the writer money and credit for it.

Department Story

People often wonder what story department of the film studios do other than reject scripts. The following may illustrate why so few ideas are generated by them.

A story editor at MGM fell in love with Theodore Dreiser's novel *Sister Carrie* and tried unsuccessfully to bring it to his bosses' attention. Finally, he decided to go right to the top, but knowing that Louis B. Mayer never read a book, he made a careful synopsis of the plot and sent it with a letter which pleaded with him to read the outline. After a while the enterprising story editor was summoned to his chief's office. From behind his desk, Mayer looked up for a moment and said:

"So, you want me to make a picture about a *hoor*," he snarled like Leo the MGM lion. And he fired the poor story editor.

(*Carrie* (1952) was made eventually by Paramount, starring Jennifer Jones and Laurence Olivier.)

Spiritual Comfort

A writer complained to Louis B. Mayer about changes imposed on his script.

"The Number One Book of the Ages," the mogul comforted him, "was written by a committee. It's called the Bible."

New Twist

Samuel Hoffenstein, a poet who earned a living as a screenwriter in the thirties and forties, was asked to rework a Tarzan story by giving it a new twist. He read through the script, did not see anything particularly wrong with it, but he put in the time to serve out the allotted number of weeks on his contract. At the end he handed in a neatly rewritten script, which had an unexpected twist. Hoffenstein had translated the whole screenplay into Yiddish.

The Color of Your Money

Damon Runyon was talking up a story to Darryl Zanuck, who was growing excited.

"Why don't you put it down on paper," he suggested, "and I'll buy it."

"Before I can do that," said Runyon, "I'll have to give it some more thought. And I can't do that, unless I get some thinking money."

The Perfect Script

A new writer at the Goldwyn Studios had turned in his first script and was surprised to get a summons to see the boss.

"This is a perfect script," Sam Goldwyn said to the writer, "in fact, it is the first time in my life that I've seen a perfect screenplay. I want you to have copies made and distributed to all the other writers on the lot as an example of what I consider a really perfect script."

The writer was walking on clouds towards the door, when he heard Goldwyn say:

"And hurry, before I start rewriting it."

Lester Cowan, the producer for whom F. Scott Fitzgerald wrote a screen version of his *Babylon Revisited,* kept hiring as many as a dozen writers to try and improve it. The thirteenth went back and read the original script by Fitzgerald and told Cowan:

"This is the most perfect film scenario I have ever seen. I don't see why you want to revise it."

"You're absolutely right," said Cowan after a moment's reflection. "I'll pay you two thousand a week to work for me and keep me from changing one word of it."

Starting to work on *Paper Moon* (1973), Peter Bogdanovich had his first meeting with Alvin Sargent, who had just completed a draft of the screenplay.

"This is a terrific script," the director greeted the writer with genuine warmth, "it just needs a complete rewrite."

An Earful

Samuel Goldwyn once asked Moss Hart how he was doing on a screenplay about Hans Christian Andersen (1952). After giving his progress report, the writer added:

"If you don't like the job I've done, I will emulate Van Gogh, cut off my ear and present it to you."

"My boy," said the producer, "in my desk I've got a whole drawer full of ears. All I ask from you is a good box-office script."

The Reader Over Your Shoulder

During his stint in Hollywood, the playwright Marc Connelly was told to read *Quo Vadis,* the biblical epic by Henryk Sienkiewicz, for a screen adaptation. Having spent several days going through conscientiously the novel, which he carried into the commissary, Connelly saw a writer come up to him.

"Marc, I think you ought to know," the colleague whispered in his ear. "There's another guy reading that book behind you."

Saga

The first writer David O. Selznick hired to write a screenplay for *Gone with the Wind* (1939) was the Pulitzer-winning playwright Sidney Howard. His drafts would have played five and a half hours. After Howard quit, Selznick worked over two years with a dozen writers, including Charlie MacArthur, John Van Druten, and F. Scott Fitzgerald. In a letter to his daughter, Scottie, the novelist called the book "not very original . . . but interesting, surprisingly honest, consistent and workmanlike throughout, and I felt no contempt for it but only a certain pity for those who consider it the supreme achievement of the human mind."

Fitzgerald and his mistress Sheilah Graham had some fun acting out key scenes between Rhett Butler and Scarlett, but this came to a grinding halt, when the writer was terminated after two weeks for using words other than those of Margaret Mitchell's, "as if it were Scripture."

Atlanta and the original director George Cukor had both been fired when Victor Fleming, the replacement director, demanded—as replacement directors tend to—a complete rewrite. Every idle day was costing David Selznick a fortune, and in desperation he offered Ben Hecht $15,000 if he could do it in a week. It was then that Selznick was appalled to learn that Hecht had not read the most admired novel of the decade, and given the time constraint, he had no intention of doing so. ("It would only have confused me," Hecht told his agent, Leland Hayward.)

Instead, in a bizarre role-reversal, the writer made the producer tell him the entire story. After an hour of Selznick's recitation, Hecht had enough.

"That's the most involved plot I've ever heard," said the doctor to the patient. "Can't you just throw it away and I write a new one?"

Plot Point

Like many a Hollywood writer today, Ben Hecht made more money as a script doctor and adviser than on his own screenplays. A desperate producer once offered to pay him anything he asked. Hecht was just about to catch a train from Los Angeles back to New York, and mentioned that he could work on it during the four days. But when the producer heard the price, he swallowed and asked: "How much would it cost to Kansas?"

In his autobiography, Hecht describes the kind of consulting he was asked to do.

I remember a phone call to Nyack from the MGM Studio in Hollywood. Bernie Hyman, then the studio head, wished my help on a plot problem that had arisen in a two-million-dollar movie being prepared for shooting.

"I won't tell you the plot," he said. "I'll just give you what we're up against. The hero and heroine fall madly in love with each other—as soon as they meet. What we need is some gimmick that keeps them from going to bed right away. Not a physical gimmick like arrest or getting run over and having to go to the hospital. But a purely psychological one. Now what reasons do you know that would keep a healthy pair of lovers from hitting the hay in Reel Two?"

I answered that frequently a girl has moral concepts that keep her virtuous until after a trip to the altar. And that there are men also who prefer to wait for coitus until after they have married the girl they adore.

"Wonderful!" said the Metro head of production. "We'll try it."

Take This Job and Shove It

For some reason, many of the highest paid film writers have a low self-esteem. They feel oppressed by a system that gives them money but very little final say about their scripts. But some of the inferiority complex comes from being treated actually as inferiors by producers and directors. One of the cherished stories from the Hollywood of the 1940s tells of the successful team of Billy Wilder and Charles Brackett, when they were loaned out by Paramount to MGM. There, an executive producer by the name of Sidney Franklin summoned the two writers to a story conference. As he described the project, Franklin would turn to Charles Brackett, and ask him to perform some menial task:

"Jack, would you lower that window?" Then he might order Billy Wilder:

"Steve, take your foot off that chair."

This went on for a while, when Brackett got up on his own accord.

"Mr. Franklin," he said with cold dignity, "my name is Charles Brackett. I am too old and too rich to put up with this sort of nonsense. If you call us once again by any other names than our own, we'll walk out that door and never come back."

MGM returned the loaned writers to Paramount three days later.

(A variation has been told of Raymond Chandler against Billy Wilder as director. In the mid-1980s the story resurfaced with William Goldman cast as the hero and Chevy Chase as the villain.)

Modest Request

In pitching a movie to be called *Decameron Nights* (1928) to Erich Pommer, head of UFA Studios in Berlin, the English producer-director Herbert Wilcox had nothing but a title and a vague idea about an atmosphere of sex. Pommer lined up a high-powered German cast, but when they asked to see a script and there was none, they walked out. Erich Pommer managed to coax them back by assuring them that the English-man *"hat es im Kopf*—had it all in his head." Lionel Barrymore was more tolerant. When Wilcox told him the story, the American star said:

"O.K.—but do me a great favor. Before we start, tell me my first and last scene!"

Help from the Stars

Even after successive producers and directors have made their suggestions, often wholesale rewrites are demanded by the prospective stars, allegedly to make the best use of their talent. Having a star as a collaborator can pose a problem in writing—and with another of the "Rs."

Nunnally Johnson was writing a movie at International Pictures for Gary Cooper. *Along Came Jones* (1945) was based on a novel. Halfway through the script, Johnson ran into Cooper at lunch and asked him if he would like to read the original novel. The star readily agreed and took away the book. The screenwriter carried on with his script. Two weeks later, John-son had almost finished the draft when he ran into the actor at the commissary:

"How did you like the book, Coop?"

"Oh, fine, I'm about halfway through," the movie star replied. "I'm reading it word by word."

Acting Problem

Alan Ladd, Sr., was stopped on the Paramount lot by a friend, who said:

"I hear your new picture starts Monday."

"Yeah," Ladd sighed, "and I haven't even read the script yet."

"That must be kind of disturbing," the friend sympathized.

"Sure is," said Ladd, "I don't know what I'm going to wear."

La Ronde

David Mamet was nominated for an Academy Award for adapting *The Verdict* (1982) for the screen. When he first turned in his screenplay to Twentieth Century-Fox, the producers did not like it and went to Jay Presson Allen to do another version.

She told them that she thought Mamet's script was brilliant, but could not persuade them to stay with it. Her version was then given to Robert

Redford, who spent a long while trying to adapt the script more to his liking. When it looked unlikely that Redford would do it, the producers went to Sidney Lumet, a friend of Jay Presson Allen, and he expressed an interest in directing.

But Lumet had just seen the off-Broadway revival of David Mamet's *American Buffalo*, which so impressed him that he asked the playwright whether he had done any writing for film. Mamet then gave Lumet the screenplay which the studio had turned down. The director liked it so much that he insisted to the producers that he would only do that version. And that is how Twentieth Century-Fox ended up—by accident—with the original script for *The Verdict*.

Script Conference

Burt Lancaster was reluctant to play Wyatt Earp in *Gunfight at the O.K. Corrall* (1957), but he was under contract to Hal Wallis, and Kirk Douglas managed to talk him into it. But Lancaster did not like the script by Leon Uris, which he found too wordy. When the producer refused to have it rewritten, the star himself hired a writer and locked him up for two weeks in Hal Wallis's office until he re-emerged with a script which had seventy fewer pages.

Seeing that the script had been reduced to pure action with hardly any characterization left, Lancaster advised Kirk Douglas that they must play Doc Halliday and Wyatt Earp as a couple of "pre-Freudian fags. We're in love with each other and we don't know how to express ourselves that way—so we just kind of look at each other and grunt."

How To Deal with Proposed Changes

Shaw did not suffer Hollywood gladly. Gabriel Pascal was trying to nego-tiate with RKO a production of *Arms and the Man*, starring Ginger Rogers, and there was discussion, as always, of a few cosmetic changes in the script. The studio wanted to change the title to *The Chocolate Soldier*, and it was worried about offending Bulgaria, where Shaw's play was set, though some three generations before. But the most serious complaint came from the star, who worried whether her role was really the leading female lead. "Tell Miss Rogers," wrote GBS to his producer, "that Raina is the star part. . . . If she suggests that the part of Louka might be made that star part, do not argue with her; just throw her out of the window and tell her not to come back."

Hollywood never made the movie.

Happy End

At the height of the Garbo-Gilbert craze, MGM was so eager to cash in on their initial success that they recast John Gilbert in Tolstoy's *Anna Karenina*. The title was considered unsuitable to describe the momentous re-teaming of the lovers of the century. At a script conference someone came up with the suggestion that it be called *Heat*. Frances Marion, who had written the screenplay, pointed out how this would look on the bill-boards:

"GILBERT AND GARBO—IN HEAT."

So the studio called the 1927 silent travesty *Love* instead, and Anna Ka-renina, instead of throwing herself under the wheels of the train, reappears five years later at the military academy her son is attending. She sees her lover Vronsky, who asks: "What has happened? Why are you wearing black?"

He finds out that MGM had decided to kill Anna's husband to give a happy twist to Tolstoy's tragic story.

Lead Balloon

During the war, Clark Gable was in an aviation picture, being shot at an old flying field in Texas. One morning as he arrived on location, the star saw the director planning to shoot a scene in which two aces were about to make a test flight. Gable glanced at the dialogue in the script and asked:

"Do you mean to send those boys up in this script?"

In a Nutshell

Herman Mankiewicz was asked during a conference at Paramount whether to purchase a screenplay called *The Marriage Mask*.

"I don't understand what the script is about," Mankiewicz began his analysis. "But it reminds me of the fear I get now and then of having to drink a glass of water without the glass."

Settled Once and for All

Thousands of words have been expended over the years by critics on the meaning of "Rosebud," the word uttered by the dying newspaper magnate in *Citizen Kane* (1941). Explanations have ranged from the obscene to the obscure. Rita Alexander, the secretary to whom Herman Mankiewicz dictated the first draft of the screenplay in 1940, remembers asking him who was Rosebud.

"It isn't a who—it's an it," the writer corrected her.

"What is Rosebud, then?" she asked.

"It's a sled," Mankiewicz explained.

Collaboration

"Nothing puts me to sleep faster," Herman Mankiewicz once declared, "than the sound of my collaborator's typewriter."

Norman Krasna was discussing with a fellow playwright a movie script they had been handed to rewrite.

"It has no story, no characterization, so what's good about it?" groaned the collaborator.

"It has some of the finest typing I've ever seen," said Krasna.

Whose Funeral Is It Anyway?

One of the bitterest stories illustrating the fate of writers in Hollywood circulated around the middle of the century. Cyril Maude, the script-writer, lay dying, but summoned enough strength to compose a few lines of verse which he asked his best friend to read at his funeral. Maude died promptly, and the friend, who happened to be a director, called up another director:

"Cyril's funeral is tomorrow at noon. Could you meet me a couple of hours before?"

"Why?"

"Cyril gave me a poem to read at his grave," said the best friend, "and frankly it stinks. I want you to help me fix it."

CHAPTER 17

Knock on Hollywood

New in Town

When Shelley Winters first came to Hollywood, she had a house up in the hills, but she was so afraid of being alone that she would ask the waiters and waitresses at Googie's, an all-night restaurant, to come up to her house and read scripts with her. They would either read or listen to her read until sunrise. As word of her various eccentricities spread around town, the actress said:

"I'm outspoken, but not by many."

Arriving from Sweden to Hollywood, Viveca Lindfors thought it must be an exceptionally clean place, because she kept hearing about so many people being washed up.

Comedian Joe Frisco arrived in Hollywood, and a friend showed him the scenery:

"Look at those hills—look at the ocean!"

"Yeah," Frisco said, looking, "b-but you can't put k-k-ketchup on it."

Later, when he got a bit more settled in, Frisco observed in his trademark stammer that Hollywood was the only town, "where you c-c-can wake up in the morning and listen to the birds c-c-coughing in the trees."

During Oscar Levant's first visit to Los Angeles, Harpo Marx drove him out to the beach. In those days there were only stark stretches of gray sand and blue water as far as the eye could see.

"There," Harpo pointed out to sea happily, "how do you like it?"

"Hey," said Levant, "a Gentile Ocean!"

Put Out More Flags

Michael Curtiz was working in Germany when Hollywood called in the person of Harry Warner, who promised to make Curtiz as famous as Coca-Cola if he came to America. It was 1927, Weimar Germany was not exactly a bed of roses, so Curtiz yielded to Warner's blandishments and signed a contract. He glimpsed the Statue of Liberty on a beautiful July morning and found the whole of New York City decked out, with flags and parades everywhere. There were photographers and reporters, and as studio representatives whisked Curtiz off towards the Manhattan office of Warner Brothers, the bewildered director raised his voice above the bands to ask:

"Never did I imagine anything quite so colossal! Tell me, does Harry Warner put on such a parade for every director he brings to America?"

"Well . . . no," said one studio man. "Just those who arrive on the Fourth of July."

Culture and Agriculture

Most people today are unaware that within recent memory Los Angeles County was number one in growing citrus in the United States. That is the context for Fred Allen's famous statement:

"Hollywood is a place where the girls have false hair, teeth and calves on their legs. The men have their shoulders pulled up and wear toupees. When two stars make love on the screen it's not two people making love; it's a lot of commodities getting together. California is all right if you're an orange."

Maurice Maeterlinck is credited with first calling Hollywood a cultural desert.

His fellow playwright Ferenc Molnár said it was "a sunny place for shady people."

"Hollywood may be thickly populated," Sir Cedrick Hardwicke found, "but to me it's still a bewilderness."

It was another Englishman, J. B. Priestley, who observed that Los Angeles "was a series of suburbs in search of a city," while Raymond Chandler thought it had the personality of a paper cup.

"Hollywood is not uncivilized," the writer Patrick Mahoney once remarked, "it is decivilized."

And script-doctor Abe Burrows complained:

"No matter how hot it gets in the daytime, there's nothing to do at nights."

Claire Bloom once said that she liked to work in Hollywood, but as for living there:

"I'm too young to die."

Humorist S. J. Perelman thought of Hollywood as "a piquant mixture of the Main Line, the Mermaid Tavern and any lesser French penal colony."

Aldous Huxley lived the last two decades of his life in Los Angeles:

"No man could find a better spot on earth," he said, "if only he had an intelligent person to talk to."

Perhaps the truest observation from a convert to Los Angeles came from Will Rogers:

"It's a great place to live, but I wouldn't want to visit there."

"In 1940, I had my choice between Hitler and Hollywood," René Clair recalled, "and I preferred Hollywood—just a little."

Fish Out of Water

Neil Simon, having made the move from New York to Los Angeles for the duration of his marriage to Marsha Mason, finally heard enough from the boosters of the Southern California climate:

"When it's 100 degrees in New York," he admitted, "it's 72 in Los Angeles. When it's 30 degrees in New York, in Los Angeles it's still 72. However, there are 6 million interesting people in New York, and 72 in Los Angeles."

D. W. Griffith, interviewed at 72 one block from Hollywood and Vine, looked out from his window at the town he helped to create.

"The most brainless people in the world live in Southern California," he said. "No one here has any brains except he comes from the East."

East Is East

William Hurt hates Southern California so much that he never packs a bag when he leaves New York for the West Coast, and if there is just one free day between shooting, he would rather spend it on planes, preferably heading East. The actor once told interviewer Larry King that he must have physical possession of his return ticket to New York during every scene, hidden in his bathing trunk or in his rags, as it was in the prison cell in *Kiss of the Spider Woman* (1985). If William Hurt ever had to play a fully nude scene, one can picture him in a hat, or he might have to fall back on his training in Method acting and use sense-memory.

Spring Fever

Edward G. Robinson and Dane Clark were lunching at the Brown Derby and conversation turned to a favorite topic of transplants: the difference between the two coasts.

"California just isn't like the East," sighed Dane Clark. "Do you remember, Eddie, those springs in Brooklyn?"

"I certainly do," said Robinson. "I'm still carrying dents in my back where they came through the mattress."

Vaudeville

Solly Violinsky, an old vaudevillian actor, was once asked why he came to Hollywood.

"To play a neat Mexican," he replied in his thickest Jewish accent.

Running into a producer who had done him a bad turn, Violinsky said:

"I'd like to buy back my introduction to you."

A State of Mind

"The only way to avoid Hollywood," Igor Stravinsky once said, "is to live there." Ben Hecht called it "the most boss-ridden place in the world," and Frank Capra summed up the town in one word: "Nervous." For really vicious insights one must go to the residents who have made the commitment, or been committed, to live there. Some of the pearls cast over the past fifty years or so still sound true about Hollywood:

- where they place you under contract instead of observation (Anon.);
- where an angle is the shortest distance between two points (Allan Dwan);
- where they shoot too many pictures and not enough actors (Walter Winchell);
- less a place where films are made than where films are made from (Arthur Knight);
- where they mix a beautiful doll with a few feet of Technicolor—and wind up with a beautiful dollar (Jack Benny);
- where you often find a combination of hot heads and cold shoulders (Gregory Peck);
- where most people have no mind but it's made up (Rube Goldberg);
- where a man can get stabbed in the back while climbing a ladder (William Faulkner);
- where your best friend will plunge a knife in your back and then call the police to tell them that you are carrying a concealed weapon (George Frazier);
- where conversation consists of ad-fibbing (Bill Demarest);
- where everyone is a genius, until he's lost his job (Erskine Johnson);
- where they have great respect for the dead, but none for the living (Errol Flynn);
- the only town where you can say, "Come up and see me some time," and not get taken up on it (Mae West);
- where if you don't find happiness you send out for it (Rex Reed);
- where the stars twinkle until they wrinkle (Victor Mature);
- where the most common illness is dementia peacock (Eddie Albert);
- where people bite the hand that feeds them only if they're convinced that it's non-fattening (Anon.).

Laugh-In

The product of a cafe society without cafes, classic Hollywood wit was one of the glories of the film colony's golden age. At a recent exhibition about the great Goldwyn at the Frances Goldwyn Library in central Hollywood, some of his sayings were blown up on large posters. An adroit mixture of self-deprecation and sincere malice towards others, the best aphorisms produced by Hollywood about its own follies are verbal cartoons crying out for some kind of permanent exhibition. They are almost tangible objets trouvés, *pleasing pebbles smoothed over decades of handling. For most of them the context is lost—who really said it to whom on what occasion— and this makes them eminently reusable.*

Howard Dietz once shut Wilson Mizner up by telling him:
  "Bill, failure has gone to your head."

Lyricist Bert Kalmar said of Herman Mankiewicz:
  "To know him was to like him. Not to know him was to love him."

An actor bragged to Charles Boyer that his latest movie had doubled the number of his fans.
  "Congratulations," said Boyer, "I didn't know you got married."

Jack Carson said of an actor who was asked to do a simple stunt:
  "He's not exactly a coward, but most of his pluck is in his eyebrows."

Oliver Hardy was attending a Broadway play and someone asked Phil Brito where the rotund comedian was sitting.
  "Try the first two rows," said Brito.

Everybody was buzzing about the latest Hollywood genius, Orson Welles.
  "That fellow is positively amazing," Ray Milland was telling Marlene Dietrich. "He can write, direct, produce, even act . . ."
  "Yes," Miss Dietrich observed, "he is a perpetual notion machine."

Actress Connie Moore must have heard this line, and she enlarged upon it to generalize about the male of the species:
  "Man is a perpetual-notion machine," she was quoted, "and it's always the same notion."

Comedian Tom d'Andrea defined what a Hollywood genius was in the forties: "A man who can write, produce, direct, make a flop—and have his option picked up."

Eddie Mannix, longtime lieutenant of L. B. Mayer, resented Irving Thalberg's pervasive influence and was not that sorry to see him shuffle off the mortal coil.
  "Irving was a sweet guy," he eulogized the boy genius, "but he could piss ice water."

Mannix began his career as a policeman in New Jersey and he policed MGM, according to writer Elliot Paul, by creating "single-handedly a class of psychos called Mannix-depressives."

One writer always refers to Israeli producer Menahem Golan, who has recently dominated the schlock-movie niche but wants to be remembered as an artist, as "the Golan Depths."

Barbara Stanwyck once described the endless round of social affairs in the movie colony as "fêtes worse than death."

The actress had one of the sharpest tongues in the movie colony. She said about a rising star:

"Her body has gone to her head."

Peter Lawford, after taking a fresh starlet out to dinner:

"The girl's so perfect that practice couldn't make her."

Observing a starlet eyeing the expensive talent at Romanoff's, actor Dennis Morgan remarked:

"I could see she had chinchillas running up and down her spine."

A starlet was telling Dorothy Parker that she had been hurt sliding down a bannister.

"Perhaps it was a barrister," mused the incredulous writer.

Which brings us to Ben Hecht's celebrated definition of a Hollywood starlet as the name given to "any woman under thirty not actively employed in a brothel."

Special Occasions

Leland Hayward was one of the top Hollywood agents when he married his client Margaret Sullavan. A friend sent him the following cable:

CONGRATULATIONS ON GETTING
THE OTHER 90 PERCENT.

Eddie Cantor received the news, along with the rest of Hollywood, that a son had been born to Norma Shearer and Irving Thalberg. Before the ceremony of circumcision, traditionally performed on Jewish male infants on the eighth day, Cantor sent a telegram to the happy father:

"Congratulations on your latest production. Sure it will look better after it has been cut."

Danny Kaye sent a wire to actress Benay Venuta after the birth of her second daughter:

> "I'm glad you lost that great big blister
> That turned out to be Patty's sister."

Feet to Print

Sid Grauman opened his Chinese Theatre on Hollywood Boulevard in 1927, trumpeting that it was an authentic recreation "in every detail," and forgetting perhaps that most Chinese pagodas do not screen movies. According to legend Grauman was the first who had walked across the wet cement in front of his brand-new building. When the chief mason bawled him out, the entrepreneur called up his friends—Douglas Fairbanks, Mary Pickford, and Norma Talmadge—and bid all three of them follow his footsteps. The cement by that time had dried and the stars had left no impression. But this was Hollywood, so Grauman arranged to have a special slab of fresh cement laid in the central courtyard just before the opening of Cecil B. De Mille's *King of Kings*. He called back the Fairbankses, who inaugurated the tradition, followed by Norma Talmadge a few days later.

Among the hundred and sixty or so prints of feet, with or without shoes, there are hands, Trigger's hooves, John Barrymore's famous profile, and Betty Grable's even more famous legs. There are also banal greetings from the stars to Grauman, of which Joan Crawford's is a good example: "May this cement our friendship," she wrote.

Another Fine Tradition

Wilson Mizner turned up at one of the typically lavish and pretentious movie premieres at Grauman's Chinese Theatre in a beat-up Model T Ford. The stars appeared in their most showy apparel and alighted from their vast automobiles, which were driven away by their private chauffeurs. When Mizner got out from his wreck, with a beautiful starlet on his arm, there was no chauffeur to drive it away.

"Just a moment, sir," said one of the eight magnificently bedecked flunkeys lining the entrance to Grauman's, "you will have to move your car." Mizner handed him the car's bill of sale and license.

"It's your car, my good man, and I wish you a thousand happy landings," and he made a dignified exit, unaware that he may just have invented valet parking.

Greek Tragedy

Michael Cacoyannis was visiting Hollywood and was taken to the set of *Irma La Douce* (1963) at United Artists, where he was introduced to Billy Wilder as the man "who directed *Electra*—you know, the Greek tragedy."

"The only Greek tragedy I know is Spyros Kouras," said Wilder referring to the boss of Twentieth Century-Fox.

Though a sophisticate, especially by Hollywood standards, Billy Wilder has always enjoyed puncturing intellectual pretentions. During a vacation in Paris in the late forties he kept hearing everybody talking about a new philosophy called Existentialism. Wilder could not make head or tale of it, especially after Jean-Paul Sartre personally tried to explain it to him. But it gave him the idea for a new twist on an old Greek plot.

"This boy falls in love with his mother and marries her," Wilder used to explain Existentialism. "They live together quite happily until one day he learns that she isn't his mother. So he commits suicide."

Stranger Than Physics

Albert Einstein was visiting the California Institute of Technology in Pasadena when Charlie Chaplin invited him for a drive down Hollywood Boulevard. Passersby recognized the great clown and began to cheer him. An embarrassed Chaplin then pointed to his companion, whose famous face had been in all the newspapers. A gathering crowd then began to cheer both of them, bringing a quizzical smile to Einstein's face.

"They're cheering me, because they understand me," Chaplin explained, "and they're cheering you, because they don't."

Chaplin loaned a book by Einstein to Ernst Lubitsch. When the director returned the book, Chaplin asked how he liked it.

"Very much," Lubitsch replied. "That fellow Einstein has many of my ideas."

On his return to Princeton, one of Einstein's colleagues asked him what Los Angeles was like.

"Can a fish describe," Einstein mused, "the murky water in which it swims?"

City Lights

In the golden age of Hollywood, before smog and freeways, there were other irritations. Ivor Montagu recalls from the early thirties playing tennis at Charlie Chaplin's house in Beverly Hills:

One night an aeroplane flew low over the twinkling lights spread over the blazing landscape, the pilot from time to time shutting off his engine and bellowing through a megaphone a call for everybody to go to the current next premiere. Seeing the blaze of our tennis court on the hillside he circled low, switched off and shouted tentatively:
"Harold Lloyd?"
Charlie was furious and yelled back at the top of his voice:
"No! 'City Lights'!"

As It Is in Heaven

Beatrice Lillie was new in Hollywood when Chaplin invited the famous English comedienne to his hilltop estate. Pointing to the lights below and the stars above, Chaplin sighed:
"Beautiful, isn't it?"
"Yes," she agreed. "Some night I just know those stars will come together and spell Marion Davies."

Beached

The Santa Monica beach house that William Randolph Hearst built for Marion Davies had fifty-five rooms and cost three million dollars. She kept open house there, and her entertaining was so lavish that an anonymous newsman concocted the headline:

MARION DAVIES CLOSES BEACH HOUSE—THOUSANDS HOMELESS.

Marion Davies was also a generous Robin Hood who took great joy in redistributing the wealth Hearst gave her. The ex-chorus girl gave a dozen monogrammed silk shirts to a prop man at the studio who picked up her handkerchief, and she paid doctors' bills for several people in need. Or she would leave a chunk of money at the studio cafeteria just in case anyone ran short of cash.
Later when Hearst ran into money trouble during the Depression, Miss

Davies lent him one million dollars that she had saved up from his gifts. The tycoon was deeply moved.

Where Alph the Sacred River Ran Dry

William Randolph Hearst frowned on alcohol, and up in his castle at San Simeon, guests were suffered to drink only in their rooms. Marion Davies kept up a polite fiction that she was abstaining for his sake, but in fact she simply did her drinking out of his sight. Once when she was sipping a cocktail closeted with her friend Joan Crawford, Hearst walked in on them unannounced. Marion had barely managed to pass her glass into Crawford's hand.

"I never saw you drink before," Hearst said in a tone of disappointment. Crawford, who had not yet entered her alcoholic period and actually disliked booze, which had destroyed her second marriage to Franchot Tone, flashed a smile:

"I thought I'd try it."

"Well, try it then," Hearst ordered.

"Anything for a friend," said Crawford gracefully and almost choked on the cocktail.

Mortgaged to the Hill

"Hollywood is divided into two classes," Jimmy Durante once said. "Those who own swimming pools—and those who can't keep their heads above water."

Philip Merivale was telling Edward G. Robinson about a new house that a mutual acquaintance of theirs had bought:

"A hilltop mansion, five-car garage, swimming pool, stables . . ."

"And on a clear day," interrupted Robinson, "he can see the finance company."

Unreal Estate

The Garden of Allah on Sunset Boulevard was originally the private home of the actress Alla Nazimova (1879–1945), hence the pun of her name. After losing her home, Nazimova described to a New York reporter the feeling common to so many of the transient visitors to the movie colony then and now.

I had a beautiful home in Hollywood. For a long time I had dreamed of how happy I should be when I could have all the things that I wanted around me. One morning I was awakened by my maid saying the houses on the hill opposite were burning, and the fire would soon reach my house. I realized I must save whatever I wanted most. I went into my bedroom and looked around. I thought, there is nothing I want in this room. I went to the library. No, I said to myself, I cannot take all my books. I went from room to room and found nothing I could not do without, nothing I felt I had to save. I wandered back into my bedroom. There was some snapshots on the bed. I took them in my pocketbook and left. I had gone down the street only a block when the maid came running to me and said they had controlled the fire and it had not reached my house. I went back, but I did not like my house any more. I had discovered that when it came down to the last test, there was nothing there that really mattered to me today. Today I have not so many things and I am happier.

The Great Outdoors

Arthur Mayer once called on Robert Benchley at the Garden of Allah on Sunset Boulevard, which became a favorite hotel with those New Yorkers who liked to believe that their visit to the Coast was purely transitory. Benchley was sitting inside his darkened room under a sun lamp with his shorts on. Mayer asked him why he wasn't outside in the plentiful sunshine.

"I don't trust nature," Benchley replied. "Out there things can fall on you. Like meteors. Or manna."

Groucho Marx was mowing his lawn in his shabbiest gardening clothes and without his famous moustache. A woman driving an expensive car stopped and asked:

"My good man, what do you get for mowing lawns?"

Without missing a beat, Groucho replied:

"The lady who lives here lets me sleep with her."

The woman then drove away.

Bing Crosby once put up a sign on his lawn in Beverly Hills:

"Keep off the grass. Remember when you, too, were struggling for recognition."

Gene Fowler dropped by W. C. Fields one day, and caught the actor in the act of violently kicking a rose bush in his garden.

"Bloom, damn you," Fields muttered.

On another day and in another part of the garden, Gene Fowler came upon W. C. Fields holding a quart of martinis in one hand and a long whip in the other. With each swig he would lash his whip at a passing swan.

"Don't look aghast," he barked at Fowler, "the so-and-so hissed at me!"

Shaken, Not Stirring

W. C. Fields used to bring a martini-shaker every day to work, claiming that it was filled with pineapple juice. One day, a fellow actor emptied the contents of the shaker and replaced it with undiluted pineapple juice. Fields did one of his famous recoils and exclaimed in horror:

"What rascal has been putting pineapple juice into my pineapple juice?"

W. C. Fields was one of the great boozers, but even he stood in awe of Mark Hellinger, the Broadway columnist turned Hollywood producer.

"I got Mark Hellinger so drunk last night," he once said, "that it took three bellboys to put me to bed."

Adolph Zukor recalled the old Hollywood as a very quiet place, with no drinking and very little smoking. The evenings were practically inaudible. "No sound at all, but the popping of the California poppies."

And in the same old Hollywood, W. C. Fields was asked once if he ever suffered delirium tremens while working there.

"Impossible to answer," rasped the bulbous-nosed comedian. "It's impossible to tell where the D.T.s end and Hollywood begins."

CHAPTER 18

Social Studies

What I Want for Christmas

William Randolph Hearst and Marion Davies gave parties not only on the West Coast but also in New York. Anita Loos recalled one Christmas party (when Hearst had given his mistress the Ritz Tower building on Park Avenue as her Christmas present) to which Mabel Normand arrived late, disheveled and without her then constant companion, none other than Samuel Goldwyn.

The star explained that as they were passing St. Patrick's Cathedral she had an impulse to go in and pray, but was prevented by a mob, which also separated her from her companion. The editor of *Photoplay* magazine, also at the party, inquired of Miss Normand what her prayer had been about.

"A thousand people on Fifth Avenue heard it," the star replied. "I prayed to Saint Anthony for Sam to get a nose operation that would make him look more like a goy."

Mank Manqué

Some of Hollywood's *nouveaux riches* invested their extra cash in art; the Impressionists were the preferred choice for the collectors. One day Joseph

Cotten was happily showing off his newly acquired Utrillo, when Herman Mankiewicz stage-whispered to his wife:

"Do you realize, Sara, that we are the only Jews west of the Mississippi who do not own an Utrillo?"

Though by no means a practicing Jew, Herman Mankiewicz despised the Hollywood grandees who claimed to be "partly Jewish" or were aping the WASP life-style. His own definition of a half-Jew was "somebody whose mother and father were Jewish."

And once when he glimpsed his Beverly Hills neighbor Sam Jaffe, meticulously dressed in white tennis gear, carrying his racket and tennis ball and off to play, Mankiewicz observed:

"Behold the outdoor Jew."

The Jewish Flyer

Louis B. Mayer saw himself as a Jewish paterfamilias, and wanted his employees—especially, beautiful young actresses—to turn to him with every problem. Asking him for help in some personal matter was the surest way to win his favor. One day, Herman Mankiewicz, who, like so many New Yorkers, could barely drive a car, decided to join Leland Hayward and his wife Margaret Sullavan in taking flying lessons. Mrs. Mankiewicz—universally called, especially by her husband, "poor Sara"—went to Mayer to talk her husband out of this latest manifestation of his death wish. The studio boss tried every argument with the stubborn and contrary writer, but to no avail. Mankiewicz was about to leave, savoring his triumph, when Mayer turned to him:

"Herman, you've ever heard of a Jewish flier? Who? Name one!"

While Mankiewicz frantically searched his mind, Louis B. made him promise—for the sake of his wife and children, of course—never to take to the skies.

(Despite his notorious contempt for the moguls, Mank had a grudging admiration for the MGM boss.

"L. B. Mayer may be a shit," he conceded once, "but not every shit is L. B. Mayer.")

More Tribulation

Herman's brother, Joseph Mankiewicz, was sitting at the Brown Derby one evening with Wilson Mizner, when in walked Rufus Le Maire from Paramount, having just attended an opening. The actor was dressed to the hilt, his theatrical outfit topped off with a huge Inverness cape. Mizner looked at Le Maire as he passed their booth, and said to Mankiewicz:

"That, my boy, sets the Jews back six hundred years."

Mama Knows Best

Hollywood screenwriter Samson Raphaelson (who wrote *The Jazz Singer* and many of the Lubitsch comedies) used some of his considerable earnings to buy a yacht. He also enjoyed dressing up, even on dry land, in yacht club clothes. According to legend, he was visiting his old Yiddische mama one day, and she asked what cap he was wearing.

"It's my captain's hat, Mama," he replied. "I've got a big boat now, and I am its captain."

"By me you're a captain," she told her son, "and by you you're a captain. But by captains, you're no captain."

Unwelcome to the Club

Most people know of Groucho Marx's celebrated resignation from the Friar's Club in Hollywood.

"I don't want to belong to any club," he wired, "that will accept me as a member."

Groucho did, however, apply to join a beach club in Santa Monica, which was well known for excluding Jews.

"My wife is a Gentile," he explained to a friend, "so maybe they will let our son go into the ocean up to his knees."

Mature Judgment

When the film people first descended on the sleepy hamlet of Hollywood, the owners of some bungalow courts posted signs that read: "No Dogs or Actors Allowed." (What offended some players was having to take second billing.) Occasionally, Jews were added to the list. In the 1940s, long after the motion-picture industry became dominant in Southern California, Victor Mature applied for membership in the exclusive Los Angeles Country Club. He was turned down because of a rule specifically excluding actors.

"I'm no actor," Mature protested, "and I have twenty-five pictures to prove it."

We Shall Overcome

Barbara Stanwyck was the star of a film which was partly shot on location in the South. In booking accommodations at the only decent local hotel, the production manager was informed that they would be honored and delighted to have Miss Stanwyck, but her maid, Harriet Coray, would have to stay at a very comfortable place at the other end of town, because she was black. The actress gave instructions to cancel her suite and to book her with Harriet into the hotel for black people.

"I don't believe they will refuse me a room," she said.

Hollywood Royalty

Ensconced in Pickfair with Mary Pickford, his fairy-tale wife, Douglas Fairbanks enjoyed being called the royalty of Hollywood. Soon he developed a weakness for the real kind and took every opportunity to hob-nob with the aristocracy or to bring their names up in conversation.

In the early thirties Fairbanks visited George Bernard Shaw in England to persuade him that he and Mary Pickford would produce *Caesar and Cleopatra* with greater sensitivity than the Hollywood moguls who periodically tried to buy the rights from him. On his return from Hollywood, Fairbanks told the British writer Ivor Montagu about the meeting.

"I had fixed up to meet Mr. Shaw, but just an hour before I was due to call somebody rang. Your prince [i.e. the Prince of Wales] wanted to play golf with me."

Charlie Chaplin, who came out of the grinding poverty of London's East End, liked to tease Fairbanks about this weakness. He would greet him sometimes with a clipped upper-crust accent:

"Hullo, Douglas, how's the duke?"

"What duke?" asked Fairbanks.

"Oh, any duke," replied Chaplin.

The Way We Were

When Hollywood's royal couple broke up, Douglas Fairbanks retreated from Pickfair to an English country home and sought consolation in the arms of Sylvia Hawkes, a model. An emissary from Hollywood sought him out, begging him to reconsider what a divorce from America's sweetheart and immediate remarriage would do to his image and to box-office receipts. The handsome star was unmoved, until the messenger let slip:

"It wouldn't be so bad," he wrung his hands, "if Miss Hawkes had not been just a mannequin—a mannequin!"

Fairbanks gave him a cold stare:

"Mary sold bananas in Toronto."

Bea Lillie, who off the screen and stage was known as Lady Peel, heard that Mary Pickford was taking French lessons. She called her on the phone and announced:

"C'est Lady Parle qui Peel!"

Good Help Is Hard To Get

Samuel Goldwyn described a dinner at Fanny Ward's, one of the earliest Hollywood stars, who was being wooed by various producers after a proposed merger of several motion-picture companies.

A representative of one of the two rival companies sat beside me while a relentless hospitality was being waged. At last he turned to me pleadingly.

"For heaven's sake," he whispered, "I want a clear head for our talk. Won't you tell that butler to stop filling my glass?"

"Butler," I whispered back, almost congealed with horror. "Sh! That's Miss Ward's husband."

This husband, by the way, was Jack Deane, her leading man, whom she married after coming to Hollywood.

The Butler Motif

As often in Hollywood, art imitates life. It was Erich von Stroheim's suggestion that the role of film-director and former husband of the fading star in *Sunset Boulevard* (1950) should be played as a butler.

Barbra Streisand garnered an early reputation for being difficult to work with. During the making of her first film, *Funny Girl* (1968), she was described by Joyce Haber as a "full-fledged monster" for treating veteran director William Wyler as if he were a butler.

Fish Story

The story is told with different casts, but it, too, probably belongs to the incorrigible wit and drunkard Herman Mankiewicz. Invited to a dinner party at the house of producer Arthur Hornblow, Jr., a gourmet and wine snob, the writer arrived already fortified, and during cocktails managed to put away a few more drinks. Then came dinner, during which choice wines, carefully selected, were correctly served to go with each course. Towards the end of the feast, Mankiewicz suddenly heaved forth, hurriedly left the table and was heard throwing up in a nearby powder room. His return, looking pale and sweaty, was greeted in silence by the rest of the dinner guests.

"Don't worry, Arthur," said Mankiewicz to his host, who looked understandably anxious, "the white wine came up with the fish."

(Hollywood columnist Edith Gwynn once wrote of Arthur Hornblow that "he not only knows what year the wine was made but he can tell you who stamped on the grapes.")

The Fake Impostor

Mike Romanoff ran the movie colony's most exclusive eatery before the Second World War; band-leader Ray Noble called it so swank that "they served pigs' feet with shoe trees in them." Sometimes the restaurateur, who was a New Yorker named Harry Gerguson, liked to refer to himself by what he claimed to be his full title: "His Imperial Highness Prince Michael Alexandrovitch Dmitri Romanoff." Some were taken in by this con-man, and many suspected his pedigree, but Herman Mankiewicz threatened to ruin Romanoff by exposing him as a real prince, trying to pass himself off as an impostor.

Advice

Like several celebrities, James Wong Howe once opened a Chinese restaurant in Los Angeles. Because of Howe's fame, as one of Hollywood's most distinguished cameramen, local newspapers gave extensive coverage. A photographer was sent down to take a picture of the proud restaurateur and his staff in front of the new establishment. Trying to fit in the whole group, the man was stepping off the sidewalk and backing into traffic, so Howe helpfully suggested that he might use a wide-angle lens for the shot. The photographer did not take kindly to the suggestion.

"Why don't you stick to your chop suey," he told the cinematographer, who had won two Oscars behind the camera, "and let me take the pictures."

Hollywood Bitch

Lady Elsie Mendl, one of the social queens of Hollywood during the 1940s, had a miniature poodle, called Blue, which she always took with her. At a party given by Louis B. Mayer at his house, Blue jumped up on a couch and snuggled up against the mogul.

"Nice dog," he said to Lady Mendl, "I'd like to buy her."

"I'd forget about her if I were you," said the British lady with aristocratic bluntness. "She's just another Hollywood bitch trying to make a connection."

Information, Please

The Hungarian beauty Marion Mill Preminger came to Hollywood in the 1930s with her then husband Otto, and quickly became known as a social butterfly. During the war, Sir Charles and Lady Mendl were giving a party for the British Minister of Information to which Mrs. Preminger had turned up in revealing décolletage.

"My dear, when I said we would like to see more of you," said Lady Mendl pleasantly, "I meant you should come more often."

"I wore this in honor of the Minister of Information," said the unfazed Hungarian, "I thought he'd like more information."

"Yes," retorted Lady Mendl, "but not about the navel base."

"If brevity is the soul of wit," said Joan Davis of somebody's party rags, "then that dress is good for a lot of laughs."

Party Lines

Sergei Einsenstein very much enjoyed parties during his visits to the West. At a reception in Paris where the director was being lionized, his boring host managed to corner Eisenstein and made a long statement about all Russians being like the gloomy, obsessed characters one reads about in Dostoyevski.

"Do the Russians ever laugh?" he asked in conclusion.

"They will," Einsenstein replied, "when I tell them about this party."

Groucho Marx, leaving a Hollywood party, said to the hostess: "I've had a wonderful evening, but this wasn't it!"

At another party Groucho was approached by a celebrity hound.

"You remember me, Mr. Marx," he said. "We met last month at the Glynthwaites."

"I never forget a face," said the comic, "but I'll make an exception in your case."

Robert Goldstein, a longtime executive at International Pictures and then at Twentieth Century-Fox, was at an unusually boring party one night.

"If this is a party," he said upon leaving, "so is the Republican."

Goldstein was having a drink at 21 with Earl Wilson, the saloon editor of the *New York Post*, when Sam Marx, the MGM producer, came in.

"Who was he before?" asked the journalist for background.

"Same guy," said Goldstein.

Columnist Earl Wilson bumped into Humphrey Bogart at a party. The actor was on the wagon, and the journalist noticed that he was standing "naked"—i.e. without a martini in hand.

"Oh, I've heard you don't drink any more?" said Wilson.

"Not any more," Bogie said for the record. "Just the same amount."

Soon after the publication of *Past Imperfect* (1945), Humphrey Bogart was introduced to its author, Ilka Chase.

"I thought it was wonderful," he said sincerely. "I can't tell you how much I enjoyed it. By the way, who wrote it for you?"

"I did," said the columnist. "But who read it to you?"

Dr. Selznick, I Don't Presume

Not content with the tremendous financial and popular success of *Gone with the Wind*, producer David O. Selznick felt that he should be awarded an honorary Doctor of Letters by a major university. This would be a relatively easy matter to arrange today, with dozens of colleges that have film departments or programs, and many of them anxious to attract funds from the movie industry. But in the early 1940s, Selznick's assistants, who put out the word, found no takers. They reported back to their boss that no major university could be found that would make him Dr. Selznick.

"Well," replied the mogul to this setback, "find me instead two minor universities who will each give me a degree, and I'll be satisfied."

Patron of the Arts

Jack Warner had commissioned Salvador Dali to paint a portrait of his wife Ann, and threw a grand party to unveil the new creation. All the Warner stars, writers, and staff turned up for the event, which was held on the great terrace that wrapped around the Warners' mansion. The studio chief stood in front of the easel, which was still covered up, and introduced the artist.

"To tell the truth," said Warner, "I haven't seen the painting yet, but I have extraordinary faith in this man's talent, and you all know how good I am at picking talent." The crowd—mostly talent he had picked—laughed appreciatively, and Jack Warner pulled the string.

The portrait revealed a striking likeness of Ann Warner. The background showed a desert with an oasis in the distance. There, very small but with surrealistic clarity, Dali had painted a cage with a monkey. The monkey's physiognomy bore an unmistakable resemblance to that of Jack Warner.

There was a painful silence as the mogul took it in, and before he remarked with a forced smile:

"I'm so glad I was included."

Everybody applauded, but as Paul Henreid observed in his memoirs: "I never saw the painting hung while Jack was alive."

Where Did We Go Wrong?

Anita Loos bumped into Paulette Goddard in New York at the Museum of Modern Art's exhibit of the Gertrude Stein collection. After they walked among the famous paintings, Loos became concerned about the sad expression on Goddard's face, and she asked what was the matter.

"I was just thinking about Gertrude," said the star. "She was ugly, fat, and a lesbian, but she collected more loot than all the jewels of Liz Taylor, Marlene, and mine rolled together."

(Paulette Goddard did not do so badly. I remember in the 1960s occasionally lining up with her at the bank in the little town of Ascona on Lago Maggiore, where she then lived with her last husband, the writer Erich Maria Remarque. One of the topics of gossip in that cosmopolitan community was the original Toulouse-Lautrec that hung above a toilet in their house.)

Vita Brevis, Ars Longa

The ruling passion in Edward G. Robinson's life was art: he built two of the finest collections of Impressionist paintings in the United States—the first and finer one he lost to divorce. Because of his fame, people would come up to him in museums and ask Robinson's advice about which unknown artist would make them money in the future.

"Money and art are not the same," Robinson would say to such people indignantly. "In fact money is nothing; art is everything."

Drew a Blank

An executive invited writer Jerry Chodorov to a dinner party.

"Sorry, but I've got a prior engagement," Chodorov excused himself. "I'm dining that evening with Louis Blank."

"Blank?" echoed the mogul with amazed contempt. "But he's *lunch!*"

Toasts

Spyros Skouras, the host of the 1959 dinner given to the Soviet party chief at Twentieth Century-Fox, toasted him:

"Look at me, Mr. Khrushchev, I was a poor Greek shepherd, and now I'm the boss of 35,000 employees. That's America."

"I was a poor Ukrainian shepherd," Khrushchev raised his glass, "and today I'm the boss of 200 million citizens. That's the USSR!

The $64,000 Question

Harold Ramis was recently invited to a birthday party for Mark Canton, production chief at Warner Brothers. He suddenly realized that he had not bought the celebrant a present, and the more he tried to think of a suitable gift, the more unsure he became. Finally the writer-director-actor called a friend.

"What do you give a man," Ramis asked, "who *wants* everything?"

CHAPTER 19

Titillations

The Golden Calf

In 1922 Will H. Hays resigned from the Harding cabinet where he was Postmaster General, accepting a salary of a $100,000 to save Hollywood's reputation from sex and drug scandals. Eventually the Hays Office evolved a Production Code, spelling out what could or could not be shown or mentioned on the screen. As a first step, the new morality czar issued a list of twelve prohibitions. The commandments were greeted by this headline in *Variety*:

"Hays Two Up on Moses!"

Upright and Uptight

One of the early pictures assigned to Irving Thalberg by Louis B. Mayer was production of a script titled *Pleasure Mad* (1924). The story involved a great deal of nudity, but the censorship imposed by the new Hays Office forced Mayer to cancel it. However, the exhibitors had already booked and promoted the film, so Thalberg was given the delicate task of finding a "wholesome" story that would be made under the title. The young producer finally bought a novel called *Valley of Content,* and when questioned by his boss whether it was really proper, he pointed out the author's name, which happened to be Blanche Upright.

"You can hardly be more wholesome than that, Mr. Mayer."

The Birds and the Bees

Arthur Mayer was about to start the promotion campaign for *Go West, Young Man* (1936), the latest Mae West vehicle, when he was summoned to a special meeting of all the picture publicists at the Hays Office. Will Hays was reading from a long list of complaints concerning sexually explicit movie posters, and lecturing the advertising men on their public duty, when two amorous pigeons alighted on the ledge of the window. The censor, sensing that the attention of the room was being diverted, asked:

"What's going on out there?" Si Seadler, in charge of advertising for MGM, lowered his eyelids in mock modesty and pointed out the window at the pigeons:

"They're violating the Production Code, sir."

Early Spice

In 1896 Thomas Edison filmed the first kiss on screen. This act, lasting a few seconds, was performed by two staid, middle-aged actors well known on the Broadway stage: May Irwin and John C. Rice. The kiss provoked violent reaction, including a comment from Herbert Stone, one of the earliest film critics, who said that "magnified to gargantuan proportions, it is absolutely disgusting. Such things call for police intervention."

As might be expected, Paris pioneered adult pictures. In June 1908, *Variety's* correspondent in the French capital reported on "men's days—when moving pictures are shown for the gaze of the male gender only." It would be wrong to suppose, however, that the subjects held no interest for the female gender. The article added that the spicy films excited "the interest of the community to such an extent that women dress in male attire to attend."

That's Why They Are Called Protestants

One of the early Biograph newsreels in 1896 showing a benevolent Pope Leo XIII smiling and waving, caused militant protest by Protestants throughout America.

Catholic Protester

Baby Doll (1956), Elia Kazan's film based on a story by Tennessee Williams, was widely condemned by the Legion of Decency and the Catholic Church, because it depicted, among other things, a marriage that remained unconsummated. Cardinal Francis Spellman of New York City, on his return from visiting the troops in Korea, preached a sermon against it in St. Patrick's cathedral. He forbade Catholics, under pain of sin, to see the film and considered it the patriotic duty of all Americans to boycott it. Asked whether he had actually seen the film, the cardinal asked rhetorically:

"Must you have a disease to know what it is? If your water supply is poisoned, there's no reason for you to drink the water."

The Land of the Free

One might think that morality was the only factor in censoring movies. But long before the Hays Office and the Legion of Decency came to regulate what may be seen on the screen in the land of the First Amendment, there was the case of *The Thief* (1905). Edwin S. Porter's film contrasted an affluent woman shoplifting at Macy's, who stole for kicks and was acquitted, with a mother who needed to steal bread to feed her baby, and was taken away in a paddy wagon. The short film ended with an image of the blind goddess of Justice with her scales, which are usually balanced. But Porter depicted one side of the scales weighed down with a dollar sign. This was excised in each and every one of the United States until fifty years later, when *The Thief* was shown uncensored on television.

Where Angels Fear To Tread

"Unfortunately it has been our experience," wrote Heywood Broun in one of his essays, "that there is a distinct affinity between fools and censorship. It seems to be one of those treading grounds where they rush in." Censorship of certain words or images can easily spill over to the suppression of ideas and the very meaning of a film. The Legion of Decency objected to the last line in *Elmer Gantry* (1960), where Burt Lancaster, emerging from the burning church, is supposed to reply to Arthur Kennedy's greeting, "See you around, brother," with "See you in hell, brother." The clerical gentlemen who controlled the Legion considered the idea of a man knowing and wishing to go to hell more vicious than a number of "damns" and "hells" in the picture.

Burt Lancaster went to New York and spent long hours with a monsignor, explaining how that line had summed up the corrupting power of

Elmer Gantry—all to no avail. The line was cut from that picture, but it kept gnawing at Lancaster, who finally said it sixteen years later to Paul Newman in *Buffalo Bill and the Indians* (1976).

Prospecting

George S. Kaufman observed that the Hays Office was so strict that when "two people were in bed they had to be either wed or dead." Producer Joe Pasternak was summoned by the censor about a scene in *Destry Rides Again* (1939). There was no problem about Marlene Dietrich dropping some gold rings down her bodice. The censor objected to the next line by one of the cowboys:

"There's gold in them thar hills."

Go West, Young Man

Hedda Hopper once asked Mae West how she knew so much about men.

"Baby," replied the sex star, "I went to night school."

Mae West came up with one of her most famous lines during the filming of *Night After Night* (1932), in which she played a minor role. The hat-check girl, admiring West's beautiful tiara, gasped, according to script, "Goodness, what beautiful diamonds!" The queen of sex, with her perfect timing, improvised the reply:

"Goodness had nothing to do with it, dearie," which, except for the last word, became the title of her autobiography.

When Marilyn Monroe became the reigning sex queen of Hollywood, a reporter asked Mae West about her.

"She's a good kid," said the once and future queen, "and they have handled her publicity well. I just don't think she has the equipment."

Pure Research

When the censor alleged that *The Outlaw* (1943) exposed too much of Jane Russell's mammary charms, Howard Hughes became interested in the question not simply as a producer but as an engineer. With his inexhaustible curiosity and empirical mind, Hughes sent cameramen into movie houses, where they secretly took pictures of Lana Turner, Hedy Lamarr, and some of the other sex goddesses then in vogue. He had blownups made and measured, with the most precise instruments, how much of the entire bust was exposed. He then went to the censor's office and argued that Jane Russell seemed to expose a greater area of her chest simply because there was more of it, and that she was actually more covered up *proportionately* than some of the other stars whose cleavage had been allowed. Faced with such scientific evidence, the censor was forced to yield on that point to Howard Hughes, though it took three years to have the film released.

After all that trouble, RKO fully intended to exploit the star's most obvious assets. "What are the two big reasons for Jane Russell's success?" asked the billboards advertising *The Outlaw*, at least in Los Angeles. Below, in smaller letters was given the lesser answer: "Her beauty and her charm."

Sightings

Soon after her rise to fame, Jane Russell was spotted walking prominently through the Stork Club. Producer Bob Goldstein was having dinner, and his companion remarked:
    "I hear she has a wonderful part in her next picture."
    "That's right," said Goldstein, "I can see it from here."

Herb Stein once remarked that Jane Russell's success was due to her having a big studio behind her. Mack Sennett retorted:
    "Son, it isn't what Miss Russell has behind her."

Lana Turner turned up one evening at Romanoff's in a low-cut gown and a miniature golden airplane of exquisite workmanship hanging from a chain around her neck. "Prince" Mike Romanoff was standing near producer-writer Charles Brackett when she passed.
    "What do you think of Lana's airplane?" he asked.
    "Lovely," said Brackett, "and what a landing field!"

Sweaters

During the sweater craze in the forties, Hazel Brooks showed up on the set wearing one.
    "Not every man is interested in seeing bosoms," she was told by the director.
    "I didn't think we were appealing to that group," replied the actress.

When Greer Garson was one of the reigning queens at MGM, she was constantly typecast as a prim and proper lady. In one picture she wanted to put on a sexy sweater for a change, but the studio was afraid it might spoil her carefully built virtuous image.

"What's the matter?" Miss Garson exploded. "Are you afraid I'll make Clark Gable look flat-chested?"

A Bust

A radio interviewer once asked Groucho Marx what he thought of a new movie starring Hedy Lamarr and Victor Mature.

"No picture," came the reply, "can hold my interest when the leading man's bust measurement is bigger than the leading lady's."

Props

After casting Vivien Leigh in *Gone with the Wind* (1939), producer David Selznick began to worry about the smallness of her breasts, as they would (not) be revealed by some of the low-cut gowns being designed for the picture. He suggested that she should wear fuller bras. Vivien Leigh dispatched her personal assistant Sonny Alexander, who came back with half a dozen samples. After trying a few in front of the mirror, the future Scarlet O'Hara inspected her equipment:

"Fiddle-dee-dee, I'm not going to wear these silly props, when I have perfectly good ones of my own!" And she didn't. But the next time Selznick welcomed her to the set, he looked and said:

"You see how much better you look now!"

Carole Lombard began acting in the twenties when being flat-chested was an asset. But she continued as a big star in the thirties, when fashions and public taste had changed. So in preparing for a scene, she always made a point of calling out very loudly to the wardrobe assistants:

"Okay! Bring me my breasts!"

To prepare Dustin Hoffman's transformation into the character of Dorothy in *Tootsie* (1982), costume designer Ruth Morley sought advice from various people about how to create the ample breasts that Hoffman wanted. Before she settled for specially made prostheses, she listened to suggestions about filling falsies with rice or bird seed.

"My big fear was," Morley told writer Susan Dworkin, "that when he began to sweat, his bosom would grow oats."

Come and Sign on the Dotted Couch

Judy Holliday went to discuss a new role with the head of a studio who began to make advances. The actress put her hand inside her dress and pulled out her pair of falsies.

"Here," she told the lecher, "I think this is what you're after."

"Betty, you're a wonderful actress," director George Seaton sincerely complimented Betty Grable on one occasion.

"Yes," replied the reigning symbol of long-legged beauty with equal sincerity, "but I'd hate to do it for a living—without my legs."

Marie Macdonald was asked once whether she was embarrassed about being continually referred to as "The Body."

"Not at all," said the star. "I found out long ago that in Hollywood a girl doesn't get anywhere by being known as 'The Brain.'"

Ripeness Is All

Remarking about the latest sex star in Hollywood, Dame May Whitty, the distinguished British actress who played many character parts in American movies, told an interviewer:

"I've got everything Betty Grable has—only I've had it longer."

It's a Dirty Job But Someone's Got To Do It

Raymond Chandler was fond of telling a story about Harry Tugend, trying to be a producer and hating it.

"You know this is a lousy job. You got to sit and talk to that bird brain seriously whether or not this part is going to be good for her career and at the same time you got to keep from being raped." Whereat a rather innocent young man piped up:

"You mean to say she's a nymphomaniac?" Harry frowned off into the distance and sighed, and said slowly,

"Well, I guess she would be, if they could get her quieted down a little."

Facing a day of shooting *La Bohème* (1926) Lillian Gish sighed:
"Oh dear, I've got to go through another day of kissing John Gilbert."

Physics

One trouble with little girls is that they grow up in the most delightful ways. One day a director, accompanied by Margaret O'Brien's mother, went and complained to Samuel Goldwyn that the child star was experimenting with a strapless gown for one of the scenes he was shooting.

"She's not old enough to wear anything so sophisticated," he argued. Mrs. O'Brien nodded vigorous agreement. Goldwyn thought for a moment.

"Let her try the gown," he finally responded with the wisdom of Solomon. "If it doesn't fall down, she's old enough."

Under a Bushel

George Lucas wrote the part of Princess Leia in *Star Wars* (1977) for a virginal teenager. Carrie Fisher was nineteen when she played it, and her physical charms were completely covered in a long white robe. Lucas even insisted on having her breasts fastened to her chest with electrical tape.

"No breasts bounce in space," the actress joked about it, "no jiggling in the Empire."

Liberation

Hollywood's self-policing of motion pictures began to fall apart in the mid-sixties, with a flood of European and American films, such as *Who's Afraid of Virginia Woolf* (1966), challenging the Production Code that had been in effect since 1930. Jack Valenti was appointed president of the Motion Picture Association of America by Lyndon Johnson, for whom he had worked as special assistant. He has held the job now for almost twenty-five years. Apart from a few controversial cases, such as *The Last Temptation of Christ* (1989), the MPAA these days is much more concerned with video piracy than the almost subliminal glimpse of pubic hair in Michelangelo Antonioni's *Blow-Up* (1967). Valenti, like Will Hays before him, came to Hollywood from Washington to enforce a make-believe morality that bore no resemblance to real life. When the Code collapsed under the assault of the sexual revolution, *Variety* in its 1967 annual issue ran an "Ode to a Revised Motion Picture Code," part of which ran:

> In urban nabes and drive-in glades,
>   The screen at last is free,
> Four-letter words, explicit verbs
>   Titillate tots of three.
> With derrieres and pubic hairs
>   Blithely exposed today,
> When they say "he went thataway,"
>   Means the hero turned gay.

And the mock-ode concluded:

> Let villains win and reward sin
>   With riches aplenty,
> Now girls can strip or take "a trip"
>   Thank you, Jack Valenti!

CHAPTER 20

Power Extensions

A Question of Casting

Many Hollywood people recalled that Ronald Reagan loved to discuss politics, especially after his marriage to Nancy Davis. Still, there was considerable surprise at the news that the former contract player from Warner Brothers would run for elected office. More surprised than anyone was his former boss Jack Warner, who was told upon returning from Europe that Ronald Reagan had been nominated as the Republican candidate for Governor of California.

"No, no, no," said the showman. "Jimmy Stewart for governor—Reagan for best friend."

Political Training

The other day [1989] former President Ronald Reagan fell off his horse, something that happens even to good horsemen, which he is. Veteran director Allan Dwan told Peter Bogdanovich about an episode during the shooting of *Cattle Queen of Montana* (1954) near Glacier National Park, when Reagan was supposed to ride towards the camera and yell a warning.

The trouble was "we got him on an Indian horse that wasn't broken and knew nothing about pictures."

The actor tried to control the beast as it danced sideways, and when he raced by the camera he was enraged, yelling at the director and crew, who were howling with laughter:

"I'm not one of those Hollywood riders," quoth Ronald Reagan, "who says he can ride and can't ride! This goddamn horse won't do what I tell him!"

Raymond Massey, in A Hundred Different Lives (1979), *recalled an earlier horse incident, while making* Santa Fe Trail (1940), *where the young Reagan was itching to be in charge and go his own way.*

The action was simply that the three troops mount and move off at a trot. Ronnie was holding forth about the direction.

"This is a scene of action. We're too apathetic. There should be a feeling of urgency. We wouldn't mount formally by the drill book. I'm going to vault into the saddle and make it look we're in a hurry." The other officers, including Errol Flynn, mindful of the potential discomfort of jumping into a McClellan saddle, indicated that they would do it as rehearsed.

"Action!" Ronnie sprang forward with a prodigious leap which carried him with sabre in its sling to an ignominious landing on his behind on the other side of his horse. Director Mike Curtiz shouted:

"Cut! Acrobat bum!"

A Question of Makeup

Throughout his presidency people wandered about the real color of Ronald Reagan's hair ("does he or doesn't he?") and whether he used makeup to look as young and fit as he did. Frank Westmore, in the chronicle of his famous family of makeup artists, says that his brother Perc (who also styled the Reagan hair into granite) refused to apply makeup to the actor in *King's Row* (1941) and had a royal row about it with director Sam Wood. Apparently the future politician never forgot that he had played one of his few memorable performances, on the screen at least, with no makeup.

"For the Reagan character to be believable," Perc Westmore argued at the time, and looking perhaps to the future, "he cannot go around looking like a department store dummy."

Field Day

Ronald Reagan was the first actor to achieve the highest office in the United States (or any other country, for that matter). Early reaction in Hollywood was amazement. English actor Michael Caine was quoted in the *New York Times:*

"President Reagan is straightforward. He was very straightforward as an actor, too, but I come from a country where an actor couldn't get elected rat-catcher."

Entertainers, most of whom knew him, had a field day. When advisers failed to wake President Reagan after the shooting down of Libyan war planes, Johnny Carson quipped on the *Tonight Show:*

"I understand there are only two reasons you wake up Ronald Reagan. One is World War III. The other is if *Hellcats of the Navy* is on the late show."

And after Reagan signed his new tax law in the summer of 1981, Johnny Carson remarked:

"I think he was in Hollywood too long. He signed it, 'Best wishes, Ronald Reagan.' "

Later that year, Nancy Reagan was getting flak for her designer clothes, and Bob Hope observed:

"Ronnie's hero is Calvin Coolidge and Nancy's is Calvin Klein."

Remember When

After Ronald Reagan became President many people recalled early signs of his political ambitions. Columnist James Bacon remembered him "moaning" in the 1940s that even though he was in some of the top-grossing Warner movies at the time, any good new script would be given first to Errol Flynn or newcomer Marlon Brando.

"Perhaps you are in the wrong business," Bacon suggested.

The actor Jean-Pierre Aumont remembered in 1981 that he ran into Reagan at a Hollywood party back in 1946. He was talking so much politics that Aumont warned him:

"You know, one of these days you're going to end up as President of the United States." And Reagan was supposed to have replied, quite casually:

"Yes."

Richard Widmark told *People* magazine in September 1982 that he had known Ronald Reagan for a long time, and that he was "a nice affable guy." When asked whether he had voted for him, Widmark added:

"Of course not. I said I've known him for a long time."

In the same week, Paul Newman was interviewed by Mimi Sheraton in the *New York Times* about his salad-dressing business.

"I've had more fun doing this than anything else I've done in a long time," Newman declared. "But remember, it's really my way of telling Ronald Reagan that his salad days are over."

When President Reagan proposed the first of his annual budget cuts to the arts, Theodore Bikel observed:

"Every profession has its John Wilkes Booth. Reagan is ours."

Once an Actor

Ronald Reagan's saving grace—to those who do not think that he was the savior of Western civilization—is his sense of humor. Immediately upon leaving the White House, a collection of his best jokes appeared under the title "Stand-up Reagan." He is the most anecdotal President since Lincoln, and his memory seemed never far from his Hollywood memories. Some claim he based many of his policy decisions on scripts which he acted out forty years before. Reagan's one-liners, most evident and welcome after the failed assassination attempt in 1981, saved the nation from prolonged trauma: it is hard to imagine what it might have been like if there had been silence or only official communiqués out of the hospital for several weeks. Instead we heard that, as he was wheeled into intensive care, the President told the group of anxious surgeons and nurses:

"Please assure me that you're all Republicans!" And coming out of surgery, he wrote a note which quoted W. C. Fields:

"All in all, I'd rather be in Philadelphia." And then came another note:

"If I had had this much attention in Hollywood, I'd have stayed there."

Even at the height of his career, Reagan was called the "Errol Flynn of the B movies," and he knew it was time to think of another profession or medium when cast against a chimpanzee as his costar in *Bedtime for Bonzo* (1951). He was once presented with a picture of himself in bed with Bonzo, and Reagan quipped:

"I'm the one with the watch."

Reagan took his oath of office as Governor of California just past midnight on January 2, 1967, to get an early start on his term (though it would be claimed twenty years later that it was due to advice from Nancy's astrologer). Spotting among the inauguration crowd fellow actor George Murphy, who had been elected to the U.S. Senate, Reagan ad-libbed:

"Well, George, here we are on the late show again!"

In March 1981 the Gridiron Club invited Ginger Rogers to its annual dinner. President Reagan was the last speaker, and he looked at the actress with whom he had starred back in 1951:

"Ginger Rogers, I'm glad you're here tonight," said the President. "You and I appeared in the film *Storm Warning*, but I was never really sure what the title meant until I met [House Speaker] Tip O'Neill."

(Since retiring from Congress Tip O'Neill himself has acted in some commercials. An actor friend of mine, Charles Kahlenberg, who often plays politicians on the screen, was asked whether he minded the competition.

"Not at all," he replied. "At least he did the politics first, and acting second.")

We All Make Mistakes

Preceding George Murphy and Ronald Reagan in turning from acting to politics, Albert Dekker was elected to the California state house.

"Occasionally," a fellow actor remarked, "an innocent man is sent to the legislature."

That Is the Question

During the early part of the Reagan administration, Ed Asner was president of the Screen Actors Guild, like Ronald Reagan before him. But when he spoke out strongly against U.S. policy in Central America, Reagan was upset, and according to Johnny Carson—or one of his writers—he is supposed to have said to an aide:

"What does an actor know about politics?"

Land of the Free

Ronald Reagan cut his political teeth during the House Un-American Committee hearings which targeted Hollywood in order to reap maximum publicity for the anti-Communist cause. Reagan was president of the Screen Actors Guild during this period, and he met his second wife when

Mervyn LeRoy directed Nancy Davis to him with a problem: how to get her name off the mailing lists of left-wing organizations. Reagan did better than that—she would soon assume his name.

The other future President to achieve national prominence during the McCarthy era was, of course, Richard Nixon. While members of the Committee would intimidate and try to silence the writers who came to be known as the Hollywood Ten, Nixon's specialty was asking leading questions from cooperative witnesses. This finely honed Nixonian sentence was put to Robert Taylor:

"As far as you are concerned, even though it might mean that you would suffer, possibly at the box office, possibly in reputation or in other ways, for you to appear before this Committee, you feel you are justified in making the appearance and would be so again if requested to do so?" To which Robert Taylor replied fearlessly:

"I certainly would, sir. I happen to believe strongly enough in the American people and in what the American people believe in to think they will go along with anybody who prefers America and the American form of government over any subversive ideologies which might be presented and by whom I might be criticized."

But the American people were confused. They heard John Howard Lawson and Dalton Trumbo appeal to the American Constitution and Bill of Rights even as they were dragged out of the hearing room and ultimately to jail. A few days after the Nixon-Taylor exchange, a newspaper columnist reported a conversation he had overheard between two fans:

"I'm not going to see any more of his pictures," said one, "I'm only watching real American stars."

"You got it wrong," the other replied, "he's an anti-Communist."

"I don't care what kind of a Communist he is," insisted the first, "I'm not watching him."

Rather Be Seen Dead Than Red

Ring Lardner, Jr., one of the Hollywood Ten who were jailed and black-listed, told the above story in a recent speech, which included also this personal footnote.

After years of writing television scripts under pseudonyms, during which time I was unable to accept job offers abroad because I was denied a passport, the Supreme Court overruled the State Department on that issue, and I was so eager I went immediately to a photographer near my home in New York who advertised passport pictures among his services. But he couldn't meet my demand for a picture the same day. I would have to go, he told me scornfully, to one of those assembly-line purveyors of photographs without negatives. (This was pre-Polaroid.)

"But," he warned me, "you'll end up looking like a Communist."

No, Mr. De Mille

The House Un-American Activities Committee and the blacklisting of some of Hollywood's major talent inflicted deep wounds on the film colony from which it has not fully recovered forty years later. One of the most dramatic showdowns was at the meeting of the Screen Directors Guild of America, on October 22, 1950, during which a faction of its board of directors, led by Cecil B. De Mille, tried to remove the Guild's president, Joseph L. Mankiewicz.

All officers of unions were required by law to sign a loyalty oath and now De Mille wanted every Guild member to do the same. He chose a time when Mankiewicz was vacationing in Europe to send out ballots to approve a new bylaw concerning the mandatory oath. The ballots were open and members had to sign their names on the principle that patriots had nothing to hide. Upon his return, Mankiewicz was appalled by this whole procedure, and insisted on calling a membership meeting to discuss it. De Mille retaliated by starting a recall drive to remove Mankiewicz. This time he sent out secret ballots, which had only the word "yes" on it, and he made sure that known friends of Joe Mankiewicz were left off the list. Finally a faction to stop De Mille began to rally and twenty-five of the most famous directors called a "Special Separate Meeting to consider the proposed recall of the president."

The ballroom of the Beverly Hills Hotel was packed as Joseph Mankiewicz outlined his opposition to the blacklist, the open ballot, and a mandatory oath for all members, as essentially un-American. De Mille rose to defend his position and to attack the directors who had called the meeting as being affiliated with subversive organizations. Many of them were foreign-born, he pointed out, and for the first time the veteran director was hissed. Then the counter-attacks began from both native and foreign-born directors. One of them said that he was fighting in France while De Mille was defending his capital gains in Hollywood. William Wyler, who had also fought in the war, said he was sick and tired of being called a Communist just because he disagreed with De Mille. George Stevens offered to resign from the board, asking De Mille to stop his recall movement. De Mille demanded in return contrition from Mankiewicz, which was not forthcoming.

A stalemate seemed to have been reached, when a man who had been silently sitting in a baseball cap and tennis shoes raised his hand.

"My name's John Ford," he said taking the pipe from his mouth. "I make Westerns." After a significant pause he continued. "I don't think there is anyone in this room who knows more about what the American public wants than Cecil B. De Mille—and he certainly knows how to give it to them. In that respect I admire him. But," said Ford, looking straight at De Mille, "I don't like what you stand for, C.B., and I don't like what you've been saying here tonight. Joe has been vilified, and I think he needs an apology."

De Mille sat in silence, and Ford introduced a resolution to remove De Mille and the entire board of directors, and to give a vote of confidence to Mankiewicz.

"And then let's all go home," said Ford, "and get some sleep. We've got some pictures to make tomorrow."

Cecil B. De Mille and the board of directors resigned and there was a unanimous vote of confidence in the president, with only four abstentions.

Robert Parrish, for whom this was his very first meeting of the Screen Directors Guild, remarked in his autobiography:

"We had saved Mankiewicz's presidency and defied the man who parted the Red Sea twice."

Witchhunt

Soon after the House Un-American Committee began its investigation of Hollywood, Billy Wilder happened to be walking with a colleague on the Paramount lot, when they smelled and saw a huge belch of smoke rising from the RKO studio next door.

"I wonder what they're burning there," said Wilder's friend.

"Probably Eddie Dmytryk," replied Billy Wilder, referring to the director RKO was about to blacklist.

Howard and Paul

Paul Jarrico was just finishing a screenplay called *The Las Vegas Story* in the spring of 1951, when he was summoned to appear before the House Un-American Committee. The same morning that he issued a statement that he would not co-operate with the Committee, Howard Hughes gave orders to have him "eliminated" from the payroll and barred from the RKO lot. On the other hand, Hughes needed *The Las Vegas Story* as the next vehicle for Jane Russell, so he further ordered that the script be rewritten and Jarrico's name removed from the credits. At this point, the Screen Writers' Guild, which had fought long battles over its jurisdiction over credits, determined that the script still had substantial portions conceived and written by the banished writer and entered the fray. It led to a lawsuit against Hughes and a countersuit from him, alleging that Jarrico had violated the morals clause of his contract by taking the Fifth Amendment during the hearing before a congressional committee.

It was a celebrated case, marking the last appearance of the litigious Howard Hughes in a public courtroom. The mood of the times was definitely on his side and RKO won on every point against the fired writer. Judge Orlando Rhodes found that Jarrico had indeed violated his contract and had "placed himself in moral obloquy." However, a few moments after his stern pronouncement, the judge warmly shook Paul Jarrico's hands and said sincerely:

"It's been a pleasure to have been associated with you."

A Common Past

During the blacklist period, writer Dalton Trumbo hardly ever turned down work and wrote many scripts under various assumed names. He was much in demand for his skill and sometimes he received so many assignments that he shared them with other blacklisted writers. One of these was Paul Jarrico, who wanted to thank his friend for passing on a commission by inviting him and his whole family to Paul's Duck Press, an expensive Los Angeles restaurant specializing in venison. The waiter who took the orders immediately recognized Dalton Trumbo, a very convivial and outgoing man:

"Mr. Trumbo, I used to be a waiter at the MGM commissary—it's so good to see you—how are you—it has been ages since I've seen you—where have you been all this time?"

"In jail," said the writer matter of factly.

"That's funny," said the waiter, "so have I."

Absolute Power

The politics of the blacklist pale next to the power wielded by a genuine dictator. My father, the Hungarian playwright Julius Hay, was in Soviet exile during Stalin's reign of terror in the thirties, and worked in one of the Moscow studios. In his memoirs, Born 1900, *he captured one of those moments when the dictator hiccuped and the film artists all but choked to death.*

One day Comrade Samsonov asked to see me but was not in his office when I arrived. No one apologized for the fact, but this was not in itself remarkable. What was remarkable was a quite unusual tension running through the entire building. Clearly no one had his mind on his work. More and more people came in—directors, actors, writers— but despite the throng it was as quiet as an empty church. I slowly gathered that somewhere in a very important place some very important films were being shown to a very important personage—and that some very important decisions depended on the upshot. It was as if we in Lychov Street must whisper lest we disturb the showing in the Kremlin.

We had been waiting for some hours when Samsonov finally appeared. He hopped in on his stumpy legs like an agitated dachshund, but his eyes behind his spectacles gleamed with an unearthly bliss. There was no doubt at all *whose* presence he had recently been in and *whose* words still rang in his ears. His voice, which was trembling with ecstasy, was in marked contrast to the content of his short speech.

"Comrades! Mammoth catastrophe! Wholesale rejection! All the films shown by the entire Soviet film industry—all slung out! Including two by Eisenstein and one by Pudovkin. Prodigious, unprecedented, utter and complete artistic débâcle!"

He paused. Then, more objectively, the tremble of ecstasy replaced by a military severity. "Government decision: this studio to be disbanded. A studio for children's films is to take its place. All the films on our books to be scrapped."

The speaker began applauding before any of us could say a word. A violent if brief storm of applause shook the room. Here and there one heard people repeating the names "Pudovkin" and "Eisenstein." Then the two greatest names in film. A dog would not have accepted a crust from their hands at that moment.

But Not the Last

Eisenstein began working on *Ivan the Terrible* (1942–46) during the evacuation of the Soviet film industry to Central Asia from the Nazi advance on Moscow. The film was inspired by patriotism, a reminder to his fellow countrymen about the glorious past when Russia stood strong. Inevitably, there were resemblances between the cruelties of the medieval autocrat and those of Stalin the Terrible. As the movie was moving toward completion, some of Eisenstein's close associates began to fear for his life. But the director shrugged off the danger:

"This will be the first time in history," he told one friend with grim humor, "that a man has committed suicide by cinema!"

We've Come a Long Way, Comrades

Director Frank Pierson was visiting the Soviet Union with a delegation of American movie-makers. Discussing the great changes that were taking place under Mikhail Gorbachev's reforms, one of the prominent Soviet film directors remarked in the spirit of *glasnost*:

"Now we can talk about the films that we are not allowed to make."

Who Cares?

Even before the film adaptation of Richard Condon's novel *The Manchurian Candidate* was completed in 1962, there was concern about releasing such an anti-Communist film. In particular, people worried about delicate negotiations going on with the Soviets about limiting nuclear tests. Frank Sinatra, the star of the movie, decided to go right to the top to find out if there might be a problem. He dropped in at the Kennedy compound in Hyannisport and, choosing his words carefully, told the President about his current project.

"That's great," said John Kennedy, an obvious fan of the book, "and who's playing the mother?"

(Angela Lansbury did, with superb evil.)

The Candidate

Robert Redford got the idea for *The Candidate* (1972) while watching on television the image-making that surrounded the 1968 presidential elections. To establish a sense of realism about a political campaign, he hired Jeremy Larner, a former speechwriter for Eugene McCarthy. Rather than hiring extras, advance men would hand out pictures of Redford as Democratic candidate for the U.S. Senate. When enough people gathered, the star appeared. Believing him to be a politician, some of them began heckling him:

"What about welfare?" asked somebody, after the camera had stopped rolling.

"Beats me," said Redford.

The movie-makers got so much into the act that they began to suggest seriously that the actor should run for office. But Robert Redford was horrified.

"What would happen if I won?" he asked.

CHAPTER 21

The Importance of Oscar

Oscar Is Born

The first Academy Awards were announced on February 18, 1929, but the dinner to hand out the statuettes was not held until three months later, on May 19, at the Blossom Room of the Hollywood Roosevelt Hotel. It took only five minutes to distribute the first Oscars. Though there was no suspense, the pattern of star behavior for the awards was beginning to show. None of the three nominated actors bothered to show up. Emil Jannings, who won the first two years, sent a telegram from his native Germany, which was read aloud by Douglas Fairbanks, Sr., first president of the Academy:

"Hand me now already the statuette award," it went, perhaps too carefully translated from the German.

Charlie Chaplin, who was nominated for *The Circus* (1928), stayed away "due to cold feet," as William C. De Mille was to remark.

Al Jolson, commenting on the fact that *The Jazz Singer* (1927) received a special Oscar for pioneering sound, got the laugh of the evening by pointing to the statuette:

"For the life of me I can't see what Jack Warner would do with one of them. It can't say yes."

Screenwriter Frances Marion (who remembers the first award night as held at the Alexandria Hotel) described Oscar "as a perfect symbol of the picture business: a powerful athletic body clutching a gleaming sword with half of his head, that part which held his brains, completely sliced off."

King Oscar

In those early days everybody was aware that the results were dictated, if not rigged, by Louis B. Mayer, who considered the awards his own brainchild. During the 1943 Academy Award presentations two MGM press agents literally knelt attendance at the side of Louis B. Mayer's chair throughout the entire dinner. It was at this same ceremony that Mayer put his arm around William Goetz, his son-in-law, and remarked publicly:

"Some day you may even be as great as I am."

The King and I

In 1939, announcing that George Bernard Shaw had won an Oscar for the screenplay of *Pygmalion*, the novelist Lloyd C. Douglas made a sly dig at the absent winner:

"Mr. Shaw's story is as original now as it was three thousand years ago."

Shaw, who had withstood Hollywood's blandishments for decades, pretended to be furious when his golden statuette was delivered in England.

"It's an insult for them to offer me any honor," he fumed, "as if they had never heard of me before—and it's very likely they never have. They might as well send some honor to George for being King of England."

Please Control Yourself

The Academy gave a special Oscar to Walt Disney in 1939 for *Snow White and the Seven Dwarfs*. Shirley Temple, who got her own special Oscar four years earlier at the age of six, stood on a chair to present one normal-sized statuette to the animator, accompanied by seven decreasingly smaller ones.

"Isn't it beautiful and shiny?" asked Shirley Temple.

"Yes, and I'm so proud of it," said Disney, "I'm going to burst."

"Oh don't do that!" Shirley exclaimed with genuine alarm.

Noises Off

Jerome Kern was the presenter for the music awards during those 1939 Oscar ceremonies.

"Of all the noises," the songwriter began, "I think music is the least annoying."

When We Were Rudely Interrupted

The dreary monotony of the over-scripted Academy Award shows is every so often interrupted by someone unforeseen, which enables some stars to display unsuspected natural wit. When Marlon Brando was announced the winner of the 1972 Best Actor Award (for his role in *The Godfather*), a woman in Apache costume—identifying herself as Sacheen Littlefeather and as president of the National Native American Affirmative Image Committee—appeared on the stage of the Dorothy Chandler Pavilion. She turned down the award on Brando's behalf and said that she would explain his reasons, but had been forbidden to read her fifteen-page speech. (Producer Howard W. Koch had in fact issued her an ultimatum backstage that he would have her physically removed if she went over forty-five seconds.)

Rock Hudson, who was to present the next award, editorialized that "often to be eloquent is to be silent," and Raquel Welch, about to announce the Best Actress nominations, was heard in a stage whisper:

"I hope they haven't got a cause."

But the best line came from Clint Eastwood, a man with very few words to waste. He introduced the Oscar for Best Picture with:

"I don't know if I should present this award on behalf of all the cowboys shot in John Ford Westerns over the years."

(Rona Barrett later reported that Ms. Littlefeather was not really an Apache, but true to Hollywood casting, an actress known by the name of Maria Cruz, who had been selected "Miss American Vampire of 1970."

Whether Brando found out about the true identity of his spokesperson, he might have been inured to such revelations. He married his first wife, Anna Kashfi, believing her to be a demure Oriental woman from Darjeeling, India. It was later disclosed that she was Joan O'Callaghan, the daughter of an Irish factory worker.)

Found Wanting

The 1973 ceremonies are remembered for the naked man who streaked by David Niven as he tried to introduce Elizabeth Taylor. While Henry Mancini and his orchestra came to the rescue by ad-libbing the strains of "Sunny Side Up," the streaker was led off by security guards.

"Just think," Niven resumed suavely, "the only laugh that man will probably ever get is for stripping and showing off his shortcomings."

(In fact, Robert Opal became a minor celebrity on the talk-show and party circuit, and he died in a somewhat lurid limelight: he was found murdered in his San Francisco sex shop.)

Battle for the Hearts and Minds

Accepting the Oscar for *Hearts and Minds* as the best documentary, Bert Schneider caused a backstage furor during the 1974 Award ceremonies. He conveyed greetings of friendship from the Viet Cong delegation to the peace talks in Paris, which were not well received by the Hollywood establishment. John Wayne and Bob Hope prevailed upon Frank Sinatra, about to go on stage, to read a disclaimer on behalf of the Academy. Schneider had his defenders, including Francis Ford Coppola and Shirley MacLaine, who said:

"Bob Hope is so mad at me, he's going to bomb Encino."*

Gone Hollywood

One of the rare experiences of recent Academy Awards when the audience was moved, not just the recipient, was the honoring of Dr. Haing S. Ngor, who played Dith Pran, the Cambodian interpreter, in *The Killing Fields* (1984). He had never acted in his life and did not seek the role. The Cambodian refugee's picture was spotted not in a casting directory but in a newspaper photograph of a wedding reception by Pat Golden, who interviewed him. Then the casting director took the 35-year-old gynecologist to see director Roland Joffe and producer David Puttnam on the Warner Brothers lot. It was an unusual audition, with the non-actor holding the film people spellbound with his own personal story of torture at the hands of the Khmer Rouge and of his escape from Cambodia.

"When he looked out the window," Joffe later remembered, "he did not see the Warners parking lot on a Sunday afternoon, which I did—he saw Phnom Penh."

By the time his performance was honored, Dr. Ngor thanked the Academy as a Hollywood professional, expressing his gratitude to Warner Brothers, God, and Buddha—in that order.

But What a Way To Go

When *Casablanca* won the Oscar for Best Picture in 1943, executive producer Hal Wallis beat his boss Jack Warner to the podium. The next

* An exclusive suburb of Los Angeles.

morning, when he came to work, basking in the afterglow of recognition bestowed by his peers, Wallis found all his personal belongings strewn on the lawn outside his private bungalow on the Warner lot. That is how one of Hollywood's ablest and most powerful producers found out that his services were no longer required. Hal Wallis went over to Paramount, where he established his own production unit.

Gone to the Dog

Robert Towne had labored eight years on the screenplay version of *Greystoke: The Legend of Tarzan, Lord of the Apes* (1984), which he had hoped to direct. But when he ran over budget in making his first film, *Personal Best* (1982), Warner Brothers repossessed the rights to *Greystoke* and gave it to Hugh Hudson. The British director, according to ancient custom, brought in his own writer, Michael Austin, to polish the script. Towne, whose reputation as screenwriter is second to none in Hollywood, was so disgusted that in the credits he replaced his name with P. H. Vazak, one of the giant Komondors he owned at the time. It was the first time that a Hungarian sheepdog, which resembles a carwash in motion, had been nominated for an Academy Award.

Career Move

Early in his career, Ernest Borgnine was working with Spencer Tracy in *Bad Day at Black Rock* (1954), when he was offered the chance to play the lead in a small black-and-white film, written by an unknown television writer named Paddy Chayefsky. Borgnine, frustrated with always being cast to play heavies, told Tracy that he was leaving for New York to do the part. As Borgnine recounted on the *Larry King Show*, Spencer Tracy thought this would be a big mistake, that he should be content to be making a good living as a character actor.

"You're gonna make a little black-and-white film," he lectured Borgnine, "no one's ever gonna hear of it, you're gonna think you're a star and you're not gonna be a star."

"Spence," Borgnine told him, "if I don't try it now, I'll never know."

Borgnine went on to make *Marty* (1955) and was nominated for an Academy Award along with Tracy. As Borgnine went up to collect his Oscar, he passed Spencer Tracy, who said to him:

"You never listen, do you?"

Compliment

Cliff Robertson was also frustrated to see a succession of roles he created on stage or on television given to other stars in the film version: Marlon Brando in *The Fugitive Kind* (the 1959 movie version of Tennessee Williams's play *Orpheus Descending*), and Paul Newman in *The Hustler* (1961). As a last straw, Jack Lemmon bought the rights to *Days of Wine and Roses* (1962), which Robertson first played on Playhouse 90. One of the more satisfying moments in his life, Cliff Robertson told a Tarrytown Film Weekend audience, was after Jack Lemmon had failed to win an Academy Award for the role and had called him.

"You son of a bitch," said Lemmon, only half-kidding, "if you hadn't done that role first, I'd have an Oscar in my hand right now."

Lure

In the French film industry there is a popular saying directors use when they keep asking the actors for another take: "Come on, let's do it again and we'll get the Oscar."

As soon as Peter Bogdanovich had cast Cloris Leachman in the role of Ruth Popper in *The Last Picture Show* (1971), he predicted that she would win the Oscar for it.

"How do you know that?" she asked taken aback.

"Because anybody who plays that role will win an Oscar," said the brash young director.

Throughout the making of the picture, Cloris Leachman would turn after each shot she completed to Bogdanovich and ask:

"Okay? An Oscar?"

(Cloris Leachman did get an Academy Award, as did Ben Johnson, to whom Bogdanovich had also promised one, after he first refused to do the picture.)

The Joy of Winning

Fed up with all the false modesty that filled the air at the Academy Awards, Donald Ogden Stewart accepted the screenwriting award in 1941 with this:

"There has been so much niceness here tonight that I'm happy to say that I'm entirely and solely responsible for the success of *The Philadelphia Story*."

Jimmy Stewart won an Oscar for his role in the same movie. He was sharing a house with Burgess Meredith at the time, and upon getting home,
late but excited, Stewart woke him up:

"Look, what I've won!" and showed him the statuette. His roommate
squinted at him and said groggily:

"What did you do . . . win at Ocean Park?"

Oscar Wylder

When he started directing, Billy Wilder was often confused in Hollywood
with his senior Central European colleague William Wyler. Introducing
Wilder as the Academy Award winner for *The Lost Weekend* (1945),
Wyler—who had won the Oscar for directing *Mrs. Miniver* a couple of
years before—quipped:

"I am delighted to acknowledge all the critical praise I received for
directing this picture."

"Thank you, Willie," Billy Wilder riposted, "and how did you like my
Mrs. Miniver?"

And Losing

Johnny Weismuller, was nicknamed "the censored Adam," and his studio
denied that "Mr. Weismuller played gin rummy with the chimpanzee on
the set and had lost three dollars to the ape."

Interviewed after one of the Academy Award presentations, where his
artistic efforts had been passed over again, the durable box-office star stayed
in character:

"Me sit in trees seventeen years," he said. "Me watch 'em come and go."

The Noscar

Being recognized by one's peers in front of the whole world is said to be
one of the peak experiences in a film artist's life. The converse can be very
painful. Over the years, for one reason or another, some of the greatest
and most popular artists—from Chaplin to Cary Grant, Barbara Stanwyck
to Steven Spielberg (so far)—have been denied the honor of an Oscar.
Because of the hype surrounding the Academy Awards, fueled largely by
the film industry itself, the letdown is so much the worse for being played
out in public.

After Paul Newman was not even nominated for his tour de force as
Rocky Graziano in *Somebody Up There Likes Me* (1956)—while his wife

Joanne Woodward had just won for *The Three Faces of Eve*—friends held a private ceremony on Oscar night for the actor on the Malibu beach. Somebody made up a special statuette and presented the "Noscar" to Newman.

Thirty years later, the Academy board voted Newman a special honorary Oscar, which has often been given to giants in the industry passed over for an award in the regular voting process. It was the first time it had been granted an actor who still considered himself in his prime. Worried about its symbolism, Paul Newman thanked the Academy via satellite hookup:

"I'm grateful this award didn't come wrapped in a gift certificate to Forest Lawn."

At Last, Something to Cheer About

Although the Oscar is mainly regarded by actors as a bankable asset, it often brings money more to the studio than to the performer. The day after Eileen Heckart had won the 1972 Academy Award for Best Supporting Actress (in *Butterflies Are Free*) she went to the unemployment office near her home.

"They cheered me when I walked in," she commented. "I'm very well known there."

CHAPTER 22

Previews and Reviews

The Long and the Short of It

Film-makers particularly resent the emphasis placed on audience research by the major studios. Director Richard Brooks once said:

"Columbus would still be in Spain, if they waited for preview cards."

Hitchcock never saw his films with an ordinary audience.

"Don't you miss hearing them scream?" someone asked him.

"No," explained the master of suspense, "I can hear them when I'm making the picture."

After the screening of A Woman Under the Influence (1975), actress Gena Rowlands was asked at a Tarrytown Film Weekend why the films of her husband, the late John Cassavetes, tended to be so long. She explained that a lot of people left during Cassavetes's films to get away from their intensity: to smoke a cigarette or eat a snack before they feel calm enough to return.

"So we try," Rowlands said with tongue firmly in her cheek, "to leave enough minutes in our movies for those who want to visit the lobby."

Collector's Item

Dore Schary finished *Lust for Life* (1956), a movie about the life of Van Gogh, and invited William Goetz, the son-in-law of Louis B. Mayer and one of the foremost collectors of Van Gogh paintings in the United States, to a preview at MGM.

"Do you think it's commercial?" afterwards Shary asked anxiously.

"Certainly," said Goetz with a straight face. "Everyone who owns a Van Gogh will simply have to see it."

Polite Fictions

In Hollywood everybody is nice to everybody's face, a skill that is most needed after industry screenings. After watching many a flop, Sid Grauman developed a line:

"Well, it should surprise everybody."

Judith Crist recalled another line in common use:

"Well, you certainly have a *picture* there."

Writer Arthur Caesar would always say:

"It'll do great in the sticks," and then start looking for his car-keys.

But Caesar was called in by the producer of an almost certain flop, and asked whether he could do anything to salvage it.

"Cut it up," the writer suggested, "and make it into mandolin picks."

Radical Solutions

Lionel Houser, an MGM executive in the 1940s, said after a preview:

"It's so bad that we will keep the picture and release the producer."

In the same period, producer-agent George Marton said of another picture:

"It was so bad, they had to make retakes in order to shelve it."

Sneak Release

William Fox was disappointed after he saw the rushes for *The Valiant* (1929), Paul Muni's first leading role at the studio.

"However did we ever sign this monkey?" he asked, forgetting that he had earlier taken sole credit for discovering the actor. Fox had so little confidence that he released the picture without fanfare and the usual audience testing.

"It wasn't a sneak preview," Bella Muni commented, "it was a sneak release."

Notable Credit

After viewing Mary Pickford and Douglas Fairbanks, Sr., in the disastrous flop *The Taming of the Shrew* (1929), one critic remarked that the only notable aspect of the film was the photoplay credit which read:

"Written by William Shakespeare. Additional dialogue by Sam Taylor."

Give Me That Old-Time Criticism

Benjamin R. Crisler, longtime movie critic for the *New York Times* before the Second World War, defined investment as a Hollywood word that denoted "that part of a picture which the producer naïvely expects a critic to be impressed by when the picture has nothing else about it to inspire respect."

In Hollywood, bad reviews tend to be blamed on the souring of a personal relationship. Ezra Goodman, longtime movie critic for *Time*, once received a concerned phone call from the affable producer George Pal:

"Ezra, what is wrong? Are you mad at me?" He simply could not fathom that something might have been wrong with his latest film.

Grace Kingsley, one of the earliest movie critics of the *Los Angeles Times* (she started in 1913), ran into hostility with theatre managers any time she gave a film a bad review. After failing to get her fired, one manager flashed a card on the screen:

"Grace Kingsley thinks this is a bad picture. What do you think?"

Unexpectedly, friends of the critic happened to be in the audience, and when the slide came on, they stood up and chanted, before walking out:

"We think Grace Kingsley was right!"

Harry Crocker, movie columnist for the Hearst papers in the forties, had an industry column called "Behind the Makeup." One day, the Los Angeles *Examiner* ran it under the headline "Makeup the Behind," prompting one Hollywood wag to remark that it was the only time the column had been accurately described.

Professional Hazards

Irving Hoffman was longtime drama critic for the *Hollywood Reporter*. As there was very little live theatre in Los Angeles, he did his reviewing from New York, a safe distance from his readers and his publisher.

Frustrated with a scalding review that Hoffman had written of *Ethan Frome* (1936), the Broadway producer Max Gordon tried the time-honored way of having the critic removed from his job for some other reason. Hoffman was notoriously short-sighted, so Gordon wrote Billy Wilkerson, Hoffman's employer:

"What's the idea of sending Hoffman to cover my shows? Hell, the man can't even see." Told about this complaint, the critic replied:

"But there's nothing wrong with my sense of smell."

A mild-mannered man, better known for falling asleep during a performance than for his critical acumen, Hoffman occasionally came to resent the hazards of his profession. In the forties, having sat through the opening of *In Bed We Cry* (1944), by the writer and film actress Ilka Chase, he simply wrote:

"It made me Ilka."

In-fighting

Roger Ebert, the Pulitzer Prize-winning critic of the Chicago *Sun-Times*, has had a difficult time living down his youthful indiscretion of having written the screenplay for Russ Meyer's soft-porn movie *Beyond the Valley of the Dolls* (1970). Although Ebert has always insisted that his script was intended as a parody of Jacqueline Susann's novel and the movie based on it, Alexander Walker did not buy it. With some glee, the acerbic critic of London's *Evening Standard* placed *Beyond the Valley of the Dolls* on his "best-ever 'worst' film," writing that it was "the kind of movie that a maladroit Mack Sennett might have made if he had worked in a sex shop, not a fun factory."

Portrait of a Has-Been Critic

Bosley Crowther, film critic of the *New York Times* for more than three decades, was clearly out of touch with the movies of the mid-sixties. He called *The Dirty Dozen* (1966), among other things, 'a studied indulgence of sadism that is morbid and disgusting beyond words." And he wrote of

Bonnie and Clyde (1967): "It is a cheap piece of bald-faced slapstick that treats the hideous depredations of that sleazy, moronic pair as though they were as full of fun and frolic as the jazz-age cut-ups in *Thoroughly Modern Millie.*"

When other critics defended the film, Crowther attacked them. Penelope Gilliatt counter-attacked her aging colleague in the *New Yorker*: " 'Bonnie and Clyde' could look like a celebration of gangster glamour only to a man with a head full of wood shavings."

Not long afterwards, after giving a favorable review to *The Graduate* (1967), he resigned from the *Times* and took on a vaguely defined consulting job with Columbia Pictures, which invited him to attend the Academy Awards. The studio had promised the retired critic first-class treatment, but when he arrived at the Los Angeles airport, he looked vainly for the stipulated limousine, or the reserved bungalow at the Beverly Hills Hotel. Fellow critic Rex Reed described, more with glee than sorrow, how the veteran Crowther sat on Oscar night "on top of his luggage at three o'clock in the morning looking for a place to stay."

From Prostate to Prostrate; or, How To Get a Good Review

Katharine Hepburn's early career both on stage and in pictures was marred by bad reviews, and she soon became known as poison at the box office. The social historian Cleveland Amory read a very favorable notice which appeared about Miss Hepburn in Hartford, Connecticut, which was her home town. He ran into Dr. Hepburn, a well-known urologist in Hartford, and remarked on the divergence in journalistic opinion of his daughter.

"Do you know what I do?" asked Dr. Hepburn with a steady gaze.

"No," replied Armory.

"I specialize in what is known as the 'Old Man's Operation.' I have operated on half the newspaper publishers of this city already, and I fully expect to operate on the other half."

Free Law School

Bad reviews, in fact criticism of any kind, stir up inchoate feelings of helplessness and revenge in film people. Not inconsiderable money, time, and especially ego are invested in making movies. After months—sometimes years—of frustration, but also basking in the haze of mutual admiration that envelops most projects, the first critical comments are about as welcome as a kick to an empty stomach. Herbert Wilcox, one of the founders of the British film industry, had this experience, fortunately early enough in his career to live to tell about it in his memoirs:

I had produced a film which the *Daily Mail* film critic tore to pieces. I was furious. He had exceeded his province as a critic, I felt confident.

I told my solicitor to consult counsel. I was right, and according to counsel, bound to win. The writ was issued and I was licking my chops.

Sir George Sutton (Lord Northcliffe's right-hand man) asked me to come and see him. I did—but remained firm.

"Come and have a word with the chief," he suggested.

I found myself feeling a midget facing a man who appeared to be ten feet tall.

"I'm told you've taken action against the *Daily Mail*."

"Yes, sir, I have, and I'm assured I shall win," I replied.

"You're very young and new to your job. I'm old in mine—I'm giving you some advice. Never reply to criticism, never."

That was the end. I left. I was incensed, and, with my solicitor, saw our counsel, Mr. Jowitt, later Lord Jowitt. He listened and smiled.

"Can I also give you some advice?"

"Why—of course."

"Never litigate."

I telephoned Sir George Sutton telling him of my decision and asked him to pass information on to Lord Northcliffe that I had dropped the case.

"That won't be necessary," replied Sir George. "Lord Northcliffe told me when you left him there would be no lawsuit!"

Whenever I have ignored Northcliffe's advice, it has always been to my detriment. But I have *never* ignored Jowitt's.

Welles 1, Hearst 0

William Randolph Hearst tried everything within his considerable power to prevent the making and distribution of *Citizen Kane* (1941), thereby only drawing further attention to the similarities between himself and the subject of Orson Welles's masterpiece. Having attacked Welles for being a menace to freedom of speech and assembly, the press lord forbade any of his newspapers ever to mention the name of the actor-director again. This worked until the Los Angeles *Examiner* began a campaign to collect relief funds for the victims of an earthquake in Colima, Mexico, and offered to print the name of every contributor.

"The impish Mr. Welles," reported an equally impish anonymity in the *New Yorker*, "as alert as the next man to the misfortunes of a Mexican, sent the *Examiner* twenty-five dollars. The editorial suffering caused by this kindly action was indescribable. . . . Finally they included Welles in the daily list, thus: 'O. Welles, $25.00. "

Paper Trading

What Hollywood most likes to read are "the trades"—chiefly *Daily Variety* and the *Hollywood Reporter*. They are long on insider gossip about deals, executive appointments, and exits; they carry the messages of the powerful in full-page ads, and they are mercifully short on criticism. One old local saw defined it thus:

"Maybe you can call them trade papers because you can trade an ad for a nice notice."

As self-congratulatory advertisements in the trades became commonplace, some serious artists in the movie colony saw their own work debased. After an avalanche of sycophantic endorsements greeted David O. Selznick's *Duel in the Sun* (1944), Billy Wilder wanted to make a point. He had recently completed *Double Indemnity*, which he announced in paid advertisements in the trades, citing a certain George Oblath, "as the greatest picture I have ever seen." Everybody in Hollywood knew, of course, that Oblath owned a beanery near Paramount Studios.

Selznick was so furious that he threatened to withdraw all his advertising from the paper—and almost did.

The Eleventh Plague

To announce his remake of *The Ten Commandments* (1956), Cecil B. De Mille bought the front cover of the bulky and glossy annual edition of the *Hollywood Reporter*. Milton Epstein, ad salesman for the trade paper, sent a mockup of the planned ad to the director, who complained that the representation of Moses did not look majestic enough. After a shouting match on the telephone, De Mille had his way, but the salesman got in the punchline:

"All right," he shouted at the mogul, "we'll put more silver in Moses's hair!"

Did He Who Make the Lamb Write Thee?

McDaniel's Market used to advertise in the trade papers as "the grocery store to the stars." When actor Sonny Tufts made headlines in 1954 for biting a couple of young ladies in the thighs, the store rose to the occasion. In the best Hollywood taste it advertised leg of lamb in the *Hollywood Reporter* as a "Sonny Tufts special."

Breakthrough

Trade papers were not always so tame; they became domesticated. Barely one month after it had been launched, Harry Cohn banned the *Hollywood Reporter*, as he would do many times later, especially for crashing sneak previews and publishing critical comments before the official premiere. Founding publisher Billy Wilkerson ran a headlined box on the front page:

"Thanks, Mr. Cohn—the *Hollywood Reporter* has finally become important enough to be barred from the Columbia lot. Thanks, Mr. Cohn, for making the boast possible."

Sidney Skolsky went from Broadway to Hollywood in 1933. The diminutive newsman became one of Tinseltown's most powerful columnists. One day Skolsky ran into Harry Cohn at some Hollywood function.

"Sidney," the mogul said affably, "I'm going to lift the one-year ban barring you from my studio, because of what you'd said about *Lost Horizon* (1937)." Skolsky was completely unaware that he had been barred:

"I simply never have any reason to come on the Columbia lot," he told the studio head. Cohn was stumped, but only for a moment:

"From today, then," he decreed, "you'll be barred for one year."

A Matter of Honor

The relationship between the press and the studios was mostly one of mutual parasitism. On another occasion Sidney Skolsky was not only on the Columbia lot, but he was pitching *The Jolson Story* (1946) to Harry Cohn, trying to reassure him that having a gossip columnist inside would not result in leaks.

"I'll never print anything I shouldn't," Skolsky promised, "unless I get it on the outside. You'll have to trust me."

"I love the honor system," Cohn smiled. "But who can you practice it with in this industry?"

All the studios maintained large publicity departments, not just to promote movies but for damage control. Some went to obsequious lengths to ingratiate themselves with the powerful columnists. Harry Brand, when he was publicist at Twentieth Century-Fox in the 1940s, ran into a door and had himself photographed with a prominent black eye. In a conscious parody of his trade, he then sent a print to his good friend Sidney Skolsky with the inscription:

"Nobody can talk that way about you when I'm around!"

Louella & Hedda

Hollywood in the forties was dominated by the syndicated gossip columnists, none more powerful than Louella Parsons and Hedda Hopper. The latter was ten years younger and started her news career under Louella, having been an actress first. She described the difference between them:

"Louella Parsons is a reporter trying to be a ham; Hedda Hopper is a ham trying to be a reporter."

The two women became bitter rivals, constantly trying to scoop each other. Hollywood legends abounded about their power. One couple began to elope, but they mislaid Louella's phone number and had to call the whole thing off.

Another time Louella published a false item about an actress being pregnant. The story went that the star's husband was coerced into doing his duty to prove the columnist correct.

Bob Hope was leaving on a bomber flight for one of his USO tours and he gave the name of Louella Parsons as his next of kin, to be notified in case of a mishap.

"She'd be mad," said Hope, "if she wasn't the first to know."

Both columnists thought themselves above mere gossip and aspired to be regular film critics. Once Hedda Hopper expressed the opinion that George Burns had given the worst performance of his life in his latest movie. The next morning, Louella rang him:

"George, we've been friends for a long, long time," she said with total seriousness. "Next time you have an item like that you give it to me."

Joan Bennett was angered by an item Hedda Hopper ran about her. So the star had her chauffeur deliver a live, deodorized skunk to Hopper's home.

The powerful gossip columnist received the message with good humor. She promptly announced to reporters that the skunk was beautifully behaved.

"I christened it Joan, of course," she smiled sweetly.

That's No Lady

Constance, another of the Bennett sisters, remarked to Sheilah Graham, early in her career as a gossip columnist:

"It's hard to believe that a girl as pretty as you could be the biggest bitch in Hollywood."

"Not the biggest," Graham retorted, "the second biggest."

The Hollywood correspondent for the New York *Daily News* was an extraordinary character. Florabel Muir had red hair and an equine face. Once while she was tracking down mobster Mickey Cohen, she was shot in the posterior by a bullet during a shoot-out on the Sunset Strip. The *Daily News* gave her a bulletproof corset. This did not protect her on another occasion, when a drunk Franchot Tone spit bullseye in her face at Ciro's nightclub. Muir had the actor arrested and jailed. He was fined $500, but never did apologize to the lady. It would not have done him any good.

"I'm not a lady," Florabel Muir once remarked, "I am a columnist."

Etiquette

Errol Flynn once put out to sea on his yacht *Sirocco*, when he noticed that his beloved dog named Arno was missing. The distraught actor called the Coast Guard, which found the drowned body of the pet and offered to bring it to him.

"No, no," Flynn declined, "please just send me his collar." The grieving star then buried the collar in a pet cemetery.

The following morning he read in Jimmy Fidler's gossip column: "Errol Flynn, whose love for his dog Arno has been much heralded, didn't even bother to go get his body when it was washed ashore. That's how much he cared for him."

A few weeks passed, and Fidler saw Errol Flynn enter the Mocambo night club, and rose to greet him, as if nothing had happened. The actor hit the reporter so hard with his open hand that Fidler fell between the dancers on the floor. An instant later, Flynn felt a sharp pain in his ear. Fidler's wife had reached for the nearest fork and stabbed the star with it. The columnist then brought assault charges against the star, but the case was settled out of court. The two became good friends, especially after Flynn told Fidler:

"Your wife has good table manners. She used the right fork."

Real Fame

Following a Broadway play in 1932, called *Blessed Event*, that parodied Walter Winchell, the columnist himself sold a somewhat autobiographical story idea to Darryl F. Zanuck about a love triangle made up of a gangster, a chorus girl and a columnist. In *Broadway Thru a Keyhole* (1933), the character of the newspaperman was changed to that of a popular singer, which led Louella Parsons to mention in her column that Winchell had based his story on the romance between the middle-aged Al Jolson and the 18-year-old Ruby Keeler whom Jolson had won away from a hoodlum named Johnny Irish.

Jolson read the column, and the next time he spotted Winchell, at a boxing match held in the Hollywood Legion Stadium, he stopped him in the aisle, and knocked down the newspaperman with a blow at his neck. Jolson, who was one of America's most-loved entertainers at the time, got a big hand from the crowd. Winchell told the Associated Press that "a bunch of gorillas hired by a major studio were supposed to give me a shellacking, but they didn't show," and that it was not Jolson but a hitman who had sent him to the floor. The columnist, who was just beginning his climb to the pinnacle of journalistic power, wrote that "anybody else who wants to emulate Mr. Jolson can do so, but we're warning them that they will have to wait their turn in line."

The singer fanned the flames further when he challenged the columnist to a duel; Winchell would only accept it if there was a fee involved which he could give to charity. The publicity generated from this fracas was enormous, and a grateful Zanuck, who was already in production with Winchell's story, gave him a bonus of $10,000. Although Jolson did not need to become any more famous, he did remark after the incident:

"You can sing 'Mammy' for a hundred years, wear your poor old knee-caps out on splintery stages, and talk on the radio till you're hoarse as a bullfrog, but you have to sock Winchell before you really become famous."

Rumor

Walter Winchell once broadcast a rumor that Bette Davis was dying of cancer. After the actress had issued a firm and lengthy denial, one of the press agents joining his regular gathering at Lindy's restaurant on Broadway said:

"If Bette Davis doesn't have cancer, she's in real trouble!"

Her lawyer called Bette Davis to check the rumor she had died.

"During a newspaper strike," the star declared, "I wouldn't even consider it."

A Woman's Body Ought To Be Her Own

Bette Davis once had a press agent fired because he told the press that she was having a baby, and she claimed it wasn't true. A little while later, when her pregnancy became official, publicist Leo Guild asked her why at first she had denied it. Bette Davis replied that the press agent in fact knew about the pregnancy before she did. It turned out that this was the truth. The publicist was friendly with a nurse who worked on the lab test.

With or Without Catherine Deneuve

Eight hundred reporters and photographers turned up at the press conference at London's Savoy Hotel to hear the announcement that Laurence Olivier and Marilyn Monroe would work together on *The Prince and the Showgirl* (1957).

"What do you wear when you go to bed?" was one of the questions typical of the British press. Marilyn Monroe glanced at her husband, playwright Arthur Miller, and said:

"Chanel No. 5."

Showman

Journalist Ezra Goodman wrote that in Hollywood a "masterpiece is usually a movie made by someone without talent but with a talented press agent." Mike Todd was the only one of the old-time showmen who managed to transfer the magic of Broadway to making films. "He was," wrote the columnist Radie Harris, "P. T. Barnum, Diamond Jim Brady, Florenz Ziegfeld, Billy Rose, Alexander H. Cohen all rolled into one." She also described Todd as a "male Elsa Maxwell," for the extravagant parties he gave.

Despite his marriage to Elizabeth Taylor, Mike Todd remained a Hollywood outsider, celebrating his greatest triumph, *Around the World in Eighty Days* (1956), with parties in New York and London. The party in

Madison Square Garden turned out to be a disaster, with the distinguished actor Sir Cedrick Hardwicke trying to ride an elephant around the ring, and the waiters selling watered-down champagne at ten dollars a bottle to a celebrity crowd.

Following the gala opening in London, Todd and Taylor threw a huge party on the Chelsea Embankment in the middle of a downpour. Todd had planned every detail of that day with his usual flair for carnival, which he developed as a young man under Billy Rose during New York's World Fair in 1939. This time there were carousels, roller coasters, tent shows, balloons, and skywriting announcing the premiere of *Around the World in Eighty Days*. Todd wanted the whole world to know about his movie. Leaving the Dorchester Hotel that morning he asked the doorman if he had seen the balloons and the writing in the sky.

"Yes, sir," said the doorman, "but what are they for?"

"Here," Todd fished out two of the best dress circle tickets for the premiere, "use these and find out. I'm going to find my press agent and fire him!"

Egyptian Bondage

Even before he began filming *Exodus* (1960), Otto Preminger held a meeting with his press agents about marketing strategies for the epic.

"I see it promoted as Otto Preminger's *Exodus*," said the director with characteristic lack of ego.

"But, Otto," one of the flaks could not resist interjecting, "that's just what a lot of people are waiting for."

Preminger was not amused.

(Peter Lawford was asked once what he considered his best performance as an actor. "Sitting through *Exodus* seven times," was his reply.)

Too Good To Be True

Gene Autry is the only celebrity who has five stars on the Hollywood Walk of Fame. He received them for his work in motion pictures, recording, radio, television, and finally for live performance. Already a top Western star in the late 1930s, the singing cowboy kept doing one-night stands in one-horse towns all over the United States, which he once said, "were so small that even Mrs. Roosevelt hadn't been there."

Such a town was Columbia, Tennessee. If it had only one horse, Columbia advertised itself as "The Mule Capital of the World." Hours before the performance, Autry discovered that the theatre's sound system had been put out of commission. After some searching, George Goodale, the press agent, found out that the only man who might be able to repair it was in the hotel where they were staying. He was working for Western Union and would have been glad to help but could not leave his post.

"Look," said the desperate agent, "if I get you a relief operator, will you go right over to the theatre and get that thing working?"

"Yup, I'll do it," said the young man. "But where are you goin' to get another operator? I'm the only one in town."

A few minutes later, Goodale turned up in the company of his star.

"But that's Gene Autry," said the man in an accusatory tone, thinking he was being taken for a ride.

In fact, Gene Autry had started his career as a relief operator in the telegraph office in Chelsea, Oklahoma. He had the four-to-midnight shift, and to while away the hours, he strummed his guitar and sang. One evening, a customer heard him and suggested that with some hard work he might be able to develop his talent. "You ought to think about going to New York and get yourself a job in radio," said Will Rogers.

The sound system was fixed, and the show went on. When George Goodale tried to plant the story, though, it took the press agent three years to persuade a columnist finally to run an item that sounded too unusual to be true.

Digging His Own Grave

A press agent has been defined as one who takes in lying for a living. There was in the studio era at Warners' a press agent who fed a story to Harrison Carroll, gossip columnist for the old Los Angeles *Herald-Express*. The press release was created on a slow day and concerned sacred Indian burial grounds that had been discovered on the lot.

Unfortunately for the flak, Carroll was of the old school of journalism, who liked to check his stories, so he immediately offered to drive to the studio and inspect the graves himself. Having failed to talk him out of this plan, the publicist hurried to the scene shop and got the crew to rig up something like an archeological dig before the reporter's arrival.

It's Greek to Me

Trying to publicize the 1940 special-effects movie *Dr. Cyclops*, another press agent at Warner Brothers came up with an idea. He issued a release, according to which the Police Athletic League was supposed to have voted for the ten most infamous characters in history. Hitler was named in second place, and Mussolini in third; the pride of place went to Cyclops, the mythological figure who had given Odysseus so much trouble.

The press agent, breathing the intellectually somewhat thin air of Hollywood, had not counted on a conscientious copy-editor at the *New York Post*, who checked the name, if not the story. He found that Cyclops was the name given to a whole race of mythical giants, the most famous representative of which was Polyphemus. In printing the press agent's infamous list, there was no mention of Cyclops, with or without a doctorate.

The Outlaw Press Agent

The most famous of the early press agents was Harry Reichenbach, who started with the Jesse Lasky Feature Play company, at the beginning of movie-making in Hollywood. In A Million and One Nights, *Terry Ramsaye paints this admiring portrait:*

Reichenbach gave early evidence of his peculiar genius in the production of synthetic news of sensational character. A year before he went to the motion pictures he perpetrated the promotion of *September Morn,* a painting by Paul Chabas depicting a comely young woman clad in the modesty of her pose and the autumn atmosphere.

A reproduction of the painting was placed on exhibition in the window of a Fifth Avenue art shop. Reichenbach employed a gang of urchins and messenger boys to stand in front of the window and make remarks. He then telephoned the office of Anthony Comstock and let nature take its course in the newspapers. This campaign was supplemented with a cartoon for hand circulation depicting a censorial person in Puritan glasses sternly addressing *September Morn* with a command: "Hands Up!" Reichenbach was rewarded for his efforts with a fee of $25. Some years later, with advancing technique, Reichenbach duped New York with the story of *The Virgin of Stamboul* for Universal Pictures Corporation. He set the police to dragging a lake in Central Park for the virgin's body, and maintained a mysterious official Turkish high commission at a downtown hotel. The Turkish notables concerned were recruited from East Side coffee houses and sequestered in the Hotel Navarre while being trained in their parts. The largest item of expense in this campaign was $400 for French pastry served the Turks.

In recognition of Reichenbach's work on this picture the State of New York passed a law forbidding the giving of false information to the press. Reichenbach retaliated with a circular to the legislature threatening to prosecute the members under the act for broken campaign promises.

It Seemed a Good Idea at the Time

The most famous of the press agent's nightmares concerned the campaign devised by Bill Thomas and Bill Pine at Paramount in preparation for the release of the Mae West vehicle, *It Ain't No Sin* (1934). The studio bought fifty African parrots, known for their linguistic ability, and for weeks they were subjected to a phonograph recording, playing over and over again the title: "It ain't no sin . . . it ain't no sin . . ."

Huge lobby posters with Miss West's famous figure were printed along with full-page advertisements in the papers, all coming together for that glorious moment when the fifty parrots would be unveiled in their fifty colorful cages, screeching together, if not in unison: "It ain't no sin, it ain't no sin . . ."

Everything was proceeding on schedule. Paramount, feeling the heat from the newly formed Legion of Decency and the Production Code Administration, was persuaded that sin was no laughing matter after all. Days before the premiere a decision was made to retitle the picture, *I'm No Angel*. New posters and ads were hurriedly printed, but it was too late for the parrots. Maybe somewhere in Africa, or wherever they fled, there is a flock of trained birds, still singing: "It ain't no sin . . . it ain't no sin . . ."

Some time later, Jane Russell was slated to appear in a movie titled *Tall in the Saddle*. Taking note of Hollywood's tendency to abbreviate long titles—GWTW for *Gone with the Wind*, or FWTBT instead of *For Whom the Bell Tolls*—an RKO publicist by the name of Linn Unkefer sent out a press release, daring them to apply the same principle. The title was abandoned.

CHAPTER 23

It's All Relatives

Medical Condition

In the heyday of Hollywood, it was observed, all that a producer produced was relatives. Wilson Mizner and W. C. Fields were kibbitzing one afternoon at the commissary, when a boring producer, blood relative of the studio boss, sat down at their table. Fields took one look at the intruder and exchanged glances with Mizner, who remarked:

"Gangrene sets in."

Relativity

When Albert Einstein was introduced to Jack Warner, the producer told the professor that he had a theory on relatives, too: "Don't hire 'em!"

"In Hollywood success is relative," observed the British character actor, Arthur Treacher. "The closer the relative, the greater the success."

The Son-in-Law Business

In 1950 stockholders brought suit against Warner Brothers and United States Pictures, which was run by Milton Sperling, the son-in-law of Harry

Warner. Warner Brothers financed and distributed the films made by United States Pictures. This was not the first nepotism suit, which prompted producer Jerry Wald to remark:

"If this sort of thing keeps up, the son-in-law business in Hollywood will be set back at least ten years."

Soon after Hemingway's novel *The Sun Also Rises* came out, somebody at MGM suggested that it should be made into a film about Hollywood, called *The Son-in-law Also Rises*.

Both of Louis B. Mayer's sons-in-law were producers. One wag said that the MGM initials were Yiddish for "Mayer's-Ganza-Mishpoka," translating into "Mayer's Whole Family."

David O. Selznick was one of those sons-in-law, though he also had talent and could afford to make jokes about his family connections. Playing poker one night for the high stakes common among Hollywood's highest elite, Selznick looked at his hand for a long moment, and then, throwing more chips into the pot, said:

"The overpaid son-in-law raises a thousand dollars."

Reckoning

William Wellman's wife kept at him to allow her to play a bit part in one of his movies. Finally the director cast her in a script that required her to say seven words. But, as often happens, during shooting her part was reduced by more than half. Driving home after her scene, she said to her husband:

"Bill, we've been married for thirteen years, and you know what I've gotten out of it? Five kids and three words of dialogue!"

Before and After

The wedding of Norma Shearer to Irving Thalberg was scheduled for August 1927, to allow her first to star in *After Midnight*. Thalberg, who carefully guided her career, selected Vladimir Tourjansky for the project. The Russian director had been working in Paris and was ignorant of the Hollywood romance between his boss and the star he had been assigned. After the first day, he went to see Thalberg.

"Why must I use this girl?" he complained about Shearer. "She's cross-eyed."

Thalberg immediately removed Tourjansky from the picture and banished the Russian to film a Western in the Mojave desert, where the temperature would be well above a hundred degrees.

After the honeymoon, Thalberg put his wife in *The Student Prince*, to play a waitress in old Heidelberg. The congenial Ernst Lubitsch was having a problem in getting Norma Shearer to tone down her mannerisms, and shouted at her in frustration:

"Mein Gott! I can get a waitress from the commissary who'd do better than you."

The actress, in tears, refused to try the scene again and sent a flunkey to fetch her new husband. The director waited calmly—and the rest of the company tensely—for Thalberg to arrive. The all-powerful production chief of MGM patiently listened to his bride's account, then kissed her and said:

"Darling, I'm sure we can all learn a lot from Mr. Lubitsch."

The Seven-Year Itch

The famous image of Marilyn Monroe, with her skirt swirling above a subway grating, also brought one of her marriages to an end. Billy Wilder was filming the sequence for *Seven Year Itch* (1955) in front of the Trans-Lux Theatre on Lexington Avenue. It was the middle of the night and the director had hoped the streets would be empty. But this was New York, so a crowd of several thousand had gathered. There was a problem with the electric fan that had been placed under the grating to blow up into Marilyn Monroe's skirt, and during a period of four hours there were fifty takes.

"Fifty times her skirts flew up into the air revealing frilly white panties," publicist Leo Guild narrated the event. "Each time the crowd roared. Marilyn, always aware of what people expected of her, kept smiling. Joe DiMaggio was in the crowd. He had been sitting with Walter Winchell at Toots Shor's and Winchell suggested they go to watch the scene. The two stood there and each time the wind blew through the grating sending the skirts flying, Joe became more humiliated. He never spoke, and he saw it through to the end, becoming more and more tight-lipped, more grim. This was the final humiliation of his marriage. Movie or no movie, he just couldn't see his own wife as a spectacle for a circus mob. The stunt got world-wide attention. From the point of the picture company, it was an enormous success. For Marilyn and Joe, it was the death-knell of their marriage. It never recovered equilibrium, and on October 1, 1954, they started divorce proceedings."

Balls

Clark Gable was a man's man, and in Carole Lombard he finally found more than his match. When he was courting her, the outspoken actress kidded reporters about one of the most desired men in the world:

"God knows, I love Clark, but he's a lousy lay."

The reporters took the quote back to Gable for comment, who laughed: "Guess I'll have to do a lotta practicin'."

At ceremonies to crown Clark Gable as the official King of Hollywood, Carole Lombard was overheard telling friends in a stage whisper:

"If Clark had an inch less he'd be called Queen of Hollywood."

Maculate Conception

During a previous marriage, Clark Gable, who was famous for his big ears, fell in love with the unmarried Loretta Young while filming *Call of the Wild* (1935) in a remote part of Washington State. She announced a few months later that she would give up films for a year due to health problems. Every gossip columnist assumed she was pregnant, but she denied it to save her career. Young continued the denial even after she reappeared with a baby girl.

"I saw her in a San Diego orphanage, and fell in love," said Miss Young of her new baby, oblivious of California state laws which did not permit a single parent to adopt.

Director William Wellman, who saw his work disrupted by the romance, wryly observed:

"All I know is Loretta disappeared when the film was finished and showed up with a daughter who had big ears."

Once a Catholic

Loretta Young was a voluble Catholic, which made her affair with Clark Gable even more awkward. Joan Crawford, who had enjoyed a much longer affair with the King of Hollywood, took delight in teasing Miss Young. At a party in her house, Crawford saw a guest about to sit down on a chair that had just been vacated by Loretta Young.

"Oh you can't sit there," she grabbed the guest and explained, making sure her voice carried: "Miss Young was just sitting there, so it still has the mark of the cross on the seat."

When or Where

L. B. Mayer took an intense personal interest in his stars' morals, and intervened in Joan Crawford's affair with Clark Gable which would have broken up both their marriages. His real reasons had more to do with the image of staid probity that the film industry tried to put over to a disbelieving public, and with possible damage to box-office receipts. But Mayer was shrewd enough to know that a substantial portion of Joan Crawford's appeal to the public derived from her image as a beautiful tramp.

"I don't care what she does," the mogul once declared, hearing about her latest escapade, "as long as she doesn't get laid on Sunset."

Word of this reached the star, who wanted clarification whether her boss meant the boulevard or simply the time of day.

Romancing the Sphinx

Although the romance between John Gilbert and Greta Garbo was the talk of Hollywood and helped to sell their pictures, all of Gilbert's plans to take the Swedish beauty to the altar were frustrated. At the reception following one of these attempts in 1927, when Garbo simply failed to show up at her wedding, John Gilbert encountered Louis B. Mayer in the men's room. The head of MGM, famous for his moralizing about the virtues of family life, said to the groom:

"Don't marry her; just screw her."

Gilbert, who was drunk as usual, knocked his employer to the floor. It was Louis B. Mayer's desire for revenge, rather than the advent of sound, as some believe, which was John Gilbert's undoing. As the silent-movie star faded from favor, his boon companion John Barrymore composed the epitaph of Gilbert's career:

"From Garbo to limbo," he said.

The Bees, the Birds, and the Bears

During Tallulah Bankhead's contract with MGM some of her off-screen activities, involving stagehands and grips of both sexes, quickly reached the ears of Louis B. Mayer, who declared his outrage at the way she "had been hibernating with everybody."

"I've heard it called everything but that," said the literate actress.

Trouble with Tallulah

Already a great star of the stage on both sides of the Atlantic, Tallulah Bankhead came to Hollywood with the advent of sound. On being introduced to Irving Thalberg, she immediately got down to business.

"Dahling," she intoned, "how does one get laid in this dreadful place?"

"I'm sure you'll have no difficulties," Thalberg told Tallulah. "Ask anyone."

Losing no time, Tallulah Bankhead went to Gary Cooper, with whom she was about to make *Thunder Below* (1932), and informed her reticent co-star.

"Dahling, my high school days are over. I've got a very normal desire to go to bed with you."

Ladies and Gentlemen

One of the stories that still linger about the outrageous Tallulah in Los Angeles concerns the time she was attending a function at the late, lamented Ambassador Hotel, and Nature called her to another function. Unable to find toilet paper, La Bankhead wandered about inside the ladies' room, knocking on every other booth, and waving a bill.

"Can anyone," she asked repeatedly, "break a ten?"

After a few drinks at Lucey's, near Paramount studios, John Barrymore stumbled by mistake into the ladies' room. He was happily finding relief, when a woman entered.

"How dare you!" she scolded the intruder. "This is for ladies!" Barrymore turned towards the woman and gestured towards the business in hand:

"And, madam, so is this!"

Priorities

The juiciest scandal to rock Hollywood in the thirties was the apparent suicide of Paul Bern, a top executive at MGM, only two months after his marriage to Jean Harlow.

"Dearest dear," he wrote her in his suicide note, "unfortunately this is the only way to make good the frightful wrong I have done you, and to wipe out my abject humiliation." Nature had forgotten to make Bern, to put it delicately, a man of parts, and the night of his suicide he was trying to satisfy Hollywood's reigning sex-goddess with mechanical substitutes.

All the facts did not surface except as rumor for years, because the whole of MGM was mobilized, even before the police were notified, to cover up the scandal that could have damaged one of the studio's most tangible assets—Jean Harlow. Apparently, Louis B. Mayer called a meeting of his top brass to discuss how to dispose of his former lieutenant's body.

"Get him buried," he said to Howard Strickling, his chief of publicity. "See that only sympathetic stories about the little bastard appear in the press. Send plenty of flowers."

Irving Thalberg asked: "What if we're faced with a choice between bad publicity for Jean or the studio?"

"Irving, don't be an ass," Mayer said without a beat. "Then we'll bury her, too."

Despite his physical shortcomings, Paul Bern was known as a man to whom young women trusted their confidences. He also seemed to have a secret life. Just after he died, his first wife also committed suicide and another woman turned up, claiming to have been legally married to Jean Harlow's husband. And a few years before, Paul Bern was a well-publicized item with Barbara La Marr, who had had six husbands by the time she was thirty and died of a drug overdose. According to Hollywood gossip, after La Marr turned him down, the unhappy producer tried to drown himself in the toilet, but his head got stuck and a plumber had to be called to unscrew the seat.

"He looked like he'd just won the Derby," commented one wag.

Hollywood on the Rocks

An inveterate gossip asked Ben Hecht why the marriage of a Hollywood couple was being dissolved.

"They have found," said the cynical writer, "that mutual hatred is not sufficient basis for a successful marriage. There has to be a little more."

"There's a good reason why so many Hollywood girls get married in the morning," Cornel Wilde once remarked. "They want the afternoon free to plan their divorces."

Following her divorce from Orson Welles, well known for his total self-absorption, Rita Hayworth remarked:

"All's Welles that ends Welles."

Hedy Lamarr divorced John Loder because he fell asleep watching one of her pictures.

"That wasn't in the marriage vows," the husband complained to publicist Leo Guild.

In 1960, during one of his repeat performances in an alimony suit, Mickey Rooney complained in a Santa Monica courtroom:
"I have so many wives and so many children I don't know who to visit at Christmas time."

On hearing about Gloria Swanson's fifth marriage, her first husband, the actor Wallace Beery, exclaimed:
"Damned if she didn't keep on getting married! I got her into an awful bad habit."

Hearing that a famous Hollywood couple was breaking up, Joan Bennett gave her analysis:
"He fell in love with a pair of big, blue eyes—then made the mistake of marrying the whole girl."

On the short-lived marriage of a Hollywood celebrity, Barbara Stanwyck commented:
"He found out there were a lot of things he couldn't say with flowers."

If at First You Don't Succeed

Barbara Stanwyck had an unhappy marriage to the comic Frank Fay. Soon after their bitter parting, Fay suddenly became the toast of Broadway in *Harvey* (1944). The title refers to a six-foot white rabbit that only the drunk Elwood P. Dowd (played by Frank Fay) could see. Asked by the columnist Earl Wilson whether she would go and see her former husband perform in this hit show, Barbara Stanwyck shook her head.
"I've already seen," said the star, "all the white rabbits Frank Fay has to offer."

Another of Barbara Stanwyck's brief marriages was to Robert Taylor, a flying enthusiast. One day the actor boasted, probably not for the first time, about the number of flying hours he had under his belt.
"Now you can do everything that the birds do," his wife remarked coolly, "except sit on a barbed wire fence."

Midlife Crisis

Producer Sam Spiegel went through a phase when he changed his name to S. P. Eagle. During this midlife crisis he also eloped with a starlet, Lynn Baggett. Arriving in Las Vegas, there was a telegram waiting from his friend Billy Wilder:

YOUR MARRIAGE LEAVES THIS TOWN
S. P. EECHLESS.

Truth Is Its Own Reward

Like many an artist Ingmar Bergman depends on his friends and those close to him for their frank opinions. He once told of showing his new film, *Winter Light* (1962), to his wife, the pianist Käbi Laterei.

"It's a masterpiece, Ingmar," Mrs. Bergman said afterward. "But it's a dreary masterpiece."

Soon afterward she wasn't his wife.

All My Wives

Some people, like Oscar Wilde, have put only talent into their work; they reserve their genius for life. Roger Vadim is one of those enviable men who have been married to several of the most desirable women of the silver screen and continue on good terms with them, as this coda in a book about his ex-wives illustrates.

Many people keep telling me, "You should make a film starring all your ex-wives."

It's an amusing idea but impossible for reasons one can easily imagine. Once, however, chance brought all these goddesses together, at the peak of their beauty, on the same set.

I had just met Jane Fonda and was making *Circle of Love* (1965) with her at the studio in Saint-Maurice.

I was showing Serge Marquand how to fall from a window onto the pavement of a street during a fight scene. But my demonstration was too realistic and I broke my shoulder.

Annette Stroyberg, who was passing through Paris, had come to see us on the set. She was present when I had the accident. Jane, told of the incident in her dressing room, ran over immediately. The two women supported me and did their best to comfort me while we were waiting for the ambulance.

It so happened that Catherine Deneuve was rehearsing on another set. She heard about my accident and came to find out how I was.

When the ambulance arrived, Jane, Catherine and Annette got in with me. By extraordinary coincidence, Brigitte Bardot was driving into the courtyard of the studio as we were leaving. You wouldn't dare allow this kind of coincidence to happen in a novel or screenplay—but in real life such things do occur.

The guard asked Brigitte to make way for the ambulance and told her the name of the patient. In a panic, Brigitte got out of the car and jumped into the ambulance.

I saw the anxious faces of four women leaning over me, and despite the terrible pain in my shoulder I was able to savor that moment to the fullest.

"He's completely green," worried Brigitte.

"That's normal for a Martian," explained Catherine.

They all looked at me for an instant—Brigitte, Annette, Catherine and Jane—and burst out laughing.

Her Name in Lights

Making a state visit to France, as the queen of the silent movies, Gloria Swanson fell in love with a titled gentleman by the name of Henri Marquis de la Falaise. When her mother heard that her daughter had married a marquis, she called her lawyer at once.

"What on earth is a markee?" she demanded to know.

"It's one of those things," the attorney enlightened her, "that is hung in front of the theatre to keep the rain off the customers."

"My god," cried the anguished mother-in-law, "Gloria married one of them this afternoon!"

Something To Do

Stan Laurel had a great number of marriages, most of them unhappy. During one of his three marriages to Ruth—whom he finally divorced for the third time—the sad-faced clown was asked about his hobbies.

"I married all of mine," he replied.

CHAPTER 24

The End—That's All Folks!

It's Not My Funeral

Jack Warner feuded so much with his brother Harry that in 1958, when Jack's car collided with a truck on the French Riviera, word spread through Hollywood that Harry must have been driving it.

In the end, it was Harry who died first. After fifty years of working together, Jack did not attend his brother's funeral.

Another pair named Jack and Harry ran Columbia Pictures. Jack Cohn managed the business side in New York, while his brother Harry made pictures in Hollywood, managing to look trim well past middle age. Someone who spotted him eating heartily at Lindy's asked what kind of exercising made him look so good after thirty years in the motion-picture racket.

"The only exercise I get," Cohn answered, "is attending the funerals of friends I have outlived."

The most beloved funeral story has been attached to the passing of several moguls of the studio era, including Harry Cohn, Hollywood's favorite sonofabitch. After Cohn's funeral in March 1958 drew a record crowd of two thousand, Red Skelton told his television audience:

"It only proves what they always say—give the public something they want to see, and they'll come out for it."

Longevity

Unlike some of his fellow moguls, Adolph Zukor remained throughout his extraordinary life a modest man. The founder of Paramount Pictures, who had come to America as a penniless teenager from a small Hungarian village, was in his eighties when he said at the opening of a new building:

"This is not a monument dedicated to me, as some of you gentlemen have suggested, but rather a monument to an America which could give a chance to a boy like me to be connected with an institution like this."

Zukor, who worked almost until he dropped, declared on his hundredth birthday:

"If I knew I was going to live this long, I'd have taken better care of myself."

And shortly before his death at the age of 103, the pioneer producer was asked for the secret of his longevity.

"I gave up smoking two years ago," said Zukor.

Final Payment

It is a common practice in making movies, especially small ones, to ask actors and other creative talent to defer their salaries or fees until after a picture is released and money starts coming in. My friend Steve Kovacs was producing *On the Line* (1983), a Spanish-Mexican-American co-production, for which he wanted to hire Sam Jaffe for two days. Jaffe's agent asked for $5,000, a reasonable sum but beyond the budget. The producer suggested paying $2,000 and defering the balance.

"Sam is ninety years old," said the agent, "just how long do you think he can wait?"

Like most actors, Sam Jaffe never did see the rest of his money; within six months he was dead.

You Do Know How To Whistle?

Humphrey Bogart and Lauren Bacall fell in love during the filming of her first picture, *To Have and Have Not* (1944), where she speaks the line: "If you want me, just whistle."

As a first hint that he was interested, Bogart gave her a gold whistle inscribed with the line and signed "Bogie." Betty Bacall usually wore it around her neck. One day, hoping to attract his attention, she tried the whistle out but found no sound coming out. Then she was alarmed when several dogs rushed her. The whistle Bogie bought was pitched for a dog's ears, not for a future husband's.

Humphrey Bogart died of cancer in 1957 and was cremated. Lauren Bacall placed the gold whistle into the urn. It bore the inscription:
"If you want anything, just whistle."

And the Ship Sailed On

Ship of Fools (1965) was Vivien Leigh's last film. At an appreciation held in her memory at the University of Southern California, her director, Stanley Kramer, remembered:

On the set one morning she was making up for a scene when she fooled around at the makeup table for a long time and made life pretty miserable for all the makeup people for a period of about two and a half hours—the whole morning, really. Suddenly she looked up and must have looked at me for ten seconds, which is a long time when someone is piercing you, and said:

"I . . . Stanley, I can't do it today." And I knew that she was ill and that she couldn't do it. I'll never forget that look. That was the look of one of the greatest actresses of our time.

From that moment on I became, I think, probably the most on-purpose, understanding and patient person that I could possibly be. She was ill and had the courage to go ahead—the courage to make the film was almost unbelievable. What is then that one can say? I say this, and I mean it: I think having briefly touched hands with Vivien Leigh, I will always, working with another actress, think I can ask the same thing, and only very rarely be able to get it.

Flights of Angels

John Barrymore spent the days of his final breakdown from alcoholism in Errol Flynn's house in the Hollywood Hills. In Ladies' Man, *Paul Henreid tells the story how his boon companions bade goodnight to their sweet prince.*

I was making *Casablanca* with Peter Lorre the day of Barrymore's death, and he took Humphrey Bogart, me, and two other friends aside. "I have a fantastic idea," Lorre said, his bulging eyes glistening. "For very little, maybe two or three hundred dollars, I can get Barrymore's body away from the mortuary."

"What the hell for?" I asked.

"Yeah," Bogart seconded. "Why would you want his body?"

"Now get this. We take the body into Flynn's house—I know he's shooting and gets home late, and we arrange it in that chair in the living room he always used to sit in, then we hide and watch Flynn's face. Is that or isn't it fantastic?"

We looked at each other and then at Lorre, and our immediate shock gave way to uncontrollable laughter. We all chipped in, and Lorre set out to dicker with the mortuary. Later, thinking it over, I found that I just couldn't go through with it. "I'm sorry," I told Bogie and the others. "I'll contribute the money, but I can't go along. It goes against my grain."

The others accepted my excuses, but they went through with the stunt. They smuggled Barrymore's body out of the mortuary and into Flynn's house. "We had a hell of a job getting him to look natural in that chair." Lorre giggled when he told me about it later. "He was so stiff!"

They hid behind the doors and waited. Finally they heard Errol's car pull into the driveway, then his key in the lock. He opened the door and flicked on the lights and came in, threw his hat and coat on a chair and walked across the room, past Barrymore's chair to the bar. He nodded at Barrymore and took about three steps, then froze. That moment was fantastic! There was a terrible silence, then he said, "Oh my God!" and he hurried back and touched Barrymore, then jumped. Barrymore was ice cold.

"I think in that second, he realized what was happening," Lorre said, "and he shouted, 'All right, you bastards, come on out!'"

"Was he mad?" I asked.

Lorre shook his head. "Partly mad, but at the same time realizing how funny it was and trying not to laugh. I think, like you, he felt the whole thing was in bad taste. Anyway, he offered us a drink, but wouldn't help us take the body back!"

Intimations of Mortality

In his memoirs, Blessings in Disguise, *Sir Alec Guinness gave a strange twist to the ending of an American legend.*

In the autumn of 1955 I went to Los Angeles to make my first Hollywood film, *The Swan,* with Grace Kelly and Louis Jourdan. I arrived, tired and crumpled, after a sixteen-hour flight from Copenhagen. Thelma Moss, who had written the film script of *Father Brown (The Detective* in the USA), had said she wished to take me out to dinner my first night in town. We arrived at three restaurants of repute at each of which we were refused admission because she was wearing slacks (ah, far-off days), and finally settled for a delightful little Italian bistro, where she was confident of a welcome. When we got there— Los Angeles is an endless city to drive through—there was no table available. As we walked disconsolately away I said, "I don't care where we eat or what. Just something, somewhere." I became aware of running, sneakered feet behind us and turned to face a fair young man in sweat-shirt and blue-jeans. "You want a table?" he asked. "Join me. My name is James Dean." We followed him gratefully, but on the way back to the restaurant he turned into a car-park, saying, "I'd like to show you something." Among the other cars there was what looked like a large, shiny, silver parcel wrapped in cellophane and tied with ribbon. "It's just been delivered," he said, with bursting pride. "I haven't even driven it yet." The sports-car looked sinister to me, although it had a large bunch of red carnations resting on the bonnet. "How fast is it?" I asked. "She'll do a hundred and fifty," he replied. Exhausted, hungry, feeling a little ill-tempered in spite of Dean's kindness, I heard myself saying in a voice I could hardly recognise as my own, "Please, never get in it." I looked at my watch. "It is now ten o'clock, Friday the 23rd of September, 1955. If you get in that car you will be found dead in it by this time next week." He laughed. "Oh, shucks! Don't be so mean!" I apologised for what I had said, explaining it was lack of sleep and food. Thelma Moss and I joined him at his table and he proved an agreeable, generous host, and was very funny about Lee Strasberg, the Actors' Studio and the Method. We parted an hour later, full of smiles. No further reference was made to

the wrapped-up car. Thelma was relieved by the outcome of the evening and rather impressed. In my heart I was uneasy—with myself. At
four o'clock in the afternoon of the following Friday James Dean was
dead, killed while driving the car.

Stranger Than Fiction

*Hollywood deaths tend to have a dramatic quality, or perhaps those who
tell them know how to wring irony out of the stories. Elia Kazan directed
Natalie Wood in* Splendor in the Grass *(1961) and in his recent autobiography gave this masterly foreshadowing of her doom.*

There is a scene in this film where the character Natalie played tries,
in her desperation, to drown herself in a lake. Some days before this
scene was scheduled, Natalie took me aside and explained to me that
she had a terror of water, particularly dark water, and of being helpless
in it. Of course, I thought how perfect for the scene she had to play,
but I reassured her. The next day she told me that the fear would
paralyze her in the water of the small lake I'd chosen, and she wasn't
sure she could play the scene. Couldn't we do it in a studio tank? I
assured her it was a very shallow lake and that her feet would always
be close to the bottom. She said that even if her feet were *on* the
bottom, she'd be in a panic of fear about it. So I asked my assistant,
Charlie Maguire, to get into the water with her, just out of camera
range, while she played the scene of struggling to save herself. This
didn't entirely reassure her, but she did the scene and did it well—then
clutched Charlie. "Cut!" I cried. On dry land she continued to shake
with fear, then laughed hysterically, with relief.

Years later I was to remember Natalie's problem with that scene
when I read the newspaper accounts of her death. "The actress may
have been panicked, missed a step and slipped into the water while
trying to board the yacht's dinghy. . . . About midnight, a woman in
a boat anchored nearby heard someone calling from the darkness.
'Help me! Somebody help me!'"

The name of the yacht from which she'd stepped into the dark
water was *The Splendour.*

I'll Never Forget What's His Name

Somebody talking to John Ford towards the end of his life mentioned
Ingmar Bergman to him.

"Ingrid Bergman?" asked Ford.

"No, Ingmar Bergman—the great Swedish director."

"Oh, *Ingmar* Bergman," said Ford. "He's the fella that called me the greatest director in the world."

The Easy Part

Jack Lemmon visited the dying Edmund Gwenn, a character actor who had won an Oscar as Santa Claus in *Miracle on 34th Street* (1947). Clifton Fadiman recounts the young actor asking the older one how hard it was to be facing death.

"Oh, it's hard," Gwenn whispered in his Welsh lilt, "very hard indeed. But not as hard as doing comedy."

Famous Last Words

Walt Disney was dying in 1966 at St. Joseph's Hospital in Burbank, next door to his studio.

"Hazel," he said to the Disney Studio nurse attending him, "I hope I am remembered for more important things than inventing a mouse."

Sadness

Ernest Lubitsch was Billy Wilder's mentor and idol, and the master's death in 1947 hit him hard.

"No more Lubitsch," Wilder remarked sadly after the funeral to William Wyler.

"Worse," said his colleague. "No more Lubitsch pictures."

Real Value

David Wark Griffith died on July 23, 1948, at the Knickerbocker Hotel in the heart of Hollywood, totally ignored if not forgotten by the industry that he, as much as anyone, had made into a major force in the twentieth century. His honorary pall-bearers included Samuel Goldwyn, Cecil B. De Mille, Mack Sennett, Jesse Lasky, and Charlie Chaplin. All the powerful had turned out to the funeral of the man who a week before, observed Ezra Goodman, the last journalist to interview Griffith, "probably could not have gotten any of them on the telephone."

On April 22, 1959, the distribution rights to thirty of his films and scenarios—including *The Birth of a Nation, Intolerance, Way Down East,* and *Broken Blossoms*—were acquired at auction by the Killian Company of New York from the Griffith estate. The total price paid was $21,000 and there were no other bidders.

The Last Question

French film-makers were sent a questionnaire in which they were asked their attitudes toward their profession. The last question ran:

"What do you think about the future of the French cinema—are you optimistic, pessimistic or marking time?" Jean-Luc Godard wrote back:

"I await the end of Cinema with optimism."

Bibliography

BOOKS CITED AND CONSULTED

Achard, Marcel. *Rions avec eux*. Paris: Arthème Fayard, 1957.

Adams, Joey. *From Gags to Riches*. New York: Frederick Fell, 1946.

Adler, Bill. *The Cosby Wit*. New York: Carroll & Graf, 1986.

Adler, Bill, and Jeffrey Feinman. *Mel Brooks—The Irreverent Funnyman*. Chicago: Playboy Press, 1976.

Agee, James. *Agee on Film*. Boston: Beacon Press, 1964.

Agel, Jerome (ed.). *The Making of Kubrick's 2001*. New York: New American Library, 1970.

Alden, Debby. *If I Touch a Star Will I Sparkle Too?* Sunnyvale, California: Dublin Press, 1980.

Allen, Fred. *Much Ado About Me*. Boston: Little, Brown, 1956.

Allen, Steve. *Funny People*. New York: Stein & Day, 1981.

Almendros, Nestor (translated by Rachel Phillips Belash). *A Man with a Camera*. New York: Farrar, Straus, Giroux, 1984.

Alpert, Hollis. *The Dreams and the Dreamers*. New York: Macmillan, 1962.

——————. *Fellini—A Life*. New York: Paragon House, 1988.

Anger, Kenneth. *Hollywood Babylon*. New York: Dell, 1981.

Angst-Nowik, Doris, and Jane Sloan. *One-Way Ticket to Hollywood—Film*

Artists of Austrian and German Origin in Los Angeles. Los Angeles: Max Kade Institute, n.d.

Annan, David. *Cinema of Mystery & Fantasy.* London: Lorrimer Publishing, 1984.

Arce, Hector. *Gary Cooper—An Intimate Biography.* New York: William Morrow, 1979.

Arliss, George. *Up the Years from Bloomsbury.* New York: Blue Ribbon Books, 1927.

Arnold, William. *Frances Farmer—Shadowland.* New York: McGraw-Hill, 1978.

Astor, Mary. *A Life on Film.* New York: Delacorte Press, 1971.

Atkins, Dick (ed.). *Method to the Madness—(Hollywood Explained).* Livingston, N.J.: Prince Publishers, 1975.

Atwan, Robert, and Bruce Forer (eds.). *Bedside Hollywood: Great Scenes from Movie Memoirs.* New York: Moyer Bell & Nimbus Books, 1985.

Aylesworth, Thomas G. *Broadway to Hollywood—Musicals from Stage to Screen.* New York: W. H. Smith, 1985.

Bacall, Lauren. *By Myself.* New York: Knopf, 1978.

Bach, Steven. *Final Cut.* New York: Morrow, 1985.

Bacon, James. *Hollywood Is a Four-Letter Town.* Chicago: Contemporary Books, 1976.

————. *Made in Hollywood.* Chicago: Contemporary Books, 1977.

Baker, Fred, with Ross Firestone. *Movie People.* New York: Douglas Book Corporation, 1972.

Balaban, Bob. *Close Encounters of the Third Kind Diary.* n.p. Paradise Press, 1977.

Balio, Tino. *The American Film Industry.* Madison: University of Wisconsin Press, 1976.

Balshofer, Fred J., and Arthur C. Miller. *One Reel a Week.* Berkeley: University of California Press, 1967.

Bankhead, Tallulah. *Tallulah—My Autobiography.* New York: Harper & Brothers, 1952.

Barlett, Donald L., and James B. Steele. *Empire—The Life, Legend, and Madness of Howard Hughes.* New York: W. W. Norton, 1979.

Barnett, Lincoln. *Writing on Life—Sixteen Close-ups.* New York: William Sloane Associates, 1951.

Barnett, Luke, told to George E. Kelly. *Between the Ribs.* Philadelphia: Dorrance & Company, 1945.

Barrett, Rona. *Miss Rona.* Los Angeles: Nash Publishing, 1974.

Barrymore, Ethel. *Memories—an Autobiography.* New York: Harper & Brothers, 1955.

Barrymore, John. *Confessions of an Actor.* Indianapolis: Bobbs-Merrill, 1926.

Barrymore, Lionel (told to Cameron Shipp). *We Barrymores.* New York: Appleton-Century-Crofts, 1950.

Bauersfeld, F. S. *Tales of the Early Days as Told to Mirandy*. Hollywood: The Oxford Press, 1938.

Behlmer, Rudy, and Tony Thomas. *Hollywood's Hollywood*. Secaucus, N.J.: Citadel Press, 1975.

Behlmer, Rudy (ed.). *Inside Warner Bros.* (1935–1951). New York: Viking, 1985.

——————. *Memo from: David O. Selznick*. New York: Viking, 1972.

Behrman, S. N. *People in a Diary—A Memoir*. Boston: Little, Brown, 1972.

——————. *The Suspended Drawing Room*. London: Hamish Hamilton, 1966.

Békés, István. *Legújabb Magyar Anekdotakincs*. Budapest: Gondolat, 1966.

Bel Geddes, Norman. *Miracle in the Evening*. New York: Doubleday, 1960.

Bennett, Joan, and Lois Kibbee. *The Bennett Playbill*. New York: Holt, Rinehart & Winston, 1970.

Berg, A. Scott. *Goldwyn*. New York: Knopf, 1989.

Bergan, Ronald. *Sports in the Movies*. London: Proteus Publishing, 1982.

Bergman, Ingmar (translated by Paul Britten Austin). *Bergman on Bergman—Interviews with Ingmar Bergman by Stig Björkman, Torsten Manns and Jonas Sima*. New York: Simon & Schuster, 1986.

—————— (translated by Joan Tate). *The Magic Lantern*. London: Hamish Hamilton, 1988.

Bergman, Ingrid, with Alan Burgess. *My Story*. New York: Delacorte Press, 1980.

Berrigan, Daniel. *The Mission—A Film Journal*. San Francisco: Harper & Row, 1986.

Berton, Pierre. *Hollywood's Canada*. Toronto: McClelland & Stewart, 1975.

Betts, Ernest. *Heraclitus, or the Future of Films*. New York: E. P. Dutton, 1928.

Biberman, Herbert. *Salt of the Earth*. Boston: Beacon Press, 1965.

Bishop, Jim. *The Mark Hellinger Story—A Biography of Broadway and Hollywood*. New York: Appleton-Century-Crofts, 1952.

Black, Shirley Temple. *Child Star—An Autobiography*. New York: McGraw-Hill, 1988.

Bock, Audie. *Japanese Film Directors*. New York: Kodansha International, 1978.

Bogarde, Dirk. *Snakes and Ladders*. London: Chatto & Windus, 1978.

Bogdanovich, Peter. *Allan Dwan: The Last Pioneer*. New York: Praeger, 1971.

——————. *Pieces of Time*. New York: Arbor House, 1973.

Boller, Jr., Paul F., and Ronald L. Davis. *Hollywood Anecdotes*. New York: Morrow, 1987.

Bonomo, Joe. *The Strongman*. New York: Bonomo Studios, 1968.

Bosworth, Patricia. *Montgomery Clift*. New York: Harcourt Brace Jovanovich, 1978.

Boyd, Malcolm. *Christ and Celebrity Gods*. Greenwich, Conn.: Seabury Press, 1958.

Boyer, Deena (translated by Charles Lam Markmann). *The Two Hundred Days of 8½.* New York: Macmillan, 1964.

Braude, Jacob M. *Braude's Second Encyclopaedia of Stories, Quotations and Anecdotes.* Englewood Cliffs, N.J.: Prentice-Hall, 1957.

——————. *Braude's Treasury of Wit and Humor.* Englewood Cliffs, N.J.: Prentice-Hall, 1964.

Brenner, Marie. *Going Hollywood.* New York: Delacorte Press, 1978.

Brosnan, John. *The Horror People.* New York: St. Martin's Press, 1976.

——————. *Movie Magic—The Story of Special Effects in the Cinema.* New York: St. Martin's Press, 1976.

Brown, Peter Harry. *Such Devoted Sisters—Those Fabulous Gabors.* New York: St. Martin's Press, 1985.

Bruno, Michael. *Venus in Hollywood.* New York: Lyle Stuart, 1970.

Burke, John. *Rogue's Progress—The Fabulous Adventures of Wilson Mizner.* New York: Putnam, 1975.

Burns, Ernest D. *Cinemabilia Catalogues.* New York: Cinemabilia, Inc.

Cahn, Sammy. *I Should Care.* New York: Arbor House, 1974.

Caine, Michael. *Michael Caine's Moving Picture Show.* New York: St. Martin's Press, 1988.

Canaille, Caro. *Étoiles en pantouffles.* Paris: André Martel, 1954.

Cannom, Robert C. *Van Dyke and the Mythical City Hollywood.* Culver City: Murray & Gee, 1948.

Cantor, Eddie, as told to David Freedman. *My Life Is in Your Hands.* New York: Harper & Brothers, 1928.

Capra, Frank. *The Name Above the Title.* New York: Macmillan, 1971.

Carey, Gary. *Brando!.* New York: Pocket Books, 1973.

Carpozi, Jr., George. *The Great Ladies of Hollywood.* New York: Manor Books, 1978.

Carr, William H. A. *Hollywood Tragedy.* Greenwich, Conn.: Fawcett, 1976.

Celebrity Research Group. *The Bedside Book of Celebrity Gossip.* New York: Crown, 1984.

Cerf, Bennett. *Anything for a Laugh.* New York: Grosset & Dunlap, 1946.

——————. *Laugh Day.* New York: Doubleday, 1965.

——————. *Laughter Incorporated.* Garden City, N.Y.: Garden City Books, 1950.

——————. *The Laugh's On Me.* New York: Doubleday, 1959.

——————. *The Sound of Laughter.* New York: Doubleday, 1970.

Chaplin, Charles. *My Autobiography.* London: The Bodley Head, 1964.

Chaplin, Lita Grey, with Morton Cooper. *My Life with Chaplin.* New York: Bernard Geis, 1966.

Chevalier, Maurice, told to Eileen and Robert Mason Pollock. *With Love.* Boston: Little, Brown, 1960.

Chierichetti, David. *Hollywood Director—the Career of Mitchell Leisen.* New York: Curtis Books, 1973.

Clurman, Harold. *All People Are Famous*. New York: Harcourt Brace Jovanovich, 1974.

Cocroft, Thoda. *Great Names and How They Are Made*. Chicago: The Dartnell Press, 1941.

Cocteau, Jean (translated by Ronald Duncan). *Diary of a Film (La Belle et la bête.)* New York: Roy Publishers, 1950.

Cohn, Art. *The Nine Lives of Michael Todd*. New York: Random House, 1958.

Colombo, John Robert (ed.). *Popcorn in Paradise—The Wit and Wisdom of Hollywood*. New York: Holt, Rinehart & Winston, 1979.

Cook, Bruce. *Dalton Trumbo*. New York: Scribner's, 1977.

Coppola, Eleanor. *Notes*. New York: Simon & Schuster, 1979.

Corliss, Richard (ed.). *The Hollywood Screenwriters*. New York: Avon Books, 1972.

Cotten, Joseph. *Vanity Will Get You Somewhere*. San Francisco: Mercury House, 1987.

Cowing, George Cecil. *This Side of Hollywood*. Pasadena: Shaw Press, 1938.

Crist, Judith. *Take 22*. New York: Viking, 1984.

Cronkite, Kathy. *On the Edge of the Spotlight*. New York: Morrow, 1981.

Crowther, Bosley. *Hollywood Rajah—The Life and Times of Louis B. Mayer*. New York: Holt, Rinehart & Winston, 1960.

Dalio. *Mes Années folles*. Paris: Éditions J.-C. Lattes, 1976.

Dardis, Tom. *Harold Lloyd—The Man on the Clock*. New York: Viking, 1983.

David, Saul. *The Industry—Life in the Hollywood Fast Lane*. New York: Times Books, 1981.

Davidson, Bill. *The Real and the Unreal*. New York: Harper & Brothers, 1961.

Davis, Bette. *The Lonely Life*. New York: Putnam's, 1962.

Davis, Bette, with Michael Herskowitz. *This 'n That*. New York: Putnam's, 1987.

Davis, Owen. *I'd Like To Do It Again*. New York: Farrar & Rinehart, 1931.

Davis, Jr., Sammy. *Hollywood in a Suitcase*. New York: William Morrow, 1980.

Day, Beth. *This Was Hollywood*. New York: Doubleday, 1960.

De Mille, Cecil B., and Donald Hayne (ed.). *The Autobiography of Cecil B. De Mille*. Englewood Cliffs, N.J.: Prentice-Hall, 1959.

De Mille, William C. *Hollywood Saga*. New York: Dutton, 1939.

Delmont, Joseph. *Wild Animals on the Films*. London: Methuen, 1925.

Derek, Sean Catherine. *Cast of Characters*. New York: Leisure Books, 1982.

Dimick, Howard T. *Photoplay Making*. Ridgewood, N.J.: The Editor Company, 1915.

Dody, Sandford. *Giving Up the Ghost—A Writer's Life Among the Stars*. New York: M. Evans, 1980.

Dunne, John Gregory. *Quintana & Friends*. New York: E. P. Dutton, 1978.

———. *The Studio*. New York: Farrar, Straus & Giroux, 1969.

Dworkin, Susan. *Making* Tootsie—*A Film Study with Dustin Hoffman and Sydney Pollack*. New York: Newmarket Press, 1983.

Ebert, Roger. *A Kiss Is Still a Kiss*. Kansas City, Kan.: Andrews, McMeel & Parker, 1984.

———. *Two Weeks in the Midday Sun—A Cannes Notebook*. Kansas City, Kan.: Andrews and McNeel, 1987.

Eells, George. *Ginger, Loretta and Irene Who?* New York: Putnam's, 1976.

———. *Hedda and Louella*. New York: Putnam's, 1972.

Eisenstein, Sergei. *Film Form*, and *The Film Sense*. Cleveland: World Publishing, 1957.

Evans, Charles. *The Reverend Goes to Hollywood*. New York: The Crowell-Collier Press, 1962.

Fadiman, Clifton (ed.). *The Little, Brown Book of Anecdotes*. Boston: Little, Brown, 1985.

Feinman, Jeffrey. *Hollywood Confidential*. Chicago: The Playboy Press, 1976.

Fields, W. C. *By Himself*. Englewood Cliffs, N.J.: Prentice-Hall, 1973.

Finch, Christopher. *Rainbow—The Stormy Life of Judy Garland*. New York: Grosset & Dunlap, 1975.

Finch, Christopher, & Linda Rosenkrantz. *Gone Hollywood*. New York: Doubleday, 1979.

Fisher, Charles. *The Columnists: A Surgical Survey*. New York: Howell, Soskin, 1944.

Flamini, Roland. *Scarlett, Rhett, and a Cast of Thousands—The Filming of* Gone with the Wind. New York: Macmillan,1975.

Fontaine, Joan. *No Bed of Roses*. New York: Morrow, 1978.

Fowler, Gene. *Father Goose—The Story of Mack Sennett*. New York: Covici-Friede, 1934.

———. *Good Night, Sweet Prince*. New York: Viking, 1944.

Fowler, Will. *The Second Handshake*. Secaucus, N.J.: Lyle Stuart, 1980.

French, Philip. *The Movie Moguls*. London: Weidenfeld & Nicolson, 1969.

Frewin, Leslie. *Dietrich*. New York: Stein & Day, 1967.

Friedrich, Otto. *City of Nets*. New York: Harper & Row, 1986.

Fuller, Edmund. *A Thesaurus of Anecdotes*. New York: Crown, 1942.

Gardner, Gerald (ed.). *The I Hate Hollywood Joke Book*. New York: Ballantine, 1982.

Garnett, Tay, with Fredda Dudley Balling. *Light Your Torches and Pull Up Your Tights*. New Rochelle, N.Y.: Arlington House, 1973.

Geduld, Harry M. (ed.). *Authors on Film*. Bloomington: Indiana University Press, 1972.

Gerber, Albert B. *Bashful Billionaire*. New York: Lyle Stuart, 1967.

Gershuny, Theodore. *Soon To Be a Major Motion Picture*. New York: Holt, Rinehart & Winston, 1980.

Giesler, Jerry, told to Pete Martin. *Hollywood Lawyer—The Jerry Giesler Story*. New York: Simon & Schuster, 1960.

Gish, Lillian, with Ann Pinchot. *The Movies, Mr. Griffith and Me.* Englewood Cliffs, N.J.: Prentice-Hall, 1969.

Glyn, Anthony. *Elinor Glyn.* New York: Doubleday, 1955.

Gobbi, Hilda. *Közben* . . . Budapest: Szépirodalmi Kiadó, 1982.

Golden, Milton M. *Hollywood Lawyer.* New York: New American Library, 1960.

Goldman, Herbert G. *Jolson—The Legend Comes to Life.* New York: Oxford University Press, 1988.

Goldwyn, Samuel. *Behind the Screen.* New York: George H. Doran, 1923.

Goodman, Ezra. *The Fifty Year Decline and Fall of Hollywood.* New York: Simon & Schuster, 1961.

Grace, Dick. *I Am Still Alive.* New York: Rand, McNally, 1931.

Grady, Billy. *The Irish Peacock—The Confessions of a Legendary Talent Agent.* New Rochelle, N.Y.: Arlington House, 1972.

Graham, Sheilah. *Confessions of a Hollywood Columnist.* New York: William Morrow, 1969.

—————. *The Garden of Allah.* New York: Crown, 1976.

—————. *Hollywood Revisited.* New York: St. Martin's Press, 1985.

—————. *A State of Heat.* New York: Grosset & Dunlap, 1972.

Green, Abel, and Joe Laurie, Jr. *Show Biz—From Vaude to Video as Seen by VARIETY.* New York: Holt, 1951.

Greene, Graham. *The Pleasure-Dome—The Collected Film Criticism (1935–40);* edited by John Russell Taylor. Oxford, Eng.: Oxford University Press, 1980.

Griffith, Richard (ed.). *The Talkies—Articles and Illustrations from Photoplay Magazine 1928–1940.* New York: Dover, 1971.

Guild, Leo. *Hollywood Screwballs.* Los Angeles: Holloway House, 1962.

Guiles, Fred Lawrence. *Norma Jean—The Life of Marilyn Monroe.* New York: McGraw-Hill, 1969.

—————. *Legend—The Life and Death of Marilyn Monroe.* New York: Stein & Day, 1984.

—————. *Zanuck—Hollywood's Last Tycoon.* Los Angeles: Holloway House, 1970.

Guinness, Alec. *Blessings in Disguise.* London: Hamish Hamilton, 1985.

Gussow, Mel. *Don't Say Yes Until I Finish Talking.* New York: Doubleday, 1971.

Hagen, John Milton. *Holly-Would!* New Rochelle, N.Y.: Arlington House, 1974.

Halliwell, Leslie. *Halliwell's Filmgoer's Book of 'Quotes.'* London: Granada Publishing, 1978.

—————. *Halliwell's Filmgoer's Companion* (8th ed.). New York: Scribner's 1985.

Hamblett, Charles. *The Hollywood Cage.* New York: Hart Publishing, 1969.

Hanna, David. *Robert Redford—The Superstar Nobody Knows.* New York: Nordon Publications, n.d.

Hardwicke, Sir Cedric, with James Brough. *A Victorian in Orbit*. New York: Doubleday, 1961.

Harmetz, Aljean. *The Making of the* Wizard of Oz. New York: Knopf, 1977.

——————. *Rolling Breaks and Other Movie Business*. New York: Knopf, 1983.

Harriman, Margaret Case. *Take Them Up Tenderly: A Collection of Profiles*. New York: Knopf, 1944.

Harris, Radie. *Radie's World*. New York: G. P. Putnam's, 1975.

Hasty, Jack. *Done with Mirrors*. New York: Ives Washburn, 1943.

Haun, Harry. *The Movie Quote Book*. New York: Lippincott & Crowell, 1980.

Hawkins, Jack. *Anything for a Quiet Life*. New York: Stein & Day, 1974.

Hay, Julius (translated by J. A. Underwood). *Born 1900*. London: Hutchinson, 1974.

Hayes, Helen, with Sandford Dody. *On Reflection*. New York: M. Evans, 1968.

Hayman, Ronald. *Fassbinder—Film Maker*. New York: Simon & Schuster, 1984.

Hays, Will H. *The Memoirs of Will H. Hays*. New York: Doubleday, 1955.

Hayward, Brooke. *Haywire*. New York: Knopf, 1977.

Head, Edith, and Jane Kesner Ardmore. *The Dress Doctor*. Boston: Little, Brown, 1959.

Hecht, Andrew. *Hollywood Merry-Go-Round*. New York: Grosset & Dunlap, 1947.

Hecht, Ben. *Charlie: The Improbable Life and Times of Charles MacArthur*. New York: Harper & Brothers, 1957.

——————. *A Child of the Century*. New York: Simon & Schuster, 1954.

Heilbut, Anthony. *Exiled in Paradise*. New York: Viking, 1983.

Henderson, Kathy. *First Stage—Profiles of the New American Actors*. New York: Morrow, 1985.

Henreid, Paul, with Julius Fast. *Ladies' Man—An Autobiography*. New York: St. Martin's Press, 1984.

Hepburn, Katharine. *The Making of the* African Queen. New York: Knopf, 1987.

Hershey, Lenore. *Between the Covers—The Lady's Own Journal*. New York: Coward-McCann, 1983.

Herzberg, Max. *Insults—A Practical Anthology of Scathing Remarks and Acid Portraits*. New York: Greystone Press, 1941.

Heston, Charlton. *The Actor's Life*. New York: E. P. Dutton, 1978.

Higham, Charles. *Celebrity Circus*. New York: Delacorte Press, 1979.

——————. *Hollywood at Sunset*. New York: Saturday Review Press, 1972.

Higham, Charles, and Joel Greenberg. *The Celluloid Muse—Directors Speak*. Chicago: Henry Regnery, 1969.

——————. *Hollywood in the Forties*. New York: A. S. Barnes, 1968.

Hodges, Bart. *Life's Little Dramas, As Told to Bart Hodges*. New York: Duell, Sloan and Pearce, 1948.

Hope, Bob. *I Owe Russia $1200*. New York: Doubleday, 1963.

——————. *They Got Me Covered*. Hollywood: Self-published, 1941.

Hopper, DeWolf, with Wesley Winans Stout. *Reminiscences of DeWolf Hopper*. Garden City, N.Y.: Garden City Publishing, 1927.

Hopper, Hedda, and James Brough. *The Whole Truth and Nothing But*. New York: Doubleday, 1963.

Hotchner, A. E. *Choice People—The Greats, Near-Greats and Ingrates I Have Known*. New York: Morrow, 1984.

Houseman, John. *Front & Center*. New York: Simon & Schuster, 1979.

Howard, Ronald. *In Search of My Father—A Portrait of Leslie Howard*. New York: St. Martin's Press, 1981.

Hughes, Eileen Lanouette. *On the Set of Fellini Satyricon*. New York: Morrow, 1971.

Hughes, Robert (ed.). *Film: Book 1—The Audience and the Filmmaker*. New York: Grove Press, 1959.

Huston, John. *An Open Book*. New York: Knopf, 1980.

Hyams, Joe. *Bogart & Bacall*. New York: Warner Books, 1976.

——————. *Bogie*. New York: New American Library, 1966.

——————. *Mislaid in Hollywood*. New York: Peter H. Wyden, 1973.

Irwin, Will. *The House That Shadows Built*. Garden City, N.Y.: Doubleday, Doran & Co., 1928.

Jackson, Clyde O. *In Old Hollywood*. New York: Exposition Press, 1977.

Jessel, George. *So Help Me*. New York: Random House, 1943.

——————. *Jessel, Anyone?*. Englewood Cliffs, N.J.: Prentice-Hall, 1960.

Jewell, Richard B., with Vernon Harbin. *The RKO Story*. New York: Arlington House, 1982.

Johnson, Dorris, and Ellen Leventhal. *The Letters of Nunnally Johnson*. New York: Knopf, 1981.

Johnstone, Iain. *The Man with No Name—The Biography of Clint Eastwood*. London: Plexus Publishing, 1981.

Jones, Lon (ed.). *Barabbas*. Bologna, Italy: Cappelli, 1962.

Kael, Pauline. *Going Steady*. Boston: Little, Brown, 1970.

Kahn, Gordon. *Hollywood on Trial*. New York: Boni & Gaer, 1948.

Kaminsky, Stuart M. *American Film Genres*. New York: Dell, 1977.

Kanin, Garson. *Cast of Characters*. New York: Atheneum, 1969.

——————. *Hollywood*. New York: Viking, 1974.

——————. *Together Again!—Stories of the Great Hollywood Teams*. Garden City, N.Y.: Doubleday, 1981.

——————. *Tracy and Hepburn*. New York: Viking, 1971.

Kaplan, Mike. *Variety's Who's Who in Show Business*. New York: Garland Publishing, 1985.

Kardish, Laurence. *Reel Plastic Magic*. Boston: Little, Brown, 1972.

Kazan, Elia. *A Life*. New York: Knopf, 1988.

Keaton, Buster, with Charles Samuels. *My Wonderful World of Slapstick*. New York: Doubleday, 1960.

Kelley, Kitty. *Elizabeth Taylor—The Last Star*. New York: Simon & Schuster, 1981.

Kennedy, Harold J. *"No Pickle, No Performance"—An Irreverent Theatrical Excursion from Tallulah to Travolta.* New York: Doubleday, 1977.

Ketchum, Richard M. *Will Rogers—His Life and Times.* New York: American Heritage Publishing, 1973.

Keyes, Evelyn. *Scarlett O'Hara's Younger Sister.* Secaucus, N.J.: Lyle Stuart, 1977.

King, Larry with Emily Yoffe. *Larry King by Larry King.* New York: Simon and Schuster, 1982.

Kleiner, Dick. *ESP and the Stars.* New York: Grosset & Dunlap, 1970.

——————. *Hollywood's Greatest Love Stories.* New York: Pocket Books, 1976.

Klumph, Inez and Helen. *Screen Acting—Its Requirements and Rewards.* New York: Falk Publishing, 1922.

Knight, Arthur. *The Liveliest Art.* New York: Macmillan, 1957.

Kobal, John. *Gods & Goddesses of the Movies.* New York: Crown, 1973.

——————. *Gotta Sing Gotta Dance—A Pictorial History of Film Musicals.* London: Hamlyn, 1971.

——————. *People Will Talk.* New York: Knopf, 1985.

Koch, Howard W. *As Time Goes By.* New York: Harcourt, Brace, 1979.

Kohner, Frederick. *The Magician of Sunset Boulevard.* Palos Verdes, Cal.: Morgan Press, 1977.

Korda, Michael. *Charmed Lives.* New York: Random House, 1979.

Koszarski, Richard (ed.). *Hollywood Directors 1941–1976.* New York: Oxford University Press, 1977.

Kozintsev, Grigori (translated by Mary Mackintosh). *King Lear—The Space of Tragedy.* Berkeley: University of California Press, 1977.

Kracauer, Siegfried. *From Caligari to Hitler.* Princeton: Princeton University Press, 1947.

Lahue, Kalton C. *Continued Next Week—A History of the Moving Picture Serial.* Norman: University of Oklahoma Press, 1964.

Lake, Antony B. *A Pleasury of Witticisms and Word Play.* New York: Bramhall House, 1975.

Lamparski, Richard. *Whatever Became of . . . ?.* New York: Crown, 1967.

Lányi, Victor. István Rado, and Held Albert (eds.). *A 25 Éves Mozi.* Budapest, 1920.

Lasky, Jr., Jesse L. *Whatever Happened to Hollywood?.* New York: Funk & Wagnalls, 1975.

Lasky, Jr., Jesse, with Pat Silver. *Love Scene—The Story of Laurence Olivier and Vivien Leigh.* New York: Thomas Y. Crowell, 1978.

Latham, Aaron. *Crazy Sundays: F. Scott Fitzgerald in Hollywood.* New York: Viking, 1971.

Lawrence, Jerome. *Actor—The Life and Times of Paul Muni.* New York: Samuel French, 1974.

Leaming, Barbara. *Orson Welles.* New York: Viking Penguin, 1985.

Lenburg, Jeff. *The Great Cartoon Directors.* London: McFarland, 1983.

Lengyel, Menyhért. *Életem Könyve*. Budapest: Gondolat, 1987.

Lerner, Alan Jay. *The Street Where I Live*. New York: W. W. Norton, 1978.

Levant, Oscar. *The Memoirs of an Amnesiac*. New York: Putnam's, 1965.

—————. *A Smattering of Ignorance*. New York: Doubleday, Doran, 1940.

Levin, G. Roy. *Documentary Explorations—15 Interviews with Film-Makers*. New York: Doubleday, 1971.

Levin, Martin (ed.). *Hollywood and the Great Fan Magazines*. New York: Castle Books, 1970.

Lewis, Arthur H. *It Was Fun While It Lasted*. New York: Trident Press, 1973.

Leyda, Jay. *Kino—A History of the Russian and Soviet Film*. London: George Allen & Unwin, 1960.

—————. *Voices of Film Experience*. New York: Macmillan, 1977.

Lieberman, Gerald F. *The Greatest Laughs of All Time*. Garden City, N.Y.: Doubleday, 1961.

Lillie, Beatrice (with James Brough). *Every Other Inch a Lady*. Garden City, N.Y.: Doubleday, 1972.

Lindfors, Viveca. *Viveka . . . Viveča*. New York: Everest House, 1981.

Lockwood, Charles. *The Guide to Hollywood and Beverly Hills*. New York: Crown, 1984.

Logan, Joshua. *Movie Stars, Real People, and Me*. New York: Delacorte Press, 1978.

Longstreet, Stephen. *All Star Cast—An Anecdotal History of Los Angeles*. New York: Thomas Y. Crowell, 1977.

Loos, Anita. *Kiss Hollywood Good-by*. New York: Viking, 1974.

—————. *The Talmadge Girls*. New York: Viking, 1978.

McBride, Joseph (ed.). *Filmmakers on Filmmaking—The American Film Institute Seminars on Motion Pictures and Television*. Los Angeles: J. P. Tarcher, 1983.

McCabe, John *Mr. Laurel and Mr. Hardy*. New York: Doubleday, 1966.

MacCann, Richard Dyer. *Film and Society*. New York: Scribner, 1964.

McClelland, Doug. *Hollywood on Hollywood—Tinsel Town Talks*. Boston: Faber and Faber, 1985.

—————. *Hollywood on Ronald Reagan*. Winchester, Mass.: Faber & Faber, 1983.

McClintick, David. *Indecent Exposure—A True Story of Hollywood and Wall Street*. New York: Morrow, 1982.

McCrindle, Joseph F. (ed.). *Behind the Scenes: Theatre and Film Interviews from the* Transatlantic Review. London: Pitman Publishing, 1971.

McGilligan, Pat (ed.). *Backstory—Interviews with Screenwriters of Hollywood's Golden Age*. Berkeley: University of California Press, 1986.

Macnee, Patrick, and Marie Cameron. *Blind in One Ear—The Avenger Returns*. San Francisco: Mercury House, 1989.

MacShane, Frank (ed.). *Selected Letters of Raymond Chandler*. New York: Columbia University Press, 1981.

Madsen, Axel. *Gloria and Joe*. New York: Arbor House, 1987.

——————. *The New Hollywood.* New York: Thomas Y. Crowell, 1975.

Maeder, Edward. *Hollywood and History—Costume Design in Film.* London: Thames and Hudson (with the Los Angeles County Museum of Art), 1987.

Mahoney, Patrick. *Barbed Wit and Malicious Humor.* New York: The Citadel Press, 1956.

Malatesta, Joe. *Incognito in Hollywood.* Los Angeles: Wetzel Publishing, 1935.

Maltin, Leonard (ed.). *The Real Stars.* New York: Curtis Books, n.d.

——————. *The Whole Film Sourcebook.* New York: New American Library, 1983.

Mankiewicz, Joseph L., and Gary Carey. *More About All About Eve.* New York: Random House, 1972.

Mario, Frances. *Off with Their Heads!* New York: Macmillan, 1972.

Martin, Olga J. *Hollywood's Movie Commandments.* New York: H. W. Wilson, 1937.

Martin, Pete. *Hollywood Without Make-up.* Philadelphia: Lippincott, 1948.

Marx, Arthur. *Goldwyn.* New York: W. W. Norton, 1976.

——————. *Son of Groucho.* New York: David McKay, 1972.

Marx, Samuel. *A Gaudy Spree—Literary Hollywood When the West Was Fun.* New York: Franklin Watts, 1987.

——————. *Mayer and Thalberg—The Make-Believe Saints.* New York: Random House, 1975.

Massey, Raymond. *A Hundred Different Lives.* Boston: Little, Brown, 1979.

Maugham, Somerset. *A Writer's Notebook.* London: Heinemann, 1949.

Mayer, Arthur. *Merely Colossal—The Story of the Movies from the Long Chase to the Chaise Longue.* New York: Simon & Schuster, 1953.

Mayersberg, Paul. *Hollywood—the Haunted House.* New York: Stein & Day, 1967.

Medved, Harry and Michael. *The Hollywood Hall of Shame.* London: Angus & Robertson, 1984.

Mellen, Joan. *Voices from the Japanese Cinema.* New York: Liveright, 1975.

Meryman, Richard. *Mank—The Wit, World and Life of Herman Mankiewicz.* New York: Morrow, 1978.

Messick, Hank. *The Beauties and the Beasts* (retitled: *The Mob in Show Business*). New York: David McKay, 1973.

Millner, Cork. *Santa Barbara Celebrities—Conversations from the American Riviera.* Santa Barbara: Santa Barbara Press, 1986.

Milner, Michael. *Sex on Celluloid.* New York: Macfadden Books, 1964.

Milton, Billy. *Milton's Paradise Mislaid.* London: Jupiter Books, 1976.

Minnelli, Vincente, with Hector Arce. *I Remember It Well.* New York: Doubleday, 1974.

Moger, Art. *Some of My Best Friends Are People.* Boston: Challenge Press, 1964.

Moldea, Dan E. *Dark Victory—Ronald Reagan, MCA and the Mob.* New York: Viking, 1986.

Montagu, Ivor. *Film World.* Harmondsworth, Eng.: Penguin Books, 1964.

————————. *With Eisenstein in Hollywood.* New York: International Publishers, 1967.

Moorcock, Michael. *Letters from Hollywood.* London: Harrap, 1986.

Moore, Colleen. *Silent Star.* New York: Doubleday, 1968.

Morella, Joe, and Edward Z. Epstein. *Paul and Joanne: A Biography of Paul Newman and Joanne Woodward.* New York: Delacorte Press, 1988.

Morgan, Thomas B. *Self-Creations—13 Impersonalities.* New York: Holt, Rinehart & Winston, 1965.

Mortimer, Hilda, with Chief Dan George. *You Call Me Chief.* Toronto: Doubleday, Canada, 1981.

Moseley, Roy. *My Stars and Other Friends.* London: Heinemann, 1982.

Munshower, Suzanne. *The Diane Keaton Scrapbook.* New York: Grosset & Dunlap, 1979.

Murray, Kathryn. *Family Laugh Lines.* Englewood Cliffs, N.J.: Prentice-Hall, 1966.

Narboni, Jean, and Tom Milne (eds.). *Godard on Godard.* New York: Viking Press, 1972.

Nathan, George Jean. *Art of the Night.* New York: Knopf, 1928.

Navasky, Victor S. *Naming Names.* New York: Viking, 1980.

New York Times Directory of the Film. New York: Arno Press, 1971.

Newquist, Roy. *A Special Kind of Magic.* New York: Rand, McNally, 1967.

Niven, David. *Bring on the Empty Horses.* Putnam's, 1975.

————————. *The Moon's a Balloon.* New York: Putnam's, 1972.

Norman, Barry. *The Film Greats.* London: Hodder and Stoughton and the BBC, 1985.

O'Brien, P. J. *Will Rogers—Ambassador of Good Will, Prince of Wit and Wisdom.* Chicago: John C. Winston Company, 1935.

Orlando, Guido, told to Sam Merwin. *Confessions of a Scoundrel.* Philadelphia: John C. Winston, 1954.

Otash, Fred. *Investigation Hollywood!* Chicago: Henry Regnery, 1976.

Parker, Ruth. *Hollywood Shortcuts to Glamour.* Culver City: Murray & Gee, 1949.

Pascal, Valerie. *The Disciple and His Devil.* New York: McGraw-Hill, 1970.

Pashdag, John. *Hollywoodland U.S.A.—The Moviegoer's Guide to Southern California.* San Francisco: Chronicle Books, 1984.

Pasternak, Joe, told to David Chandler. *Easy the Hard Way.* New York: Putnam's, 1956.

Paul, Elliot. *Film Flam.* London: Frederick Muller, Ltd., 1956.

Payne, Robert. *The Great Garbo.* New York: Praeger Publishers, 1976.

Peary, Danny (ed.). *Close-Ups—The Movie Star Book.* New York: Workman, 1978.

Poitier, Sidney. *This Life.* New York: Random House, 1980.

Polanski, Roman. *Roman by Polanski.* New York: William Morrow, 1984.

Pollock, Dale. *Skywalking: The Life and Films of George Lucas.* New York: Harmony Books, 1983.

Porges, Irwin. *Edgar Rice Burroughs—The Man Who Created Tarzan*. New York: Ballantine, 1976.

Pratt, William. *Scarlett Fever*. New York: Macmillan, 1977.

Preminger, Erik Lee. *Gypsy & Me—At Home and on the Road with Gypsy Rose Lee*. Boston: Little, Brown, 1984.

Preminger, Marion Mill. *All I Want Is Everything*. New York: Funk & Wagnalls, 1957.

Preminger, Otto. *Preminger—An Autobiography*. New York: Doubleday, 1977.

Probst, Leonard. *Off Camera*. New York: Stein & Day, 1975.

Pudovkin, V. I. (translated by Ivor Montagu). *Film Technique and Film Acting*. New York: Lear Publishers, 1949.

Pye, Michael. *Moguls—Inside the Business of Show Business*. New York: Holt, Rinehart & Winston, 1980.

Ramsaye, Terry. *A Million and One Nights*. New York: Simon & Schuster, 1926.

Ransan, André. *En Déjeunant avec* . . . Bruxelles, Belgium: L'Ecran du Monde, n.d.

Reader's Digest Treasury of Wit and Humor. Pleasantville, N.Y.: The Reader's Digest Association, Inc., 1958.

Reagan, Ronald, with Richard G. Hubler. *Where's the Rest of Me?* New York: Duell, Sloan & Pearce, 1965.

Reed, Rex. *Do You Sleep in the Nude?* New York: New American Library, 1968.

————. *People Are Crazy Here*. New York: Delacorte Press, 1974.

————. *Travolta to Keaton*. New York: Morrow, 1979.

Renoir, Jean. *My Life and My Films*. New York: Atheneum, 1974.

Rivkin, Allen, and Laura Kerr. *Hello, Hollywood!* New York: Doubleday, 1962.

Robertson, Patrick. *The Guinness Book of Movie Facts and Feats*. Enfield, Eng.: Guinness Books, 1988.

Robinson, Edward G., with Leonard Spielgass. *All My Yesterdays*. New York: Hawthorn Books, 1973.

Rosen, Marjorie. *Popcorn Venus—Women, Movies and the American Dream*. New York: Coward, McCann, 1973.

Rosenberg, Bernard, and Harry Silverstein. *The Real Tinsel*. New York: Macmillan, 1970.

Rosenblum, Ralph, and Robert Karen. *When the Shooting Stops . . . the Cutting Begins*. New York: Viking, 1979.

Rosenstein, Jaik. *Hollywood Leg Man*. Los Angeles: The Madison Press, 1950.

Ross, Lillian. *Picture*. New York: Rinehart & Company, 1952.

Rossotti, Renzo. *Hollywood Nera*. Torino, Italy: Edizioni M. E. B., 1970.

Rosten, Leo C. *Hollywood—The Movie Colony, The Movie Makers*. New York: Harcourt, Brace, 1941.

Russell, Rosalind, and Chris Chase. *Life Is a Banquet*. New York: Random House, 1977.

St. Johns, Adela Rogers. *The Honeycomb*. New York: Doubleday, 1969.

——————. *Love, Laughter and Tears—My Hollywood Story*. New York: Doubleday, 1978.

——————. *Some Are Born Great*. New York: Doubleday, 1974.

Sann, Paul. *Fads, Follies and Delusions of the American People*. New York: Bonanza Books, 1967.

Sargeant, Winthrop. *Geniuses, Goddesses and People*. New York: E. P. Dutton, 1949.

Sarlot, Raymond, and Fred E. Basten. *Life at the Marmont*. Santa Monica: Roundtable Publishing, 1987.

Sarris, Andrew. *Interviews with Film Directors*. New York: Bobbs-Merrill, 1967.

Scharf, Walter, with Michael Freedland. *Composed and Conducted by Walter Scharf*. London: Vallentine, Mitchell, 1988.

Schulberg, Budd. *Moving Pictures—Memories of a Hollywood Prince*. New York: Stein & Day, 1981.

Schumach, Murray. *The Face on the Cutting Room Floor*. New York: Morrow, 1964.

Schwartz, Nancy Lynn. *The Hollywood Writers' Wars*. New York: Knopf, 1982.

Shearer, Lloyd (ed.). *Walter Scott's Personality Parade*. New York: Grosset & Dunlap, 1971.

Selznick, Irene Mayer. *A Private View*. New York: Knopf, 1983.

Seton, Marie. *Sergei M. Eisenstein—A Biography*. New York: A. A. Wyn, Inc., n.d.

Sharaff, Irene. *Broadway & Hollywood*. New York: Van Nostrand, 1976.

Shows, Charles. *Walt*. Huntington Beach, Cal.: Windsong Press, 1979.

Shulman, Irving. *Harlow—An Intimate Biography*. New York: Bernard Geis Associates, 1964.

Signoret, Simone. *Nostalgia Isn't What It Used To Be*. New York: Harper & Row, 1978.

Silverman, Stephen M. *Public Spectacles*. New York: Dutton, 1981.

Sinclair, Upton. *Upton Sinclair Presents William Fox*. Los Angeles: Published by the Author, 1933.

Skolsky, Sidney. *Don't Get Me Wrong—I Love Hollywood*. New York: Putnam's, 1975.

——————. *Times Square Tintypes*. New York: Ives Washburn, 1930.

Slide, Anthony, with Paul O'Dell. *Early American Cinema*. New York: A. S. Barnes, 1970.

Smith, Grover (ed.). *Letters of Aldous Huxley*. New York: Harper & Row, 1969.

Smith, H. Allen. *The Compleat Practical Joker*. New York: Morrow, 1980.

——————. *The Life and Legend of Gene Fowler*. New York: Morrow, 1977.

Spanier, Ginette. *It Isn't All Mink*. New York: Random House, 1960.

Spencer, Donner, and Eve Paige. *A Treasury of Trivia*. Saratoga, Cal.: Doneve Designs, 1978.

Stallings, Penny, with Howard Mandelbaum. *Flesh and Fantasy*. New York: St. Martin's Press, 1978.

Steen, Mike. *Hollywood Speaks!—An Oral History*. New York: Putnam's, 1974.

Steinberg, Cobbett. *Reel Facts—The Movie Book of Records*. New York: Random House, 1978.

Stelzer, Dick. *The Star Treatment*. New York: Bobbs-Merrill, 1977.

Stein, Ben. *Hollywood Days, Hollywood Nights*. New York: Bantam, 1988.

Stempel, Tom. *Screenwriter—The Life and Times of Nunnally Johnson*. San Diego: A. S. Barnes, 1980.

Stewart, Jack. *The Fabulous Fondas*. New York: Belmont Tower Books, 1976.

Stine, Whitney, with Bette Davis. *Mother Goddam*. New York: Hawthorn Books, 1974.

————. *Stars & Star Handlers: The Business of Show*. Santa Monica: Round Table Publishing, 1985.

Stoker, Charles. *Thicker 'n Thieves*. Santa Monica: Sidereal Company, 1951.

Street-Porter, Janet. *Scandal!*. New York: Dell, 1983.

Sullivan, Edward Dean. *The Fabulous Wilson Mizner*. New York: The Henkle Company, 1935.

Sumner, Robert L. *Hollywood Cesspool*. Murfreesboro, Tenn.: Sword of the Lord Publishers, 1955.

Swanberg, W. A. *Citizen Hearst*. New York: Scribner's, 1961.

Swanson, Gloria. *Swanson on Swanson*. New York: Random House, 1980.

Swindell, Larry. *Spencer Tracy*. New York: World Publishing, 1969.

Tajiri, Vincent. *Valentino—The True Life Story*. New York: Bantam Books, 1977.

Talbot, Daniel (ed.). *Film: An Anthology*. Berkeley: University of California Press, 1966.

Talmadge, Margaret L. *The Talmadge Sisters*. Philadelphia: Lippincott, 1924.

Talmey, Allene. *Doug and Mary and Others*. New York: Macy-Masius, 1927.

Taylor, John Russell. *Hitch—the Life and Times of Alfred Hitchcock*. New York: Pantheon, 1978.

Taylor, Robert Lewis. *W. C. Fields—His Follies and Fortunes*. New York: New American Library, 1967.

Taylor, Theodore. *People Who Make Movies*. New York: Doubleday, 1967.

Thomas, Bob. *King Cohn—The Life and Times of Harry Cohn*. New York: Putnam, 1967.

————. *Marlon—Portrait of the Rebel as an Artist*. New York: Random House, 1973.

————. *Selznick*. New York: Doubleday, 1970.

————. *Walt Disney—An American Original*. New York: Simon & Schuster, 1976.

Thomson, David. *America in the Dark*. New York: Morrow, 1977.

Tomkins, Calvin. *Living Well Is the Best Revenge*. New York: Viking, 1971.

Tyler, Parker. *Classics of the Foreign Film*. New York: Citadel Press, 1967.

Tynan, Kenneth. *Show People*. New York: Simon & Schuster, 1979.

Ustinov, Peter. *Dear Me*. Boston: Little, Brown, 1977.

Vadim, Roger. *Bardot, Deneuve and Fonda*. New York: Simon & Schuster, 1986.

Varconi, Victor and Ed Hornbeck. *It's Not Enough To Be a Hungarian*. Denver: Graphic Impressions, 1976.

Vermorel, Fred and Judy. *Starlust—The Secret Fantasies of Fans*. London: W. H. Allen, 1985.

Vidor, King. *A Tree Is a Tree*. New York: Harcourt Brace Jovanovich, 1953.

Vizzard, Jack. *See No Evil—Life Inside a Hollywood Censor*. New York: Simon & Schuster, 1970.

Von Sternberg, Josef. *Fun in a Chinese Laundry*. New York: Macmillan, 1965.

Walker, Alexander. *The Celluloid Sacrifice*. London: Michael Joseph, 1966.

——————. *Double Takes—Notes and Afterthoughts on the Movies 1956–76*. London: Hamish Hamilton, 1977.

Walt Disney's Goofy the Good Sport. Tucson: HPBooks, 1985.

Wananaker, Marc (ed.). *The* Hollywood Reporter *Star Profiles*. London: Octopus Books, 1984.

Wanger, Walter, and Joe Hyams. *My Life with Cleopatra*. New York: Bantam Books, 1963.

Warner, Jack L., with Dean Jennings. *My First Hundred Years in Hollywood*. New York: Random House, 1965.

Warren, Doug, with James Cagney. *James Cagney*. St. Martin's Press, 1983.

——————. *Double Takes—Notes and Afterthoughts on the Movies, 1956–76*. London: Elm Tree Books, 1977.

Wayne, Jane Ellen. *Crawford's Men*. New York: Prentice Hall, 1988.

——————. *Gable's Women*. New York: Prentice Hall, 1987.

Webb, Richard, and Teet Carle. *The Laughs on Hollywood*. Santa Monica: Roundtable Publishing, 1985.

Weinberg, Herman G. *Josef von Sternberg—A Critical Study*. New York: E. P. Dutton, 1967.

Wellman, William A. *A Short Time for Insanity*. New York: Hawthorn Books, 1974.

West, Mae. *Goodness Had Nothing To Do with It*. Englewood Cliffs, N.J.: Prentice-Hall, 1959.

Whalen, Richard. *The Founding Father—The Story of Joseph P. Kennedy*. New York: New American Library, 1966.

Whittemore, Don, and Philip Alan Cecchettini. *Passport to Hollywood*. New York: McGraw-Hill, 1976.

Wilcox, Herbert. *Twenty-five Thousand Sunsets*. London: The Bodley Head, 1967.

Wiley, Mason, and Damien Bona (edited by Gail MacColl). *Inside Oscar—The Unofficial History of the Academy Awards*. New York: Ballantine Books, 1986.

Wilk, Max. *The Wit and Wisdom of Hollywood: From the Squaw Man to the Hatchet Man*. New York: Athenaeum, 1971.

—————. *Every Day's a Matinee—Memoirs Scribbled on a Dressing Room Door.* New York: W. W. Norton, 1975.

Williams, Chester. *Gable.* New York: Fleet Press, 1968.

Wilson, Earl. *Hot Times—True Tales of Hollywood and Broadway.* Chicago: Contemporary Books, 1984.

—————. *Let 'em Eat Cheesecake.* New York: Doubleday, 1949.

—————. *Pikes Peek or Bust.* New York: Doubleday, 1946.

—————. *Show Business Laid Bare.* New York: Putnam's, 1974.

—————. *The Show Business Nobody Knows.* New York: The Cowles Book Company, 1971.

—————. *Sinatra—An Unauthorized Biography.* New York: Macmillan, 1976.

Wood, Leslie. *The Miracle of the Movies.* London: Burke Publishing, 1947.

Yablonsky, Lewis. *George Raft.* New York: McGraw-Hill, 1974.

Young, Jordan R. *Let Me Entertain You—Conversations with Show People.* Beverly Hills: Moonstone Press, 1988.

Yule, Andrew. *Fast Fade—David Puttnam, Columbia Pictures, and the Battle for Hollywood.* New York: Delacorte, 1989.

Zavattini, Cesare (translated by William Weaver). *Sequences from a Cinematic Life.* Englewood Cliffs, N.J.: Prentice-Hall, 1970.

Zec, Donald. *Some Enchanted Egos.* New York: St. Martin's Press, 1973.

Zeltner, Irwin F. *What the Stars Told Me.* New York: Exposition Press, 1971.

Zinsser, William K. *Seen Any Good Movies Lately?* Garden City, N.Y.: Doubleday, 1958.

Zolotow, Maurice. *Billy Wilder in Hollywood.* New York: Putnam, 1977.

—————. *Marilyn Monroe.* New York: Harcourt, Brace, 1960.

—————. *Shooting Star—A Biography of John Wayne.* New York: Simon & Schuster, 1974.

Zukor, Adolph, with Dale Kramer. *The Public Is Never Wrong.* New York: Putnam's, 1953.

Zsuffa, Joseph. *Béla Balázs—The Man and the Artist.* Berkeley: University of California Press, 1987.

NEWSPAPERS AND MAGAZINES CONSULTED

American Cinematographer, American Film, Cahiers du Cinéma, Esquire, Film Comment, Film Quarterly, Focus on Films, Hollywood Reporter, Life, The Los Angeles Times, Newsweek, The New York Times, The New Yorker, Photoplay, Playboy, Premiere, Sight and Sound, Stage Magazine, Take One, Time, Vanity Fair, Variety.

Index of People, Films, and Studios